POLITICS AND LANGUAGE

IN DRYDEN'S POETRY

Politics and Language in Dryden's Poetry

THE ARTS OF DISGUISE

Steven N. Zwicker

PRINCETON UNIVERSITY PRESS

Copyright © 1984 by Princeton University Press

Published by Princeton University Press, 41 William Street, Princeton,
New Jersey 08540

In the United Kingdom: Princeton University Press, Guildford, Surrey

All Rights Reserved

Library of Congress Cataloging in Publication Data will be found on the
last printed page of this book

ISBN 0-691-06618-3

Publication of this book has been aided by a grant from the
Louis A. Robb Fund of Princeton University Press

This book has been composed in Linotron Galliard

Clothbound editions of Princeton University Press books are printed
on acid-free paper, and binding materials are chosen for strength and
durability. Paperbacks, while satisfactory for personal collections,
are not usually suitable for library rebinding.

Printed in the United States of America by Princeton University Press,
Princeton, New Jersey

In memory of my father,
WILLIAM ZWICKER

Contents

List of Figures

All figures are reproduced from *The Works of Virgil* translated by John Dryden (London, 1697), large paper copy held by the William Andrews Clark Memorial Library, University of California at Los Angeles.

List of Abbreviations

DNB	*Dictionary of National Biography*
ECS	*Eighteenth-Century Studies*
ELH	*Journal of English Literary History*
HJ	*Historical Journal*
HLQ	*Huntington Library Quarterly*
JEGP	*Journal of English and Germanic Philology*
JHI	*Journal of the History of Ideas*
MLN	*Modern Language Notes*
MLR	*Modern Language Review*
PLL	*Papers on Language and Literature*
PBSA	*Publications of the Bibliographical Society of America*
PMLA	*Publications of the Modern Language Association of America*
RES	*Review of English Studies*
SEL	*Studies in English Literature, 1500-1900*
SP	*Studies in Philology*
TLS	*Times Literary Supplement*

Acknowledgments

IT IS A PLEASURE to record the friendships and guidance that have helped shape this book. To Barbara Lewalski and Allen Mandelbaum, my thanks for their interest, their critical reading of the manuscript, and their very generous encouragement in this work. At Washington University I have been fortunate in circumstance, colleagues, and students; first for the chance to listen to and read John Pocock on political theory and political history—Professor Pocock's exposition of these subjects transformed my sense of literary study—and then in Professor Pocock's successor, Derek Hirst, who has shared his encyclopedic knowledge of seventeenth-century history and with whom I have taught and written on the literature and politics of seventeenth-century England. My debt to Derek Hirst is especially evident in the first half of Chapter 4, which began as an essay that we wrote together in the fall of 1978. To Richard Davis, my thanks for the pleasure of the seminars that we have taught on Augustan England; and to Gerald Izenberg, a special thanks for his efforts to increase my self-awareness in theory and method and for listening to me talk through subjects not primarily in his own field of interest. To colleagues in my own department, my appreciation for the encouragement of Naomi Lebowitz, Jarvis Thurston, and Richard and Sondra Stang.

This work has been generously supported by several institutions; my thanks to the deans of the faculty and graduate school of Washington University; to the librarians and staff of the Olin Library of Washington University, the William Andrews Clark Memorial Library of the University of California, and the Firestone and Rare Book Library of Princeton University; to the National Endowment for the Humanities; and to the Institute for Advanced Study, its director, Dr. Harry Woolf, and its professor of early modern history, John Elliott. Much of this book was written at the Institute, and I am very grateful to have been given the opportunity to work there. I am, as well, indebted to the Institute for my colleagues in 1981-1982; my thanks to Professor Elliott for his comments on this work; to Marshall Cohen for reading the opening chapter; to Frank Oakley for his help with French and English Roman Catholic dogma in the Renaissance; to Martin Ostwald for help with Dryden's translation of book 1 of the *Iliad*; and especially to Kevin Sharpe, who read several of these chapters, who listened attentively to my talk about this work, and whose understanding of court culture and seventeenth-century politics was of very great benefit; the manuscript has been much improved by his erudition.

My work on seventeenth-century literature has benefited from contact with a number of scholars; among them I should particularly like to thank Earl Miner, Annabel Patterson, and Paul Korshin. For permission to reprint in altered form Chapter 1 and the first half of Chapter 4, I am grateful to the editors of *Annals of Scholarship* and the *Journal of British Studies*. The manuscript itself has received very careful attention from several readers and from Mrs. Arthur Sherwood of the Princeton University Press. My thanks to Michael Seidel and Michael McKeon, who read this book for the press; to Carol Kay for her timely reading of Chapter 1; to David Bywaters, whose comments were especially helpful in Chapter 5, allowing me to see a distinction between the politics of the "middle way" in Dryden's earlier work and the poet's stance in *The Hind and the Panther*; and to Tom Schweitzer, whose very astute comments helped to sharpen and clarify arguments and expression throughout the manuscript.

My thanks finally to the support of my family; to Judith, whose commitment to this work and good judgment have helped at every turn; to my children for their indulgence; and to my mother, Golde Zwicker, whose encouragement in this work has been unfailing.

POLITICS AND LANGUAGE
IN DRYDEN'S POETRY

1. Language as Disguise

POLITICS AND POETRY IN THE LATER
SEVENTEENTH CENTURY

POLITICAL thought of the later seventeenth century is often
studied as the history of and ideologies implied by such words
as "property," "liberty," and "prerogative." Nor is it surpris-
ing that students of political thought should have isolated these
terms for special attention; they appear prominently and re-
peatedly in the writing and recorded speech of nearly every
political actor of the age. In fact, they appear so frequently
and in such contradictory contexts that we must wonder not
only what meaning such words had but if indeed they had
any meaning at all, or rather if meaning was their most im-
portant function. Since the study of political language often
stresses its conceptual character to the neglect of the polemical
circumstances of its expression, I should like here to redress
the balance. My intention in doing so is to supplement what
is already understood about meaning with an argument about
polemic, about the character of such key words as "property"
and "liberty" and such central terms of political self-definition
as "moderation" not exactly as noise but as reflexive response,
as the invocation of a nearly uniform set of calling cards whose
presentation seems to have been demanded of all those en-
gaged in political discourse in the later seventeenth century. I
am concerned, then, with the extent to which key words in
the later seventeenth century are dysfunctional as a description
of behavior and belief; I am concerned, in other words, with
lying.

Scattered widely through the political documents of this
age are indicators of moderation, dispassion, flexibility, and
compromise. The words "enthusiasm" and "fanaticism" are
frequently used as terms of slander and abuse, implying as

3

they do extremity and rigidity in politics and religion. Yet the years between the return of Charles II and the end of the century yield little real evidence of moderation and dispassion; they are, in fact, years marked by a high pitch of verbal abuse, by steady threats to civic stability from extremes of the left and right, by political dissension and political polarities. The legacy of the civil wars was an ineradicable partisanship which turned in the later decades of the century to bitter party politics and an equally powerful denial of partisanship and party in obeisance to a fiction of patriotic conformity to civic stability. Politics in these years became a spectacle of men declaring moderate goals, often engaging in immoderate designs, apprehending such deceit, and hurling at one another accusations of disguise and masquerade.

Wing's *Short-Title Catalogue* gives some evidence for my contention.[1] Under such headings as "true," "faithful," "plain," and "character" fall a very large number of titles purporting to be documents of political analysis and political revelation. Indeed, the sheer number of these entries raises a question of whether there is any literature so wholly given over to unmasking and unveiling, to the discovery of hidden character and true motive as the political pamphlet of the later seventeenth century. Wing's entries for "character" include, for example, such items as "The character of a popish successor," "The character of a biggoted prince," "The character of a protestant jesuit," "The character of an agitator," "The character of an antimalignant," "The character of a modern sham-plotter," "The character of a church-papist," "The character of two protestants in masquerade." And first-word entries locate only the most obvious and most accessible source for such language. In an atmosphere so highly charged with suspicion, the very expression of political opinion was taken as a sign of party, sect, or political obligation. Accusations of covertness and deceit are so widespread that the artless denial of partisanship had itself become an automatic and a nearly pointless gesture. Honesty and politics were virtually exclusive conditions.

Nor is political masquerade confined to broadside and pamphlet. The most important crisis of the age, the most significant treaty of the later seventeenth century, and the most far-reaching political revolution in this age of revolutionary change are themselves indisputable and brilliant examples of masquerade, of the nation caught in its every turn and gesture by the habits and compulsions of deceit. The Popish Plot was in large part the incredible fiction of one man playing on the political gullibility of the nation; the Treaty of Dover was a double bluff hinged on secret clauses; and the Glorious Revolution was carried off by men willing to pretend that James II had abdicated and that William of Orange sailed to England with 12,000 troops merely to supervise free parliamentary elections.

For immediate cause, we need not seek far in explaining why men felt impelled to adopt disguise, to cling tenaciously to the fiction of constitutional conservatism in an age of frequent and violent assault on that constitution. The fact of change itself and the extremes to which political change had run impelled men to seek the stance and language of centrist politics. To what degree men intended to deceive one another by doing so and to what degree they deceived themselves as they justified radical or absolutist solutions to political problems under the pretense of constitutional legalism, it is difficult to say.[2] What is certain, however, is that the number of accusations of such deceit and hence the level of suspicion of politics was very high; we may safely assume that actual examples of concealment were also widespread.

But disguise in Restoration politics, whether self-delusion or deliberate malfeasance, was seldom a matter of shallow cover or simply verbal habit. It was a deeply felt political imperative that influenced the ways in which men used and conceived language. Of course, the study of politics in any age reveals discrepancies between language and behavior. And the presence of disguise as political stance and political theme over the whole of the century is underscored by the striking parallels between earlier and later seventeenth-century political crises, parallels relentlessly uncovered and exploited by Restoration politicians. Moreover, the religious and philosophical skepticism of Donne's satires, the riddling of language and literary conventions in the *Songs and Sonnets*, the brilliant anatomies of masquerade in the *Alchemist* and *Volpone*, and the critique of court life in the lyrics of Gascoigne, Greville, and Raleigh suggest the continuity of the theme and the sophistication with which men had thought on the implications of disguise in the earlier English Renaissance.

And yet the degree to which disguise permeates and defines national life in the Restoration is not fully to be explained by contemplating deceit as a universal in politics or by citing the literary themes and tropes of earlier generations. There are, as well, specific short- and long-range conditions that help account for its character and intensity in these years. The fear and suspicion of politics and of constitutional speculation in the aftermath of the civil wars, and the precarious balance between king and parliament throughout the Restoration, heightened the need for political disguise. Moreover, the long history of conspiracy mentality in post-Reformation England;[3] the transformation of Royalist politics into Royalist conspiracy during the Commonwealth and Protectorate years;[4] the repeated partisan uses of plots and alarms following the return of Charles II;[5] and the Jacobite conspiracies and steady threat of counterrevolution in the last decade of this century sharpened both the accusations and awareness of disguise in national politics.[6]

Political revolution and the repeated fears of such revolution drove men to the exigencies of disguise, but revolution in the seventeenth century was not confined to politics. Not only was there a fundamental and self-conscious change in political relationships over the course of this century, there occurred, as well, a revolution in language theory that changed the ways in which men thought about language.[7] The revolution in the theory of meaning turned language from divine fiat to arbitrary social pact, heightening men's awareness of the often inconvenient alignment of words and things and allowing new resolution to such troubling imperfections. At the beginning of this century, language theorists—nor were they alone—acknowledged such imperfection yet insisted on the God-given integrity of words and things.[8] By the end of the century, many of those who speculated on the nature of language were willing to assert that this relationship was arbitrary, that there was "no divine ordinance and governance of language."[9] Hobbes had so insisted at mid-century,[10] and in 1690 Locke described the connection between words and things as a *"perfectly arbitrary Imposition."*[11] Locke did not intend "irrational" to follow from "arbitrary"; the thrust of language theory throughout this century was to codify and systematize, to reduce error, confusion, and ambiguity. Such was the aim of the Royal Society; and the work of both Adamic theorists and those who argued against innatist principles was meant to rescue language from the babel of hectoring, parsing, allegorizing, and warfare that had reduced words to such confusion.[12]

But it is to simplify the course of political language over the later seventeenth century and the impact of language reform to assume a sudden resolution, a modification of all language in the direction of clarity and precision. In political discourse, language became more rather than less complex; words, the counters of political argument, needed to be weighed more exactly as the impulse to hide and repress became increasingly powerful over the second half of the century. And in the realm of theory, the move toward arbitrary language principles may have been a reaction against the abuses and unsteadiness of language, but it was, to begin with, an assertion of the fundamentally arbitrary character of language itself. The theory of language as arbitrary sign aimed at correction not by denying that words had been loosened from things but by acknowledging that those moorings were unsteady, that language was social convenience. How striking that in the later seventeenth century, men should have simultaneously explored the possibilities of construing both the sources and forms of governance and language not as inviolable gifts of heaven, unalterable truths, but as social contract, contingent arrangement. And the presence of both philosophical and political issues, the fact that the heightened drive toward political masquerade took place at a time of intense philosophical speculation on the source, character, and fixity of meaning in language helps us to grasp the singular complexity of disguise in this age. By the close of the century, disguise was at once political cover, an acknowledgment of the profoundly contingent character of political experience, and an effort to negotiate the difficult currents of language and meaning at a time when their relation had undergone a radical change. It is such a set of crosscurrents that we can feel in the debates of the Convention Parliament, in Dryden's complex and brooding translation of Virgil's political epic, and in the delicate and enigmatic lyrics from *Fables*.

But the Convention Parliament and the strategies of Dryden's late poetry are the climax of a story that began long before the Glorious Revolution. It began, I believe, with the Protestant reform of 1532. The legacy of that reform in England was twofold: a conviction that spiritual history was national destiny—hence the idea of England as Elect Nation[13]— and a dedication to the recovery of the primitive condition of the church and the purity of God's word. The impulse to cleanse and strip bare was turned by practicing reformers into a program of systematic recovery and revelation; sacred language was decoded by translation, priests shorn of cassock and surplice, churches cleansed of false ceremony and idolatrous sign. In such a program of decoding and divesting, it is not difficult to see the political implications of reform or its polemical character. The witch hunt of Protestant reformation endowed seventeenth-century religion and politics with a belief in conspiracy as historical explanation. In the long confrontation with Rome, spiritual impulses became fixed as principles of political perception: the Roman imposition of false signs and ceremonies was but one aspect of an eternal program of deceit. But conspiracy was hardly confined to the explanation of Jesuit intrigue. It was, in fact, a prism through which all events might be filtered, a device for seeing connections among disparate historical experiences and for giving them the shape and coherence of prophetic time. Conspiracy was, in effect, the handmaiden of providence, explaining those temporary defeats and setbacks in the program of godly reform and national salvation. As God spun out the great web of human history, the devil supplied a counterset of plots, alarms, and treasons. Such was Milton's vision of foreknowledge, history, and sin; such was Marvell's strategy in linking prophecy and conspiracy in *The First Anniversary*; such too was the assumption of innumerable writers of pamphlets and sermons on the civil wars, the Popish Plot and Exclusion Crisis, and the Glorious Revolution.

The one constant in all conspiracy theory was disguise. Only by fraud could conspiratorial aims be effected; only by dissimulation could men carry out concealed and nefarious designs. Such an assumption made it possible to impute intentions where none were expressed and to assign meaning where evidence was incomplete. Given this license, conspiracy theory, like Scripture, had the flexibility to fit all crises; it provided as much comfort to king as to parliament in interpreting the particulars as well as the whole course of the civil wars. None was content to leave those shattering and often inexplicable events in random or mechanical disposition. They were brooded over by Royalists and Parliamentarians, pressed by exegetes of both parties until they could be made to yield a coherent pattern, a narrative guided by the twin forces of providence and conspiracy. Providence needed simply to be endured; but conspiracy in its most obvious symptoms—suspicions and fear—might be countered.

And to such a task the Restoration government turned when in its first order of business, the Act of Oblivion, Charles forbade the use of "any reproach or term of distinction."[14] By such legislation the king would quell mistrust and create circumstances that might lead to forgiveness and political order. The specter of civil disorder and the extremes to which such disorder might run were so disturbing that the fragile structure of civic peace imposed by the restoration of Charles Stuart was erected on foundations of pretended political order and willed forgetfulness. Indeed, the very wording of the Act was an effort at healing and settling by altering and diminishing the past. The most destructive struggle in the history of the state had become, in the Act of Oblivion, "the late differences."[15] With the Act of Oblivion the stage was set for the adoption, almost by reflex, of a language of political discourse that was palliative and normalizing in the face of religious and political conditions that repeatedly led to political crisis through the end of the century.

The first condition of political quiescence was cleansing the political vocabulary; the second was altering and forgetting the past; the third was the reestablishment of civic themes to which all men might adhere, themes of wide ideological appeal: the defense of liberty, the rights of property, and religion by law established, phrases that run like colored threads through the entire fabric of political discourse in this age. Whatever their real political conviction, men paid homage to these common values. At the extremes stood the hated poles of absolutism with its implications of popery and arbitrary government, and republicanism with its associations of regicide and uncontrolled leveling. In the center stood the common good, the ancient constitution with its balance of parliamentary privilege and kingly prerogative. Throughout his reign, Charles made a special effort to fix his identity with the true Protestant faith and with the assertion and maintenance of the laws and liberties of his subjects, a code established in 1660 and repeatedly invoked by Charles, by James II, by William and Mary, by exclusionists and Tory loyalists, by Williamites and nonjurors, indeed by politicians of all stripes and colors.

Despite the lavishing of mutual esteem by king and parliament, despite their joint expressions of thankfulness and humility, of moderation and peaceableness, there was from the beginning of Charles's reign a nervous awareness that the personal and political bitterness that had divided the nation would not disappear. Men understood that political opinion must never again carry them to the extremes of civil war, yet the return of the exiled court brought a renewal of vindictiveness.[16] The lesson of the past was that such convictions must now appear tempered; the implication of such a lesson was that wary politicians would not be alone in concealing forbidden convictions. From the beginning of the Restoration, accusations of covertness and disguise were rife. Clarendon early sniped at the morose manners of the godly, their affected austerity in looks, taking outward signs of godliness as mere affectation;[17] and Venner's rising in 1661 alarmed a nation that knew the word religion to cover a variety of motives. In the same year the king issued a proclamation against "all unlawfull and seditious meetings and conventicles under the pretence of religious worship,"[18] and the lord chancellor, in proroguing parliament in May 1662, warned against the political consequences of pretense and convertness:

> Remember how your peace hath been formerly disturbed, by what contrivance and artifices the people have been alarmed with unreasonable and unnatural Fears and Jealousies. . . . Remember how near monarchy hath been dissolved, and the law subverted, under pretence of reforming and supporting government. . . . There is an enemy amongst us . . . in comparison of whom we may reasonably undervalue all other enemies; that is the Republicans and Commonwealth's Men, who are every day calling in aid of the law, that they may overthrow and abolish the law, which they know to be their irreconcileable enemy. Indeed, my lords and gentlemen, there is a very great party of those men in every faction of religion, who truly have no religion but as the pretence serves to advance that faction.[19]

Nor, of course, were all accusations of deceit and all suspicion of motives directed against those sectaries who would use conscience to mask sedition. From near the beginning of his reign, Charles's intentions in religious matters were regarded with suspicion by both his Anglican and his dissenting subjects; his efforts at religious toleration were assumed by many to be attempts at masking indulgence for papists under the more acceptable guise of toleration for Protestant dissent. Nor can we doubt Charles's awareness of the need for disguise if he intended indulgence or ease for his Roman Catholic subjects. Such indulgence would have to be flanked on all sides by assertions of Protestant zeal. And the king's efforts at such indulgence were repeatedly couched in terms whose ambiguity would allow the blurring of intentions and the conflation of religious conscience of all sorts. The Declaration of Breda (1660) promised, with neat ambiguity, a "liberty to tender consciences, and that no man shall be disquieted or called in question for differences of opinion in matter of religion which do not disturb the peace of the kingdom."[20] And in the Worcester House Declaration (1660), the king reaffirmed his intention to grant such a liberty; but now he felt the need to surround such a declaration with affirmations of his own zealously Protestant convictions, "neither the unkindness of those of the same faith towards us, nor the civilities and obligations from those of a contrary profession (of both which we have had abundant evidence) could, in the least degree, startle us, or make us swerve from it; and that nothing can be proposed to manifest our zeal and affection for it, to which we will not readily consent."[21] Yet ready consent from the king was not forthcoming for the Act of Uniformity (1662); indeed that repressive measure was tempered at the king's own request for provisions and dispensations that favored English Catholics. Moreover, while the king assured the nation of his Protestant zeal, there is evidence that he signaled Catholic listening posts of intended leniency in the enforcement of laws against the Catholics. Indeed, Charles's whole effort to establish "supreme power and authority in ecclesiastical affairs" was aimed at freeing his hand to deal with penal laws and exclusions from the Uniformity Act at his own discretion. While Charles maneuvered to achieve toleration for Catholics, he acted defensively against those who saw in such maneuvering the old specter of popery and arbitrary government. The suspicion that the king himself was a Roman Catholic and aimed to introduce popery was directly combatted by parliamentary decree that made it an offense to charge the king with popery and by the king's repeated assertions of Protestant zeal, "As to the most pernicious and injurious scandel so artificially spread and fomented, of our favour to Papists, as it is but a repetition of the same detestable arts by which all the late calamities have been brought upon this kingdom in the time of our royal father of blessed memory, we conceive all our subjects should be sufficiently prepared against that poison by memory of those disasters, especially since nothing is more evident than the wicked authors of this scandel are such as seek to involve all good Protestants under the odious name of Papists or popishly affected."[22]

It is as difficult now as it seems to have been in the 1660s to know exactly what degree of disinterestedness or sincerity to attach to Charles's plea for liberty of tender conscience; yet the consistent efforts during the early 1660s and the renewed campaign for Catholic toleration later in the decade, the rumor of the deathbed confession, and the reign of James II provide some evidence that the charges of "popish affectation" were not entirely misplaced. Charles understood the difficulty of his position, and it is hardly surprising to find evidence of double dealing in his handling of religious toleration. What I should like to emphasize here and what becomes quite evident during the renewed efforts at toleration in the early 1670s (and, of course, in the Exclusion Crisis) is that concealment and masquerade were fundamentals of political discourse and political action, and that they were perceived as such. The most spectacular example of such disguise is the Popish Plot, a fabrication so complex, used to so many ends, compounded of such an assortment of truths, half-truths, and falsehoods that it seems improbable that we shall ever be able to sift the legitimate from the imposture. But that baroque fabrication is not an isolated incident, no accidental and inexplicable madness; it is the fulfillment of a political mentality at once credulous, susceptible to seemingly any suggestion of conspiracy, hysterical in its response to the Roman Catholic presence in the nation, and at the same time well practiced in the arts and management of political disguise.

The Great Fire of London forms its own chapter in the history of conspiracy mentality, anticipating many of the charges of Jesuit deceit and treachery elaborated at such length during the unveiling of the Popish Plot. And the Dutch Wars that began in 1664 produced a virulent climate of suspicion, compounded by the humiliating reverses and defeats suffered by the English navy, the plague that first struck London in 1665, the heavy tax burden created by the war, and the fact of the fire itself. Although the king was not the direct target of much of the criticism leveled at the court and ministries, as early as November of 1664 he was on the defensive against charges of financial mismanagement and fraud. Before parliament, Charles attempted to remove a vile jealousy "which some ill Men scatter abroad . . . that when you have given Me a noble and proportionable Supply for the Support of a War, I may be induced by some evil Counsellors to make a sudden Peace, and get all that Money for my own private Occasions."[23] As the war continued such vile jealousies naturally increased and touched all who might be implicated: the king himself, the lord chancellor, Carteret, Coventry, the duchess of York, indeed any who were perceived to have profited by diverting money from its intended course. More than once the king complained of parliamentary distrust, and more than once he felt impelled to assure parliament that "no part of those Monies that you gave me for the war have been diverted to other uses."[24]

But accusations of greed and corruption were neither the only nor the most serious charges raised by critics of the court. The war itself was seen by some as a device of Clarendon to divert attention from Bristol's efforts at impeachment,[25] and to promote his own dynastic ambitions; more tellingly, the war was perceived as an instrument in the court's program to crush dissent, manage and intimidate parliament, and raise a standing army. A catalogue of such charges appears at the close of the *Second Advice to a Painter*, where the narrator shrewdly mixes the improbable and the grotesque, musing on a war fought "we know not why, as yet, / We've done we know not what nor what we get."[26] Not only is suspicion rife that the war is a blind, a decoy to cover an assortment of nasty personal and political intentions, but such charges of deceit and masquerade are themselves mounted by an opposition that busily displays its own high-minded loyalty, its plain-dealing commitment to king and country. Vitriolic satire is presented as virtue and disinterestedness. The powerful assault on the court that closes the *Second Advice* and the charges of cowardice and dissimulation leveled at the ministry in the *Third Ad-*

vice are both counterpoised by envoys to the king which insist
on Charles's innocence of the corruption that surrounds him,
his ignorance of actions taken in his own name—a fiction that
Charles would use to his own ends in 1667 as he struggled
to disentangle himself from the disasters of court policy by
jettisoning Clarendon.

And nowhere is the atmosphere of mistrust and masquerade
in the early years of the Restoration better illustrated than in
the parliamentary proceedings against Clarendon, which show
such a sharp awareness of the ways in which the past argued
caution, indeed demanded the appearance of caution in any
proceeding that conjured the image of Strafford and Laud—
an image of the unrepeatable past. The distinction between
judicial and legislative activity was not lost on those who could
themselves remember how the Commons had turned from
impeachment to attainder in the proceedings against Straf-
ford. The accusations first drawn up in the Commons openly
charged that the lord chancellor was guilty of criminal fraud,
secrecy, and corruption; that behind the power and edifice of
his ministry he had gathered great wealth, counseled the dis-
solution of parliament, and urged the creation of a standing
army. Yet the proof of such charges was negligible, the evi-
dence gathered "hugger-mugger, third hand . . . by common
fame only."[27] The original seventeen articles were eventually
reduced to a single charge, in which light the impeachment
seems less an effort to redress infringements of the law than a
campaign to purge Clarendon from office. But in the proceed-
ings against Clarendon, few would have admitted a desire to
turn parliament into an instrument of political vengeance. Sir
Robert Howard maintained that parliament moved in a sphere
above the common law, but he was alone in that assertion.[28]
The memory of the Commons' role in Strafford's impeach-
ment and attainder warned against a repetition of the past.
The reckless and openly political character of that purge with
its abandonment of legal procedures acted as a brake on the
proceedings against Clarendon. "If reason of state be a motive
of parliament to banish one man, so it may be for many. . . .
If you go in this legislative way, you bring upon yourselves

15

all the dishonour of the business . . . as you proceed so will you be justified."[29] Strafford's impeachment hung over the debates of 1667 as did the general knowledge that the law was difficult to mend once it had been trampled. Some men urged caution out of wariness, a conviction that parliament must not repeat the mistakes of the past; others claimed deliberation and judiciousness as a cover, out of a knowledge that such an appearance was now a political imperative. For Clarendon, the proceedings against him were the most transparent of fictions, flimsy platforms from which to launch a personal attack whose motives were jealousy and bitterness. To the aspersions and reproaches hurled at him, Clarendon replied with counteraccusations of malice and deceit, of the conduct of a political vendetta under color of justice.[30] Yet such rejoinder was not Clarendon's alone. To the news of Clarendon's flight in 1667, Sir Robert Howard retorted, "Lord *Clarendon* withdrawn, for fear of tumult! Any person may pretend that; so may any malefactor."[31]

The most spectacular examples of masquerade lay in the decades ahead; but the tug of war between king and parliament over toleration, religious dissent, and the growth of popery which began anew in the late 1660s provides an illuminating episode in the politics of religious language. Late in 1667 the king requested that parliament "seriously think of some course to beget a better union and composure in the minds of my Protestant Subjects in matters of Religion";[32] by this uniformity, Charles hoped to gain political quiescence. The answer from parliament was the suppression of conventicles, but in parliament such suppression was aimed at the left and right, at Protestant dissidents and at papists. Those who opposed the suppression of Protestant dissent decried parliament's assumption of "a legislative conscience, pretending a Law from Heaven to controul the Law upon Earth."[33] Such suppression, it was argued, would only punish the true believer, "not those who use the double arts of making false representations to the king." But on the question of popery, parliament was more nearly uniform. Charles may have anticipated that his move to gain "union and composure" would work against Catholic toleration, but he surely had not intended to provoke from parliament the demand that the existing laws against popish recusants be put in execution (1669), a resolution followed (1670) by an address against popery in which parliament represented to the king in great detail the causes of "the dangerous growth of popery . . . and some present remedies," which included the banishment of popish priests and jesuits, and the conviction of practicing Catholics. The king's answer was a circumspect proclamation against papists that carefully underlined his own zeal for the religion by law established. But in an obvious turnabout, the king suspended penal legislation in the Declaration of Indulgence issued in March of 1672.

The Declaration raised important questions about the extent of the king's prerogative, but it excited an equally pressing concern for the growth of popery and the safety of the Church. And such concern is anticipated in the Declaration itself, which plays upon two of the king's favorite topoi in the management of Catholic indulgence: the ambiguity of the term dissent, and the king's professed zeal for the Protestant religion. The Declaration elaborates that zeal in the history of the king's coercion of dissenters, his express intent to preserve the Church in its doctrine, discipline, and governance; yet, in the boldest of non sequiturs, it suspended that penal legislation implemented to guarantee the health of the Church. "We do in the next place declare our will and pleasure to be, That the execution of all and all manner of penal laws in matters ecclesiastical, against whatsoever sort of non-conformists, or recusants, be immediately suspended."[34] How the king's "many and frequent ways of coercion" might seem to argue such a suspension is unexplained. The posture of coercion, like the profession of Protestant zeal, seems designed to cover the king's efforts to reverse parliament on the enforcement of anti-Catholic laws.

The king must have anticipated parliamentary disapproval. The timing of his declaration—its neat coincidence with the declaration of war against the Dutch—provided Charles with an additional coercive and covering device: the necessity for political acquiescence at home in time of war. "Some few Days before I declared War," he said, "I put forth my Declaration of Indulgence to Dissenters, and have hitherto found a good Effect of it, by securing Peace at Home, when I had War abroad."[35] And this coercive theme is played on by the king and by the lord chancellor, though not finally to much effect in securing parliamentary assent to the Declaration. Indeed the "fears and jealousies" over the king's indulgence were fast in coming. In the Declaration itself the king answered criticism already abroad: "There is one Part in it that hath been subject to Misconstruction, which is that concerning the Papists; as if more Liberty were granted to them, than to the other Recusants; when it is plain there is less."[36] But such plainness was not evident to all. Even those members of parliament who wanted limited indulgence for Catholics lacked the temerity to claim that the king's indulgence had achieved such an effect. A more cynical and less ingenuous posture is assumed at the close of the speech, where the king drops the mask of modesty and evenhandedness: "I shall take it very ill to receive Contradiction in what I have done. And I will deal plainly with you, I am resolv'd to stick to my Declaration."[37]

Such resolution did not, however, forestall parliamentary criticism; even those who granted the most wholesome intentions to the king asked for a rescission of the Declaration,[38] and as parliamentary debate on the Declaration proceeded, the need to define liberty of conscience so that it might apply to Protestant but not Catholic recusancy became apparent. One member asked that the question be moved "for Dissenters of the Protestant subjects only."[39] And here parliament found a useful wedge with which to move against the growth of popery while endorsing the fiction of the king's indulgence of Protestant dissent. Thus the debate on the character of a parliamentary address to the king ensued by way of narrowing ease or indulgence of tender conscience so that it might apply only to the tenderness of reformed conscience. As one member observed, " 'Tender conscience' is of large extent; *Turks, Jews, &c.* have consciences—would have 'uniting Protestant subjects' added to the Question."[40] "In plain *English*, would not put *Romanists* in the Bill."[41] And so the Commons moved against "Popery and Policy."[42]

The king answered this affront: "He is sure he never had thoughts of using it otherwise than as it hath been intrusted in him, to the peace and establishment of the Church of *England*, and the ease of all his subjects in general. Neither doth he pretend to the right of suspending any Laws, wherein the Properties, Rights, or Liberties of any of his subjects are concerned . . . But his only design in this was, to take off the penalties and the Statutes inflicted upon the Dissenters; and which, he believes, when well considered of, you yourselves would not wish executed, according to the rigour and letter of the Law."[43] Some members of parliament acquiesced to the veiled threat, but others read more sharply: "Shall we rest in a doubtful and ambiguous Answer, where our Rights and Liberties are concerned?"[44] As answers and declarations were considered and debated, the extent of the king's prerogative in reversing or suspending laws entangled the highly charged issue of Roman Catholic and Protestant nonconformity with the more purely political aspects of this struggle, the extent of the king's legislative powers. The king pressed for control of enforcement in what he claimed were purely ecclesiastical matters, but such control, which the king claimed by ancient precedent, was perceived as an encroachment on the privileges of parliament; and some members of the House of Commons answered the king's claim with the analogy of Ship Money.[45]

The long encounter between king and the Commons over indulgence not only illustrates the complexity of Restoration political language, it also demonstrates the principal sources of that complexity: an apprehension of political issues in ecclesiastical concerns and the adoption of public stances that did not and were perceived not to coincide with the less publicly acknowledged intentions. From the beginning of the king's encounter with parliament over toleration, Charles's desire and perhaps obligation to provide Catholics with relief from penal legislation could not be openly admitted. The most useful cover for the king in this matter was the ambiguity of the terms conscience, dissent, and nonconformity. By adopting a "liberal" stance in matters of enforcement, a fiction played to the hilt by James in his management of such indulgence, the king might—and did indeed—claim generosity, kindness, and tenderness of blood, claims quite consonant with the language and stance of the Declaration of Breda. But the king was not allowed to adopt such a stance without challenge. Some members of parliament saw toleration as an attempt to embrace nonconforming Catholics together with nonconforming Protestants under the sweep of tenderness of conscience, the toleration of Protestant dissent serving the king as a cover for Catholic relief. Once this assumption was made, the king's efforts to achieve toleration by the rescission of parliamentary legislation could be and were perceived as an attempt to promote the growth of popery, to enlarge his prerogative, to elevate the crown in its legislative capacity above parliament, hence "at one blow to destroy all laws."[46] The specter of popery and arbitrary government loomed over the debate on tenderness of conscience and endowed the language of that debate with a doubleness of meaning that the king pretended did not exist but that was openly invoked by those who saw in the guise of the king's Protestant zeal and tenderness of blood a cynical bid for political power. And, of course, the whole debate over toleration in Charles's reign anticipates the more dramatic encounter under James, in which the same claims of toleration and the same accusations of arbitrary government were advanced, now heightened and rendered more urgent by James's assault on the Anglican establishment, his bid for a standing army, his quick dissolution of parliament, and, of course, his Roman Catholicism—acts and alignments that allowed little room for the guise of Protestant zeal that Charles had so often claimed.

In the turbulent sessions of parliament that followed Charles's withdrawal of the Declaration of Indulgence in 1672, the Commons hurled one affront after another at the king, piled grievance on grievance, objecting to a standing army, to the dangers of popery, to popish councils and counsellors. "Priests," it was claimed, were "daily admitted into the king's presence, and . . . a Papist major general acting in disguise . . . sat in a council of war when the military articles were agreed to."[47] The duke of York's marriage to the Catholic Mary of Modena came under parliamentary censure, and all the while the king and his lord chancellor pressed for bills of supply, increasing what some members felt an unbearable load of taxes. So long as the king was tied to parliament for bills of supply, he had to endure these affronts, but he did not endure them without flinching. In the months following the withdrawal of the Declaration, he prorogued parliament four times. Yet in the face of this dogged struggle, the front of mutual affection, honesty, and loyalty to common principles was steadily maintained by both the court and its critics. Defending the Test Act before the Lords, the Catholic earl of Bristol characterized the Commons as a "house . . . surpassing all that ever have been, in the illustrious marks of their duty, loyalty and affection to the sovereign, both in his person and government; such a house of commons as his majesty ought to consider, and cherish always."[48] And other members represented the Test Act to the king in the same language: "as to the Bill of Popery before you, he has so great love and tenderness for the king's person, that without this bill, neither the king nor we can be safe."[49]

The Commons's Address on Grievances was prefaced with the remark that the House was "abundantly satisfied, that it hath always been your royal will and pleasure, that your subjects should be governed according to the laws and customs of this realm; yet finding, that, contrary to your majesty's gracious intentions, some Grievances and abuses are crept in; we crave leave humbly to represent to your majesty's knowledge" these grievances.[50] The fiction of the king's ignorance of measures transacted in his own name is a ploy used steadily throughout the age. The king's response to such generous caressing was to prorogue parliament after passage of a bill of supply but before a bill for the ease of dissenters could be fixed. When parliament met again they voted a censure of James's prospective marriage, and again the king responded with prorogation. Yet he greeted the same parliament a week later with the familiar language of Protestant zeal and property rights: "I hope I need not use many words to persuade you that I am steady in maintaining all the professions and promises I made you concerning Religion and Property; and I shall be very ready to give you fresh instances of my zeal for preserving the Established Religion and laws, as often as any occasion shall require."[51] The lord chancellor followed the king's words: "I can add nothing to what his majesty hath said; for, as to Religion and Property, his heart is with your heart, perfectly with your heart. He hath not yet learned to deny you any thing; and he believes your wisdom and moderation is such, he never shall: He asks of you to be at peace in him, as he is with you; and he shall never deceive you"[52]—words whose irony is of course heightened by Shaftesbury's role in Exclusion. These claims of mutual esteem and common veneration of religion, laws, and property resulted in this session of parliament refusing a supply.

Yet our discussion of the struggle between king and parliament over toleration, dispensing acts, and the growth of popery is incomplete without reference to an even subtler masquerade that lay behind the domestic encounter. If the king initiated the attempt at toleration in 1667 out of the innocent gesture of composing differences at home while war loomed abroad, over the next five years his motives and the perception of those motives did not remain so simple. During those years, the alliance with France and the duke of York's conversion complicated, at the very least, the king's advocacy of toleration. And the rumor of James's conversion and the inevitability of his ascent to the throne were not the only additional factors; there was as well the growing suspicion that the king himself had popish inclinations and wished to return the nation to Rome. Finally, there is the fact of the secret treaty of Dover, whose provision for that eventuality was rumored in the early 1670s.

Driven by the desire to augment his income, to free himself from dependency on parliament, and to increase his standing against the Dutch, the king began in 1669 negotiating a treaty with Louis XIV, the secret provisions of which included the king's intent to proclaim himself Catholic and to work to return England to Rome. For these acts, the king was to receive a stipend from France. As a cover for the secret treaty, Charles had Buckingham simultaneously negotiate a public though bogus treaty between England and France, which of course contained no clause concerning the king's or country's conversion. To parliament, Charles presented the bogus treaty and protestations of undying zeal for the Anglican church; to Louis XIV he vowed the legitimacy of the secret treaty. On the provision of Catholicism and conversion, Charles did not, in fact, perform. Perhaps the gestures toward toleration and ease for Catholics must be understood in terms of the secret treaty: public signals of secret yet, in turn, fraudulent private intent. What, one wonders, was the center really like? Were the aims and intentions purely political and the terms of exchange between both Louis XIV and parliament religious terms only because those were the current counters of negotiation—Charles cynically understanding that such counters were inevitably those of public affairs? There is evidence both to support and discredit the king's sincerity in matters of religious belief and religious toleration.

We cannot hope to gauge the sincerity of any of the players in this extended encounter over religion; nor, for our purposes, is such knowledge crucial. What is important is an appreciation of the complexity of motive, ostensible and covert, that determined moves on both sides of the question. Throughout the debate, "conscience" and "toleration" as spiritual terms, and "the ancient constitution" as a legal concept, retain public acceptability, but those who participated in public debate were not innocent of the multivalent meanings of the religious and constitutional languages that they used. The highly complex character of this political language stemmed from the interplay between ostensible meaning and implication, and from the fact that some motives were admissible and others were not, and that covered motives were in many cases more powerful determinants of political behavior than spoken intentions. In an irreversible process, toleration became linked with popery, popery with arbitrary government and political absolutism, and religious dissent with political sedition—a

23

multivalence that deprived the interlocking vocabularies of religion and politics of any simple meanings.

Such a climate was brought to crisis in 1679 by the Popish Plot. But the disclosure of the Plot itself only heightened a susceptibility, constantly present during this age of plots and alarms, to the politics of conspiracy and covertness. The pamphlets, sermons, and tracts of the years between 1679 and 1682 are filled with warnings, charges, and countercharges of conspiracy and dissimulation. The distrust of other men's motives, a psychology raised to national paranoia by the experience of the civil wars, was endemic to the conduct of the debate over Exclusion. Those who adhered to the king, to the divinity of monarchy and lineal descent, saw in the Whig claims to protect the nation from popery and arbitrary government—to defend religion, liberty, and property—the spectral figure of leveling schismatics who "pretend to new revelations, raptures, or voices from Heaven and under such specious pretences, convey cheats, delusions, and impostures to the world."[53] The exclusionists aimed to divert the legitimate succession, and, acting under the guise of defense against arbitrary government, they ultimately intended to level the very foundations of society, destroy the laws, and leave "the miserable people to the discretion and mercy of the Sword of Usurpers to be governed arbitrarily."[54]

And on the other side, exclusionists used a wide array of tactics to excite fear of a prospective Catholic king. Behind the Tory claims of loyalty and legitimacy lay the appalling specter of a Romish succession, of the expropriation of property, of Jesuit torture, murder, rape, and destruction. "The Tories indeed talk much of their loyalty, and make great Boasting of their firm resolution to live and dye at the king's feet, in defense of his power and authority, yet there is nothing in the World more plain than that they design the ruin of the king and the Protestant religion, even by those specious pretenses of Loyalty."[55] In the manner that Clarendon raised to such eloquence in *The History of the Rebellion*, partisan writing became exegesis, a searching of political language and political action for the concealed intentions and true meaning of the opposition. In an atmosphere of bitter suspicion, claims of impartiality, clairvoyance, and moderation were demanded of all those who entered the debate over Exclusion.

"If I happen to please the more Moderate sort, I shall be sure of an honest Party; and, in all probability, of the best Judges; for, the least Concern'd, are commonly the least Corrupt: And, I confess, I have laid in for those, by rebating the *Satyre*, (where Justice woud allow it) from carrying too sharp an Edge. . . . they are not the Violent, whom I desire to please" (I, 215-216, 15-34).[56] So, at the height of the Exclusion Crisis, Dryden staked out the middle ground, posing as impartial physician and scrupulous historian, a man drawing pen for party but with the sole intention of healing and settling—or so, in the meticulously constructed preface to *Absalom and Achitophel* and in the poem's many gestures of moderation and evenhandedness, the poet would, for the moment, have us believe. But the meaning of his moderate and conciliatory words and evenhanded gestures has proved no simple historical or critical matter; they have had a curious double history, exciting bitter contempt among many of Dryden's contemporaries[57] and nearly universal acceptance in our own time. To read *Absalom and Achitophel* as part of the current of political discourse in the later seventeenth century is to understand the poem as an argument and construct of a very different character than we have come to assume. Such a reading, by laying emphasis on ideology as polemic, allows us to see in Dryden's art another dimension of his political argument and an image of political discourse at once sharper and more subtle than any such image otherwise available, a heightening of politics as disguise that makes the particular example paradigmatic of the whole. Nor was this fit between art and politics lost on Dryden's contemporaries. The poem touched a very raw nerve, demonstrating the techniques of dissimulation while simultaneously decrying those techniques in others. Dryden's poem was perceived as the epitome of a mode of political discourse that had grown dominant over the two decades since the Restoration, a development paralleled by Dryden's increasing mastery of its central techniques: covertness, obliqueness, and irony. The poem represents the full coincidence of political and poetic moment, a perfect consonance of the techniques of political and literary discourse. And this consonance was powerfully felt by Dryden's contemporaries, many of whom made it their business to decry and belittle his achievement while others leaned on its perfection of poetry as politics. *Absalom and Achitophel* is central to polemic in the last two decades of the century, echoed and alluded to, derided and imitated, target of bitter assault and touchstone for Tory loyalism.

In our own time, the formulation of Dryden's politics and religion into ideology and spiritual biography has made the task of hearing the poem as political discourse unusually difficult. The burden of received opinion about Dryden's moderation and conservatism has obscured the meaning of his words as political argument. Yet to claim, as I do here, that the poem has been read too literally, too autobiographically, is, in a way, to cite a kind of success for the poem as polemic. Surely Dryden intended the professions of disinterestedness and moderation advanced by metaphor, drama, and discourse in this poem and its preface to be understood as something more than necessary scaffolding. But to read his words simply as profession is to read them with a naiveté about the character of political language in his age and an ignorance of the complexity of circumstances in which he wrote and of the kinds of response that complexity demanded. To assume throughout that Dryden is a truth-teller is to narrow our understanding of the character of his achievement both as poet and polemicist, of the ways in which art and politics are bound in *Absalom and Achitophel.*

The ostensible evenhandedness of the poem, the narrator's portrait of the king in sexual excess, his admission of Shaftesbury's judicial virtues, the seeming moderation of his constitutional address all turn out, on close inspection, not to be so straightforward as has often been supposed. The argument of the parts as well as the whole of this poem is more partisan and less philosophical than Dryden's advocates have been willing to assume. In the construction of an argument whose political implications are vindictively partisan, the need for covertness, for argument through irony and indirection, was very great indeed. At a time when the center was mobile, when many men passionately believed in stability, the veiling of partisan argument was an essential condition of political utterance.

In the aftermath of Exclusion and the resounding defeat of Whiggery, the air momentarily cleared and the repressive impulses of Tory politicians and publicists emerged from the façade of moderation. Once the balance of power had shifted to the king, the compulsive need to claim the middle ground diminished. The boldness of court politics and court poetics may be surprising, but neither, in political terms, is inexplicable. The abrupt dissolution of the Oxford parliament and defiance of the Triennial Act in 1684, the execution of Stephen College, the judicial murders of Sidney and Russell all indicate a new political mood, and court propaganda under the direction of Roger L'Estrange quickly redefined the political center: "Moderation . . . is that by which we govern ourselves in the use of things a body may have too much of . . . but it is ridiculous to talk of moderation in a case that admits of no excess. Did you ever hear of any man that was too wise, too temperate, too brave, too loyal, too pious, too continent, too charitable?"[58] In *The Observator* (nos. 240-249, Nov. 1682) L'Estrange shifts fire from Whig to Trimmer, ignoring the more extreme position and claiming that the middle is now the left.[59] By redefining the center and attempting to align religion and property rights with the sanctity of lineal succession, pamphlets such as *The Prerogative of Primogeniture* could argue that men who opposed lineal descent were disloyal and disingenuous, "perjured Pseudo-Protestants who under the specious pretense of being vogued Protestants did, and still do carry on their Diabolical Vocation and Treasonable Association."[60]

The lapse of censorship laws in the wake of the king's failure to call a parliament after 1681 partly accounts for the expression of greater polarity of opinion in the remaining years of Charles's reign, but more importantly, the decisive shift in political balance released politicians from the need to caress and persuade, from the compulsion to claim moderation and disinterestedness as a political stance. Nowhere is this more incisively demonstrated than in Dryden's verse of these years; a comparison of *Absalom and Achitophel* with Dryden's contribution to *Absalom and Achitophel* Part II makes my point, but an even sharper image is projected by the major satire of the Tory reaction, Dryden's *Medall*. No longer needing to persuade, Dryden excoriates Shaftesbury in a satire whose relentless pursuit of a politically impotent figure has long puzzled critics. The intensity and pitch of satiric attack in this poem are indeed difficult to explain if we look for motivation as political urgency or personal animosity. Like the king and like Tory pamphleteers, Dryden emerged from the politics of moderation and healing counsel only after decisive political victory. The poem is a calculated abrasion, the cool flaying of a victim powerless to retaliate. If this is a less compelling performance than *Absalom and Achitophel*, it is not because emotion has overwhelmed judgment but because political opportunity has released Dryden from the constraints of posture and indirection. Such was not to be the case for long. For quite different reasons, Dryden was again to seek after the comforts and strategies of disguise in the reigns of both James II and William III.

The Tory resurgence in the remaining years of Charles's reign was managed without alienating any politically important segment of the nation. To this skillful management, James owed the quiescence of the nation at his ascent and the overwhelming Tory majority of his first parliament. But the Catholic king who came to the throne in 1685 had neither the inclination nor the patience for careful political management. Anxious to get on with what he conceived not only as a kingship but also as a mission, James tolerated little opposition in attempting to fulfill the political and hence religious aims of his monarchy: the Bloody Assizes and subsequent elevation of Jeffries, the defiance of the Test Act in staffing the army with Catholic officers, the maintenance of a standing force, the levying of customs duties on the king's own authority, the revival of the court of high commission, and the attack on

Oxford.[61] Yet even James, who dangerously and flagrantly defied the spirit of the laws, did not entirely abandon the standard political language of his age, that familiar scaffolding of property rights and the religion by law established. While he moved forcefully to impose his will and his religion, he signaled the continuity of Stuart kingship at his accession by vowing to his first parliament "I shall make it my endeavour to preserve this government both in Church and State, as it is now by law established."[62] In the central act of his kingship, the issuing of a Declaration of Indulgence that was aimed directly at the Anglican establishment, voiding penal measures and test laws and drawing into useful alliance a wide array of the king's dissenting subjects, James repeatedly hedged his Declaration with the formulas of liberty, property, and the religion by law established. While delivering what Anglicans felt as a death blow, James declared his selfless devotion to their cause. He intended, above all else, to ensure "the perfect enjoyment of their property, which has never been in any case invaded by us since our coming to the crown."[63] The first principle of the Declaration was, in fact, to "protect and maintain our archbishops, bishops and clergy, and all other our subjects of the Church of England in the free exercise of their religion as by law established, and in the quiet and full enjoyment of all their possessions."[64] The closing words of this loving message echoed and reechoed these pledges: religion and liberty, properties and possessions, lands and properties.

The king did not, of course, go unchallenged in his use of such a vocabulary. No sooner had James vowed to his first parliament the protection of religion and property than the earl of Argyle raised the standard of rebellion: "the king being now dead, and the duke of York having taken off his masque, and having abandoned and invaded our Religion and Liberties, resolving to enter into the government, and exercising contrary to law, I think [it] not only just, but my duty to God and my country, to use my utmost endeavours to oppose and repress his usurpation and tyranny."[65] Within three years "the invasion of liberty and property" had become a central standard for those prudent and careful men who invited William of

Orange to supervise parliamentary elections; and the preservation of law, liberty, and custom was foremost in William's mind as he accepted their cordial invitation to invade England.

But the political character of James's reign was not quite so simple as conciliatory language and inflammatory acts; nor were all the inflammatory acts presented in the code of religion and property. The parliamentary address that began by assuring the nation of the safety of religion and property ended in the peremptory tone more characteristic of his kingship.[66] And in his first challenge to the Test Laws, simultaneously a slap at the militia and a violation of the principle of no standing army, James lectured his parliament, "Let no man take exception, that there are some Officers in the Army not qualified, according to the late Tests, for their employments: the gentlemen, I must tell you, are most of them well-known to me: and, having formerly served with me on several occasions, and always approved the loyalty of their principles by their practice, I think them now fit to be employed under me: and I will deal plainly with you, that, after having had the benefit of their service in such a time of need and danger, I will neither expose them to disgrace, nor myself to the want of them."[67]

Down such a road few were willing to follow the king. There were no important conversions, with the obvious exceptions of Sunderland and the poet laureate, who had been attached to the duke of York's circle from early in the Restoration and who now, with what reluctance we cannot say, converted and prepared his defense of that conversion and of as much government policy as he could bear to defend.[68] That Dryden was frightened by the direction and velocity of the king's political program is clear throughout *The Hind and the Panther*, in the oblique efforts to caution the king against rashness, in the rather more direct predictions of inevitable disaster, in the elaborate obfuscation of political problems in fable and allegory of a narrative and symbolic complexity unmatched by anything in Dryden's canon. Never had Dryden been faced with a political program as indefensible as the one that he chose to defend in *The Hind and the Panther*. The massive and intricate character of his effort is a gauge both of the poet's resourcefulness and of his sense of the difficulty of his task, the danger that he felt personally and politically.

That fable should be a crucial element in *The Hind and the Panther* and should emerge in the last decade of the century as a central narrative device, a mode of political discourse in difficult and uncertain times, shows the degree to which Dryden anticipated and shared the circumstance not only of Jacobites under William III but of the majority of writers in the last decade of the century. The 1690s were years of translation, paraphrase, and fable writing of a remarkably high order and of the composition of original verse of an astonishingly minor character. It is, I think, a crucial symptom of literary culture and its relation to politics that the last decade of the century saw the publication of more editions of fables than at any earlier time in the history of printing in England.[69] These were years of political and ideological complexity and confusion, years marked by party realignment, shifting political self-definition, and the elaboration of defenses, explanations, and apologies that sought to disguise embarrassing political facts and to discover consistency in unprincipled and inconsistent behavior.

Despite the many laments over the dislocation of language from meaning in this age, the closing decade of the century might be seen as a triumph of precisely that condition. The efforts of the Convention Parliament of 1689 were largely directed toward assigning such words to the events of the Revolution as would conceal their character; and the facility that politicians displayed in doing so is testimony to their long training in the arts of political dissimulation. How else might the prince of Orange have been transformed into the king of England; how else might James's flight have been described as an act of abdication?[70] But there was more to these proceedings than the cynical manipulation of words. In order for the efforts of the convention to triumph, to achieve permanence and fixity, men needed to believe that what they had done was both pragmatic and legitimate. Pragmatism was a necessity; but legitimacy was not wholly to be ignored in a century when men had sought for precedent, rationale, and vindication as incessantly as they had pursued any local or national interest. The careful disputation over words and the successful application of words to things represented the triumph of an art and science of language and politics that had been long in the making.

Over the course of the seventeenth century, men came to understand that if language had driven them to arms, then future conflict might be avoided by suppressing language and by changing fundamentally their understanding of its meaning and efficacy. The willingness to suppress and alter language contributed to a fundamental change in the theory of meaning and implication. The rift of words from things in the later seventeenth century allowed men to recover from the polarities to which words had driven them; to see political oppositions in a new way—not mutually exclusive positions, command posts for the Armageddon, but points on a political spectrum—and to conduct a second political revolution without a single major battle or the loss of life. The Convention Parliament had compacted together in order to find a vocabulary for the Glorious Revolution. Of course, its members would hardly have thought that they had met for a convention on the meaning of meaning; and we cannot expect them to have self-consciously articulated such a philosophy of language in order to meditate on or justify their proceedings. But it is tempting to consider that Locke's statement of the new linguistic philosophy in *An Essay Concerning Human Understanding* (1690) may have enjoyed its great popularity because it could provide philosophical legitimacy for what might otherwise seem linguistic opportunism:

> The Comfort, and Advantage of Society, not being to be had without Communication of Thoughts, it was necessary, that Man should find out some external sensible Signs, whereby those invisible *Ideas*, which his thoughts are made up of, might be made known to others. For this purpose, nothing so fit, either for Plenty or Quickness, as those articulate Sounds, with which so much Ease and Variety, he

found himself able to make. Thus we may conceive how *Words*, which were by Nature so well adapted to that purpose, came to be made use of by Men, as *the Signs of* their *Ideas*; not by any natural connexion, that there is between particular articulate Sounds and certain *Ideas* . . . but by a voluntary Imposition, whereby such a Word is made arbitrarily the Mark of such an *Idea*.[71]

The *Essay* was not an original work in language theory, but it was a book of immense and almost immediate prestige in its own time.[72] It was, moreover, a book to which Locke was willing to fix his name, and in that the contrast with the *Two Treatises* is striking. Yet despite Locke's secrecy about the *Two Treatises*, there is an analogy to be drawn between Locke's vision of men compacting together to form language and the idea of consent in the creation of civil government.[73] In both cases, the compact is not of divine origin but is a social arrangement, and in both cases Locke implies that what men willingly compacted might, by the same will, be disowned or rearranged. To look back from the perspective of 1689 to 1639 and declare that men had gone to war because of a belief in the immutable character of words is to overstate this case, but such a proposition is a significant part of Clarendon's thesis in *The History of the Rebellion*. One of the clearest themes in the first book of this subtle but nearly disinterested analysis of the origins of the civil war is that sharp words beget sharper actions,[74] that men trapped themselves into irrevocable linguistic and political positions. It was not only the imperative of sharp words that had driven men to arms, of course. The frame of sacred history that Puritans had so forcefully applied to the conflict between king and parliament implied holy war. Elect Nation was opposed only by the damned; the inauguration of Christ's thousand-year rule was impeded only by the body and agents of antichrist. But what was sacred history itself other than a language? And the decline in the political prestige of sacred history came at a time when men had begun to change their understanding of the nature and origins of language. The later seventeenth century was witness to an effort to demystify simultaneously language and politics, to discount the divine origins of political words and political institutions.[75]

The strategies and arts of disguise, while we might lay to them the triumphs of political management in these years as well as the dominance and peculiar brilliance of irony and obliqueness in Restoration literature, were not without their own cost: a melancholy conviction overlaying the whole age that whatever its usefulness, the repeated and willful dislocation of language from meaning had had a profoundly unsettling effect. It seems especially fitting that the great epic of these last years of the seventeenth century should have been a translation of Virgil that chose not to celebrate empire and conquest but to see those martial achievements in a compromised light. That this century should close on a note of compromise and irony is congruent not only with the argument that I have made about the intersection of political and literary motives but with our sense of the whole of the age, and indeed with the perception of men living through those times. That Virgil's poem should have been rendered in Dryden's brooding and melancholy translation, that the celebration of empire should turn into a lament over the inevitability of invasion and conquest, indeed that epic should become elegy argues not only that men were willing to allow literary conventions to mask political statement, but that the very conventions and forms themselves underwent translation in the process. But the change was more radical than "translation" implies, for the steady manipulation of the conventions and forms of literary and political discourse had an effect on the stability and perception of such discourse, and finally an effect on the reliability of discourse altogether. Few understood deceit and its aftermath better than those poets and politicians who were at once its most brilliant actors and victims.

2. Tropes and Strategies

To write on affairs of state in the later seventeenth century was invariably, perhaps inescapably, to participate in rhetorical masquerade; to write at all was to face a language in which the central terms of public life, politics and religion, had become instruments of disguise. Such conditions applied to politicians in the most obvious of political circumstance as well as to more refined and more exotic forms of speech, to tract and pamphlet but also to lyric and epic. Disguise was an essential condition of this culture, and its effects were visible at every turn, in comedy whose essence is deception and whose most brilliant effects are variations on disguise; in epic whose most characteristic expression is in travesty and in translation; in the dominance of satire whose social role is revelation; in the emergence of new genres that take deception as their subject and whose function is to act as screen and mask, and in the transformation of old genres to accommodate the need for indirection and masquerade. What more telling comment on political culture than the fact that not only men opposing and ridiculing the court sought cover but that those who struck from its center also felt the need for disguise?

And what more telling expression of this culture than its central literary figure, its poet laureate? Dryden was the Restoration man of letters; he defined cultural standards in criticism, in satire, in drama, and in translation. He created the idiom of Restoration literature, and for much of his life he wrote from the center of power. He was also consistently blackened as a liar, a cheat, and a hypocrite. Those accusations were hardly disinterested opinion; they were epithets hurled by political enemies who sought to discredit a public voice. But the idea that Dryden was a timeserver and a cheat was also the more measured opinion of Johnson and Macaulay.[1] They had their own ideological imperatives, but they could hardly have been fired by the intentions and passions of Dryden's contemporaries. Recent attempts to construct a more sympathetic model of Dryden's character and intellect have reconciled some of the paradoxes of his career,[2] but the contemporary accusations of deceit remain a telling commentary on Dryden's literary art and on the conditions in which he practiced it.

But rather than being an encumbrance, I suspect that the necessity for disguise was a condition in which Dryden thrived; it spurred the development of a special poetic, and focused and intensified certain gifts. Dryden became the central figure of his age because he adjusted so surely to the conditions of speech set by Restoration politics. He was at his greatest ease not in confession or praise or exhortation—though there are compelling examples of these in the poet's writing—but when political needs made the sharpest demands on his powers as strategist. Politics may have thrust this poet into habits of concealment, but disguise was a condition that he turned to high art.

The contrast with Dryden's literary contemporaries is especially instructive. Marvell is the great literary ironist of this century, and yet Marvell's powers of moral and intellectual discrimination seem dulled in the polemical mode of his Restoration satires.[3] By comparison with the pastorals, where irony is so delicate and exact an instrument of perception, the satires use irony harshly and reductively; they simplify and abuse, and the poet of the pastorals or of the *Horatian Ode* and *Upon Appleton House* must have been ill at ease with such measures. Rochester's satires reach their truest pitch not in leering innuendo, but in high and open indignation. And with Milton the necessity for obliqueness in *Samson Agonistes* produced new and powerful measures;[4] but both preface and poem make us feel that concealment went against the grain, that it was a mode which politics alone forced Milton to adopt, that pulling down the temple of Dagon was, in the end, no very hidden act of revenge.

Dryden, however, seems to have negotiated the difficult currents of public life in these years with ease. He adjusted surely and quickly to the conditions of utterance that politics and history had imposed, and that adjustment is most obvious and accessible in the poet's prefaces, forewords, and critical essays. In the prose writing the techniques are more easily detached from context than in the poetry; and with an aim to clarify habits of mind and technique in circumstances in which we can most readily observe their motives and effects, it is with the tropes and strategies of the prose that I begin. Although Dryden's habits of evasion invite biographical and psychological speculation, and I shall occasionally speculate in those ways, my central concern is to demonstrate how multiple and brilliant were the literary energies directed toward disguise. The very persistence of this habit of writing is part of my argument.

In discussing the essays and prefaces, my intention is not to discount other ways of thinking about Dryden's critical writing, but to suggest an additional dimension to his work, another way of thinking about Dryden's strategies as critic.[5] Some of what I shall say has a corrective aim; declared intentions and at times the very topics of literary criticism belong to a set of polemical gestures and must be understood in those terms. All of what I want to say stresses the complexity of Dryden's writing and the care with which we must evaluate his various poses as historian, exegete, panegyrist, and poet.

From the beginning, or nearly so, ambiguity and irony were conditions of statement for Dryden. He but gradually mastered the art of personal and political statement through these ironies; yet the concern and the stamp of his manner is characteristic from early on. The elegy *Upon the death of the Lord Hastings* uses the standard topoi of elegiac verse, but it seems to have no voice at all. The same cannot be said of the letter *To Honor Dryden*. Trifling as it is—and part of the slightness is posture—the ways in which Dryden plays ironies against the standard vocabulary of Petrarchan desire look, at least retrospectively, to be very much Dryden's own. It is, however, in the preface to *Annus Mirabilis* that Dryden's polemical methods become apparent.

Students of the poem have provided us with a detailed account of the problems that Dryden faced in writing on this "year of wonders."[6] They have persuasively argued that the poem's gestures and organization were an effort to answer the harassing and often accurate criticisms of court policy in the war efforts of 1665-1666, and to adapt the apocalyptic schemes of dissenter criticism to the ends and purposes of the king and his embattled ministry. The preface demands the same attention to rhetoric and polemical intent; and seen in a polemical context, the preface has surprising coherence and argumentative point. Here Dryden first essayed the techniques that he was to use throughout his career; here are the first examples of feigned digressiveness, of political argument through literary topoi, of polemical uses of genre, of false claims of historical accuracy and disinterestedness, of false arguments about audience, and of quickly confessed and strategically placed admissions of guile.

The apparatus that Dryden assembled for his title page included the poem's Latin title, a generic definition of the poem, some tags from Trajan and Virgil, and a dedication to "The Metropolis of Great Britain" (I, 42). The title itself signals an answer to a long series of pamphlets that bore such titles and used apocalyptic schemes to predict the demise of Stuart kingship,[7] but the engagement with such an enemy goes well beyond the title. Some of the material on the title page is an effort to establish the high tone of the poem, to signal learning and antiquity, to raise the whole of these proceedings to an altitude from which it would be easy both to ignore and to condescend to the attacks on the court. But Dryden is not content with passive measures. He strives for altitude; he enters the camp of the enemy, not, however, with the intention of blaming. He has come not to harass the enemy but to wonder at their loyalty, their invincible courage and unshaken constancy. Indeed, London has "set a pattern to all others of true Loyalty" (I, 42, 4-5). What London could Dryden have had in mind? The history of this city over the previous quarter of a century was marked by outbreaks of radicalism, by significant representation in Barebones parliament, and by a massive funding of the parliamentarian war effort.[8] These facts were not obscure and they could hardly have turned anyone's mind, especially in the face of the renewed pamphlet war on the court, toward the theme of unshaken constancy. But the point of this dedication and this language was not simply to falsify the past but wholly to ignore it, to deny the enemy his own status. The strategy is reminiscent of one of the central gestures of the king's own Act of Indemnity and Oblivion—a denial of the language and facts of opposition—and it anticipates the portrait of the king in the poem not as a man embattled by sharp criticisms but as the father of his people, suffering servant, and redemptive saint (I, 98, stanzas 260-262).

The technique of denial and misrepresentation is one that Dryden turned to throughout his career, and nowhere more brilliantly than in the opening lines of *Absalom and Achitophel*, which seem so generously to concede problems, to insist on fair-mindedness, but in fact concede only what Dryden can best address and turn to his own advantage. In *Annus Mirabilis* the techniques are not so subtly deployed, but the idea of refusing the terms of the opposition and then adopting the guise of history is a central strategy in Dryden's repertoire.

Nor, of course, is this all that the preface to *Annus Mirabilis* has to offer. What follows the dedication is a treatise on genre, versification, and literary models. But the discussion does not aim disinterestedly at literary themes. At crucial points, the materials of literary discussion are given strategic purpose, and nowhere more so than in the remarks on epic and history. "I have chosen the most heroick Subject which any Poet could desire: I have taken upon me to describe the motives, the beginning, progress and successes of a most just and necessary War . . ." (I, 44, 9-11). Perhaps this is the beginning of a new *Iliad*, another *Aeneid*; here is the matter of epic poetry, yet the poem steadfastly refuses the epic genre. "I have call'd my Poem *Historical*, not *Epick*, though both the Actions and Actors are as much Heroick, as any Poem can contain. But since the Action is not properly one, nor that accomplish'd in the last successes, I have judg'd it too bold a Title for a few *Stanza's*, which are little more in number then a single *Iliad*, or the longest of the *Æneids*. For this reason, (I mean not of length, but broken action, ti'd too severely to the Laws of History) I am apt to agree with those who rank *Lucan* rather among Historians in Verse, then Epique Poets . . ." (I, 44, 27-34). Dryden's play with these modes gives him the best of both polemical worlds; the literary distinctions allow the poet the luxury of having the poem simultaneously circumscribed by the rigorous laws of history and enhanced by the demands of epic. The epic designation serves as a justification of the Dutch wars; the historical designation determines the poet's stance. Dryden elevates the court at its most vulnerable and unheroic point ("a most just and necessary War; . . . the care, management and prudence of our King; the conduct and val-our of a Royal Admiral, . . . the invincible courage of our Captains and Sea-men" [I, 44, 10-13]), yet having achieved such elevation, Dryden then refuses the genre because of his own inadequacies. Moreover, it is not only length that would deny this poem its epic title, it is point of view, as well. "Ti'd too severely to the Laws of History" (I, 44, 32), both Dryden and Lucan must be satisfied with ranking as historians in verse. And history is what this poem would most strenuously enjoy being.

The aim throughout is single-mindedly to justify the status of the poem as history. Nor does the strategy close with the handling of genre. Dryden's claim as truth-teller is also elab-orated in terms of literary models. Somewhat against his will, this poet has chosen Virgil rather than Ovid as a model for *Annus Mirabilis*, a choice of judgment over imagination. Ovid is the poet of passions, delighting the imagination and the fancy; Virgil is praised for "accuracy in the Expression" (I, 47, 119). Ovid excels in wit and suddenness of expression; Virgil, by contrast, speaks most often in his own person (I, 47, 130). The claims for Virgil seem surprisingly humble; the contrast between Ovid and Virgil is heightened by a compar-ison of the poets' handling of Dido and Myrrha. Dido, Dry-den admits, is well described by Virgil, yet Virgil "must yield in that to the *Myrrha*, the *Biblis*, the *Althaea*, of *Ovid*. . . . *Ovid* has touch'd those tender strokes more delicately then *Virgil* could" (I, 47, 134-138). This is a curious way to prepare for claiming Virgil as your master, by humbling him below Ovid in the faculties of invention and expression. The extended comparison between Ovid and Virgil aims to establish Dryden as judicious arbiter; yet the elevation of Ovid and the praise of his faculties is itself a preparation for the meaning of the model which Dryden has claimed. Dryden chose Virgil as his master in *Annus Mirabilis* because Virgil is the poet of accurate representation: "we see the objects he represents us with in their native figures, in their proper motions" (I, 47, 140-141). How appropriate for a historian; against lure and inclination, Dryden turns from Ovid and the imagination to the humbler virtues of exactitude.

Virgil is Dryden's guide in *Annus Mirabilis*. Such a choice ought to enhance the poem's claim to epic status, but Dryden uses Virgil to reinforce his claim for this poem as history. Nor is the attempt to define the poem as history limited to the discussion of literary models and modes. Bent to the same purpose is the claim for accuracy of technical language. Dryden makes a point of insisting on the proper terms for naval warfare because he wants to claim for his poem the exactitude, down to the smallest detail, of historical writing (I, 45, 65-77). This poet has schooled himself in technical language because he aims disinterestedly at history; the poem is an exercise of judgment and not of fancy.

Even the most conventional of panegyric materials in the preface is tinged with the business of history. Toward the middle of the preface, following the discussion of naval warfare, Dryden stumbles on an occasion to do a set piece of praise for the royal family: "this I have written of them is much better then what I have perform'd on any other. I have been forc'd to help out other Arguments, but this has been bountiful to me . . . without my cultivating, it has given me two Harvests in a Summer, and in both oppress'd the Reaper" (I, 46, 82-88). More than thirty years later, in the *Dedication* to *Fables*, Dryden returned to the same figure and the same language, "I have sometimes been forc'd to amplify on others; but here, where the Subject is so fruitful, that the Harvest overcomes the Reaper, I am shorten'd by my Chain, and can only see

41

what is forbidden me to reach" (IV, 1441, 95-97). The co-incidence is arresting; it suggests something like a repertoire of figures and strategies of praise. What is especially interesting is the admission of vulnerability, here to charges of conventional excess. Such an admission is a central technique in Dryden's writing, one that he learned to exercise with considerable subtlety. By acknowledging vulnerability to charges of conventional excess, Dryden sets off this panegyric as one "extorted" from its subject. The praise has not been elaborated by the arts of the poet, it comes relentlessly "without my cultivating." The strategy of admitting to one kind of disingenuousness in order to define another statement as truth itself is an important ploy for Dryden, nowhere more cleverly used than in the admission in the preface to *Absalom and Achitophel*, where the poet allows that he has distorted his subject in order to win an audience among the "more Moderate sort" (I, 215, 15-16). Dryden admits vulnerability where it can do least damage and by such frankness aims to establish greater credibility.

Such credibility and the technique of proclaimed artlessness are the informing principles of another device in the preface to *Annus Mirabilis* and a technique repeated often in the prefatory work. For the digressiveness of the preface is, in fact, a piece of imposture. It is a way of suggesting and maintaining the pretense of uncalculated address. The "Letter to the Honorable, Sir Robert Howard" begins with poetics, but Dryden is unable to keep his mind altogether on that subject. The whole of the letter is given a loose epistolary manner; but such digressiveness is not evidence of a lack of concentration. By claiming a digressive character for the whole, a casual and associative logic, the poet argues politics under various pretexts and simultaneously urges on his audience both his honesty and disinterestedness. Dryden aims for us to feel a connection between the "artless" manner of the preface—the open confession that he aims only at truth and not at wonder—and the posture of the panegyrist who admits to artfulness on other occasions in order to stress the truth of this praise and the guileless character of the admission. And the whole is given an air of a casual digression.

The prefatory material to *Annus Mirabilis* establishes a central literary preoccupation of this poet and illustrates a number of his strategies. The preface is the first example of political writing disguised as literary discussion, and it shows us how many strategies Dryden already had in his repertoire at this early date: the engagement of the opposition by denying enmity, the pose of historical disinterestedness, the self-conscious and polemically minded choice of literary modes and models, the use of literary criticism for polemical argument, and the use of digression as a pretense for honesty and plainness.

And it is this last gesture that links the preface to *Annus Mirabilis* with Dryden's first major work of literary theory, the *Essay of Dramatic Poesy* (1668).[9] The *Essay* is literary discourse and not political argument, and I do not intend to discover political statement here.[10] There is, however, an interesting continuity of strategic manner from the preface to *Annus Mirabilis*, and this manner points to later work, as well. The preface to *Annus Mirabilis* closes with the trope of guileless digression; the *Essay* opens with a dedicatory letter to Charles Sackville: "As I was lately reviewing my loose papers, amongst the rest I found this Essay, the writing of which, in this rude and indigested manner wherein your Lordship now sees it, served as an amusement to me in the country, when the violence of the last plague had driven me from the town" (Ker I, 23, 1-6).[11] Like the appeal to Howard, "But I am sensible I have presum'd too far, to entertain you with a rude discourse of that Art, which you both know so well" (I, 48, 165-166), the stance is of the candid and artless amateur.

The claim for a rude and indigested manner is one that Dryden repeatedly made, a signal of the "artless" character of what follows. The link between this signal and the claim that Dryden makes for honesty or denial of artifice is explicit at the end of the dedicatory epistle to *The Indian Emperor*: "It is an irregular piece, if compared with many of Corneille's, and, if I may make a judgment of it, written with more flame than art; in which it represents the mind and intentions of the author, who is with more zeal and integrity, than design and artifice, Madam, Your Grace's most obedient, And most obliged servant, John Dryden."[12] In place of "jumbled and artless" read "uncalculated and honest." One set of terms is used to cover another, and the motivation for the cover is not difficult to locate. How much simpler to claim in one's own interests artlessness rather than honesty, especially when the apparently casual structure of a composition can be cited as proof. And it is exactly Dryden's manner that he should at once claim honesty, construct his own evidence, and all the while busily deny design and covertness.

The claim for such artless amateurism is one that Dryden was to find repeated occasion to make. Listen to the opening gesture of the *Preface* to *Religio Laici*: "A Poem with so bold a Title, and a Name prefix'd, from which the handling of so serious a Subject wou'd not be expected, may reasonably oblige the Author, to say somewhat in defence both of himself, and of his undertaking" (I, 302, 1-4). And, again, at the opening of the *Preface* to *Fables*: " 'Tis with a Poet, as with a Man who designs to build, and is very exact, as he supposes, in casting up the Cost beforehand: But, generally speaking, he is mistaken in his Account, and reckons short of the Expence he first intended: . . . So has it hapned to me" (IV, 1444, 1-6). The guileless amateur was an identity that situated the poet at the very fringes of expertise, disarming the controversial character of what was to follow. Amateurism was also a stylistic ploy, a conscious disavowal of artifice and guile.

The topos with which Dryden opens the *Essay*—composition away from books—was of course a signal for such amateurism.[13] It was also an echo of Sidney at the opening of the *Defence*.[14] Dryden would have us perceive the *Essay* as casual and unpolemical, a tone obviously appropriate to the character that he creates for Neander, that model of casual sobriety in the *Essay*; yet he means for us to understand that this essay is also a major literary statement, a lineal descendant of Sidney's *Defence*. The formal device of the dialogue allowed Dryden to play the artless amateur and function as master ventriloquist. It is, of course, Dryden who supplies the language and with it the exact thrust of each position in the *Essay*. Yet as he does so, he claims the stance of disinterested scribe; he himself has been unable to reconcile the differences of opinion that emerge from the dialogue. Is this genuine perplexity or a way of giving the *Essay* some critical anonymity? "I will give your Lordship the relation of a dispute betwixt some of our wits upon this subject, in which they did not only speak of plays in verse, but mingled . . . many of the modern ways of writing; . . . 'tis true, they differed in their opinions, as 'tis probable they would: neither do I take upon me to reconcile, but to relate them" (Ker I, 26-27, 32-37). And if such candor and impartiality are not sufficient, the dedicatory epistle ends with the example of Tacitus: "*sine studio partium, aut irâ*, without passion or interest; leaving your Lordship to decide it in favour of which part you shall judge most reasonable . . ." (Ker I, 27, 7-10). This is a variant of the disinterested history of the preface to *Annus Mirabilis* and of the preface to *Absalom and Achitophel*. Dryden adopted the guise of amateur and historian because such positions gave him a freedom of movement and a cover, because they were a literary and political convenience, because the screen of other men's voices and opinions was more easily disclaimed than one's own. These stylistic and strategic claims seem to me to be of a piece throughout the career; the point of departure is invariably candor and modesty. There is a psychological component to the self-presentation, but it is also a strategic move. Such modesty was one way of entering into sharp polemic; however pointedly Dryden came to engage his rhetorical and political opponents, the prefatory stance aimed to disarm.

The claims that Dryden was to make in the prefaces and criticism on such subjects as poetry and history are more telling as strategy than as theory. Often and importantly, Dryden claims the role of historian and means by that that he has eschewed fancy for judgment, interest for impartiality; yet this is not a definitive stance. Where it suits his purposes, he can negotiate between the conflicting claims of poetry and history as "truth." In the *Dedication* to *The Indian Emperor*, Dryden wrote of his subject, "[Montezuma's] story is, perhaps, the greatest which was ever represented in a poem of this nature; the action of it including the discovery and conquest of a new world. In it I have neither wholly followed the truth of the history, nor altogether left it; but have taken all the liberty of a poet to add, alter, or diminish, as I thought might best conduce to the beautifying of my work; it being not the business of a poet to represent historical truth, but probability."[15] And in the dedication of *Tyrannick Love* (1670), where Dryden paints the virtues of his patron in a manner that must have set Dr. Johnson's teeth on edge, he throws poetry and history into sharper opposition. Having dwelt on Monmouth's youth, beauty, and courage, Monmouth's great "desire to oblige," Dryden closes the dedication, "This, and all that I can say on so excellent and large a subject, is only history, in which fiction has no part; I can employ nothing of poetry in it."[16]

The rival claims for poetry and history come from the same decade, and I quote them not to show that Dryden contradicted himself but that he was perfectly willing to use conventional literary topoi or variations on such as suited his immediate purposes. He can, of course, accommodate the familiar continuities and juxtapositions of historical and prophetic truth, contrasting the example of Lucan as "religious historian" with Lucan as heroic poet "not tied to a bare representation of what is true, or exceeding probable; but that he may let himself loose to visionary objects, and . . . [have] a freer scope for imagination" (Ker, I, 153, 11-16). And yet such claims for poetry as vision are directly opposite to those Dryden felt called upon to make in the preface to *Annus Mirabilis*. In the preface to *Absalom and Achitophel*, where Dryden claims the mantle of religious historian with such stunning ingenuity, he invokes the sanctity of Scripture as prophetic truth while denying to himself anything of the prophet's vocation; the rivalries and contradictions of historical and prophetic truth are held here in a delicate tension. The traditional claims for poetry and history are made without a belief in the consistent authority of either position. I suspect that Dryden found himself capable of believing in both; he adopted whatever role suited immediate needs; usefulness dictated theory.

The point of my argument is not to deny that such models as skepticism or neoclassicism allow us to see the whole of Dryden's critical career from a perspective that assimilates contradictory positions, but to insist that Dryden was a working poet who could not in the 1670s and 1680s have seen his own career with much leisure or distance. It may not have occurred to Dryden that what came off the page as contradiction could have been, or needed to have been, reconciled in larger theoretical terms. Dryden's immediate concerns were sharp and pressing, and often of an explicitly polemical character; under such duress, theoretical consistency would not have been a very important consideration. Practical politics were, and nowhere is this more obvious than in the prefatory statement to *Absalom and Achitophel*.

" 'Tis not my intention to make an Apology for my *Poem*: Some will think it needs no Excuse; and others will receive none" (I, 215, 1-2). The opening gesture is an effort to defuse partisanship, to elevate the poem above the cross fire of a pamphlet war—a strategy that marked the opening of the preface to *Annus Mirabilis*. But in the highly polarized atmosphere of Exclusion, the idea of denying partisanship altogether could not have been effectual. Dryden's strategy is therefore to allow the unhappy fact of partisanship and to portray himself as victim rather than instrument of party. With reluctance and regret, this honest poet admits to the effects of political partisanship on literary judgment: "The Design, I am sure, is honest: but he who draws his Pen for one Party, must expect to make Enemies of the other. For, *Wit* and *Fool*, are Consequents of *Whig* and *Tory*: And every man is a Knave or an Ass to the contrary side" (I, 215, 2-5). Poetry ought to be above party, and yet in such a polemicized atmosphere, an innocent effort to heal and to settle will fall into the vortex of partisanship. The self-portrait argues the poet as judicious advocate of the middle way, friend of moderation, artless patriot who admits to softening divisive truths in order to win friends and influence enemies. Moreover, to advocate moderation while at the same time calling for repression and revenge was not necessarily to engage in a fully conscious deception. There were those who believed that Stuart kingship in the person of James, duke of York, was indeed the best way to preserve balance and liberty.[17] Whether Dryden was among them we have no way of knowing; what we do know is that this is the position that *Absalom and Achitophel* relentlessly advocates, and that Dryden chose to advocate such a position by denying partisanship as far as he was capable, representing a partisan position as the middle way, and posing as dispassionate historian.

"If I happen to please the more Moderate sort, I shall be sure of an honest Party; and, in all probability, of the best Judges; for, the least Concern'd, are commonly the least Corrupt: And, I confess, I have laid in for those, by rebating the *Satyre*, (where Justice woud allow it) from carrying too sharp an Edge" (I, 215, 15-19). Here is the familiar admission of vulnerability, here is modesty and an exemplary caution strategically posed to disarm the opponent and to attract all those whom the poet might engage by such frankness. The strategy is to represent the poet in his own person, a man among men striving for truth, liable as others to pitfalls, and eager to confess distortion. The confession of modest distortion is especially clever; not only does it allow the poet to confess vulnerability to such charges, it enables him to anticipate and by such anticipation to disarm objections to the rhetorical meaning of such confession, "if you are a Malitious *Reader*, I expect you should return upon me, that I affect to be thought more Impartial than I am. But, if men are not to be judg'd by their Professions, God forgive you *Common-wealths-men*, for professing so plausibly for the Government" (I, 215, 24-27). Dryden understood the calculus of political language in the 1680s; he knew the value and vulnerability of "confession"; he understood his own vulnerability. Who in such an exposed position could have maintained innocence for very long? Dryden's confession of impartiality is a gesture that aims to win confidence and to heighten the plausibility of a whole panoply of claims for disinterestedness that unfolds in this preface and in the poem itself. Moreover, while the poet engages in this deception and disarms suspicion by acknowledging his own awareness of the extent and plausibility of such suspicion, he launches a countercharge of deception against his partisan enemies, whom he casually labels as *"Common-wealths-men."* Commonwealthsman was a slander, an act of opprobrium; it sought to connect those who advocated the exclusion of the duke of York with the men who had sought the death of Charles I and had wrought such hideous change on the body politic. But the string of such associations is not itself the subject of Dryden's elaboration here; the epithet is casually dropped in the middle of a sentence that is busy with other effects. For Dryden's central concern here is to camouflage his own efforts at disguise with charges of deceit against his enemies "professing so plausibly." For "plausibly" read "artfully" or "disingenuously." The whole is, of course, an elaborate sleight of hand in which Dryden mounts an attack by confessing vulnerability to its very terms and then retrieves from such a confession a weapon with which to vindicate his own honesty and to engage the opponent, those professing commonwealthsmen.

The same technique of attack through denial emerges again in the penultimate and final paragraphs. This disinterested satirist, this physician to the state, harbors not so much as an uncharitable wish toward Achitophel; he writes only to prevent an amputation "which I wish not to my very Enemies" (I, 216, 61). What, however, are we to think of the first assertion in light of *The Medall*, or of the second in light of the conclusion of this poem, at which David draws the sword of justice and we contemplate the bloody effects of such justice? The poem advocates that a surgery be performed on the body politic, that a diseased limb be sacrificed in order to save the state, and that limb is not the duke of York.

But the mode of the preface is not assertion and argument; its manner is casual; the structure is associative; the self-presentation is by turns self-denying and acidulous, the tone both hesitant and combative. The whole is a concoction of paradoxical, even contradictory, elements. And the poem itself is a similar triumph of contradictions. The preface is an education for and a brilliant anticipation of the poem. Its complexity shakes our balance; its claims of honesty and even-handedness anticipate the numerous signals that the poem will make of that order. And yet for all the disclaimers of party, can either preface or poem be read with any doubt about partisanship? Dryden's contemporaries did not think so, and it is only by loosening our grip on the detailed engagement of preface and poem with partisan political issues that we might come to think that the poet's claims of disinterestedness and honesty ought to be treated as something other than gesture. Of course, the preface does not have the scope or ambition of the poem, but it is a telling exercise, and our untangling of its components and gestures is an appropriate preparation for the poem.

How the poet was interested in being perceived or what he wanted to be perceived as advocating are not necessarily the same as what his poem actually advocates. The *Essay of Dramatic Poesy* is prefaced by a letter in which Dryden poses as an innocent, a man slightly perplexed by the opinions he has recorded. He is hesitant and unsteady and eager to please. But of course there is sleight of hand here, and it resides not only in the dramatization of opinions, in the character which Dryden chooses for himself in the *Essay*, and in the thinly veiled historical references, but in Dryden's whole encounter with the subjects and characters of the *Essay*. He would have us perceive himself as diffident and naive, and yet the whole engagement with Crites is a subtle and masterful put-down. The dramatic form allowed Dryden not only to characterize through language—and through language Crites emerges as grating and self-important—but also to argue the character through dramatic action, to show his vanity and rudeness and to have such vanity defeated by the elegant dispatch of Eugenius and Lisideius.

The dramatic format of the *Essay* heightens our interest in the literary topics; the encounter among personalities animates the meaning of these theoretical positions; and the setting on the Thames is an elegant stroke of the imagination.

But what seems absolutely characteristic of this poet is that he should discover ways of indulging private agendas in the midst of high-brow business, indeed under cover of that very business. Of course, the primary impulse here is not vindictiveness, but Dryden felt no contradiction between vendetta and literary theory. Such animus can be discovered over and again, and often in rather surprising places, in the English Virgil, for example, which Dryden made in the last decade of his life, a translation whose scope embraced the demands of heroic poetry, the imperatives of ideology and politics, and also the passion for revenge; for Dryden these were not sharply different issues.

The *Preface* to *Religio Laici* is the longest introduction that Dryden wrote for an original poem, and the opening gestures are familiar indeed. Here is the characteristic modesty, the hesitant claims of the amateur, the marginal authority which a layman might claim on such a "bold" occasion.[18] Here is the familiar admission of "weakness and want of Learning" (I, 302, 9), the claims of honesty and disinterestedness, even the trick of confessing some slight infraction or imprudence. But the maneuvers that mark its opening are not sustained through the *Preface*. The emotional and rhetorical center of the *Preface* is the savage attack on dissenting politics which in tone and stance is closer to *The Medall* than to either the mock humility of the opening of the *Preface* or the cool reasonableness of the poem's first lines. The savage attack on dissenters is part of a dialectic; it appears only after elaborate preparation. The *Preface* begins with a familiar gesture, the modest disclaimer.

"A Poem with so bold a Title, and a Name prefix'd, from which the handling of so serious a Subject wou'd not be expected, may reasonably oblige the Author, to say somewhat in defence both of himself, and of his undertaking" (I, 302, 1-4). The opening sentence disarms the reader by arguing the unlikely, even untenable character of what is to follow. Here are no claims to universal truth; this poet is no judge of faith in others—though in fact he will soon enough perform in such a capacity—only a humble confessor of his own. And yet confession is the mode neither of *Preface* nor poem. On the heels of this disclaimer, the poet begins to assemble some arms with which to "Combat Irreligion" and "Enemies of Piety." And though such an arsenal is acknowledged, where there is intellectual disinterestedness and charity we can hardly expect harsh combat. Skepticism guides the intellect (I, 302, 22); charity guides the heart (I, 302, 20-21; 305, 107); hence, the reference to the poet's philosophical "Scepticism" and the long excursus on the Preface to the Creed of St. Athanasius. And despite urgings of caution and prudence, Dryden ventures into dangerous territory by allowing the rights of heathens to salvation, denying—in all due modesty—the tenets of St. Athanasius.

There is not much sense in asking whether or not Dryden believed that heathens could have achieved salvation before Christ or without knowledge of Him; there is no reason to suspect that he did not believe such.[19] What is more interesting to wonder at is the rhetorical motive that might have led him into this excursus on St. Athanasius. Of the many problems that were pressing the Anglican Church at this moment—and the subsequent attacks on Catholicism and sectarianism give ample scope to those immediate issues—there was not in the early 1680s a heated debate over the preface to this Creed as a tool with which to combat Socinianism.[20] The long excursus—and Dryden's admission of its unintended length is a variant of the familiar confession of digressive looseness—has two points. First, it allows the poet to express a personal religious conviction, one that was, despite the claim of abandoning prudence, as uncontroversial as any reader could have wanted. Who indeed would have opposed the principle of charity? Moreover, in stressing the personal character and private opinion expressed in the excursus, Dryden substantiates the claims of genre, a layman's confession of faith. Second, and more importantly, the excursus establishes, through the claims of charity, two polemical points: it prefaces the bitter attack on sectarianism with a high-minded example of personal charity; and, more diffusely, it links the poet's personal charity with a political position of the king. The whole of the long Stuart campaign against penal laws was conducted under the guise of charity. And such is the guise that James II would wear in his most injurious attacks on the Anglican Church. Charity is a hand that Dryden will play again and at greater length in *The Hind and the Panther*. Of course, in that poem, Dryden softens the attacks on dissenters and accuses the Anglican Church of the voracity with which he now charges both Catholics and sectarians. But charity was the personal banner of Charles II; charity and generosity of spirit are leitmotifs for the king in *Absalom and Achitophel*. And here in the *Preface* to *Religio Laici*, Dryden aligns himself with the court's position on salvation and religious belief through the attack on Athanasius.

There is, of course, something of a paradox in this poem of Anglican charity that is more savage toward Protestant dissenters than toward heathens, papists, and deists. But theology is not the central concern of the *Preface*, or the poem, despite its claims for theological learning and despite the exposition of what looks like theological matter. The attack on dissenters has nothing to do with belief; it is wholly a matter of politics, for Dryden means to link Protestant sectarianism with regicide and republicanism.[21] The harvest of the Protestant reformation was the execution of the martyr king, and another such crop is likely to follow, "nay I fear 'tis unavoidable if the Conventiclers be permitted still to scatter" (I, 309, 302-303). Such prophecy has little to do with the modest demurs of the opening of the *Preface*. But by the middle of the *Preface*, Dryden has turned fully from a confession of faith to politics in 1682, to the Tory revenge which was to see its culmination in the judicial murders of Russell and Sidney. Such is the mood in the second half of the *Preface*; the stance at its opening is a guise subtly elaborated through the first two hundred lines that allowed a new point of entry into political controversy.[22]

For how else might we characterize such a passage: "Thus Sectaries, we may see, were born with teeth, foul-mouth'd and scurrilous from their Infancy: and if Spiritual Pride, Venome, Violence, Contempt of Superiours and Slander had been the marks of Orthodox Belief; the Presbytery and the rest of our

Schismaticks, which are their Spawn, were always the most visible Church in the Christian World" (I, 309, 275-280). The vehemence of tone and the harshness of irony show a surprising similarity to Dryden's stance in *The Medall*. But what distinguishes this preface and poem from the tactics of assault and battery that Dryden practiced in *The Medall* is the effort to present even such attack under the guise of moderation. For that, indeed, is the tactic of even this gesture in the *Preface*.

The structure of the *Preface* is binary; one half is concerned with personal faith, the other with political behavior. The point of connection between them is Dryden's assertion that by declaring his own belief in the canon of Scripture he has "unavoidably created to my self two sorts of Enemies: The Papists indeed, more directly . . . and the Fanaticks more collaterally" (I, 306, 147-151). What follows is an analysis of these enemies in the form of dialectic. The mode of argument, pitching one extreme against another, inevitably produces a mean, which happens to be the Anglican Church.[23] Here again is the victory of the middle way, though from the savagery of the attack, moderation is a peculiar victor. The methods of *Preface* and poem show how closely aligned are the two great poems of the "middle way," *Absalom and Achitophel* and *Religio Laici*. Not only does Dryden press claims of honesty and disinterestedness in both prefaces, though they are given a different turn in the preface to the religious poem, but the whole practice of conflating the sanctity of religion with politics is a fundamental ploy in both poems. And the convenience of scriptural language, particularly the language of Protestant theology, for political argument is apparent in both works. That Dryden himself should have denounced such a ploy in other men (I, 306, 152-154) is hardly reason to believe that he would find it inconvenient to practice the same conflation for his own ends.

Not only is the self-presentation as moderate in religion and politics similar in the two prefaces, they also share the technique of veiled threat against the sectaries, for it is with such a threat that Dryden closes the attack: "They may think themselves to be too roughly handled in this Paper; but I who know best how far I could have gone on this Subject, must be bold to tell them they are spar'd: though at the same time I am not ignorant that they interpret the mildness of a Writer to them, as they do the mercy of the Government; in the one they think it Fear, and conclude it Weakness in the other" (I, 310, 328-333). The threat is a close variant of Dryden's retort in the preface to *Absalom and Achitophel*: "They, who can Criticize so weakly, as to imagine I have done my Worst, may be Convinc'd, at their own Cost, that I can write Severely, with more ease, than I can Gently" (I, 215, 19-21). And perhaps a similar topos in the dedication to *Eleonora* is an echo of the earlier stance, "They say my Talent is Satyre; if it be so, 'tis a Fruitful Age; and there is an extraordinary Crop to gather. But a single hand is insufficient for such a Harvest" (II, 584, 101-103). The implication that what has been delivered is only the shadow of what could follow is the reverse of the modesty topos. Nor is it surprising to find them both in the same work. While the first feigns impotence, the second suggests hidden power. In both cases the exaggeration is argued for tactical reasons; vulnerability and hidden power are both misrepresentations; in their rawest form I suspect that neither could have inspired much belief; but they are seldom delivered by Dryden in a very raw format.

The stylistic claims at the close of the *Preface* to *Religio Laici* are important both in their own terms and in relation to other such claims. Dryden's citation of precedent and model takes us back again to *Annus Mirabilis* where style argues kind and intent. Here Dryden claims the Horatian manner in order to argue that *Religio Laici* is a poem designed "purely for Instruction" (I, 311, 347). Here the poet eschews the florid, the elevated and figurative way; as in *Annus Mirabilis*, the function of the verse is not to move the passions but to instruct the reason. Honesty is linked with the "middle way"; the epistolary style is a midpoint between the high and low manner in rhetoric. The pitch for honesty is made in the same literary terms as the claim for historical accuracy in the preface to *Annus Mirabilis*. A tactical alignment is effected between style and the Anglican synthesis, midway between the errors of popery and sectarianism. The middle way is a stylistic moment and a theological position. And the claim is repeated at the poem's close (I, 322, 451-456). The casual epistolary manner is as careful a calculation with as sharply polemical intent as the most wicked satirical portrait in *Absalom and Achitophel*. The posture of modest confession and the techniques of dialectical reasoning that aim not at persuasion but at truthfulness do not begin to describe either the intent or the scope of *Preface* or poem; they are about as accurate a representation of the resources of *Religio Laici* as moderation is an account of the politics of *Absalom and Achitophel*.

Perhaps the relative calm of the years following the defeat of Exclusion are reflected in Dryden's stance as religious philosopher. Whatever threats the sectaries might be seen to have posed during the crisis, the Tory stability during the years of Charles's personal rule was genuine. Dryden lost no occasion to heap opprobrium on a discredited party, but the stance and manner of the poet in *Religio Laici* do not suggest a frightened man. Although the claims of modesty and philosophical disinterestedness that open the *Preface* to *Religio Laici* belie its scope and harshness—a harshness that suggests politics rather than theology has moved this layman to his confession of faith—the fact that he should have chosen the format of personal confession rather than satiric attack is itself some measure of a momentarily leisured mood. Nothing, I think, could be farther from the psychological moment of *The Hind and the Panther* than such ease.

Dryden's longest and most elaborate invention is *The Hind and the Panther*; there are no close seconds, and length is only the beginning. The poem has three main divisions and subsections within those parts; we find fables hidden within fables, talking beasts, satiric portraits, hidden morals, allegories, and enigmas. This is the most complicated of Dryden's works, and there is a direct relation between this poem's complexity and the political difficulties that Dryden faced as he took up his defense of James's Declaration of Indulgence, the king's reign in general, and his own conversion to Rome. Dryden claimed personal confession in *Religio Laici*; it came to be the case in *The Hind and the Panther*, not the least of whose many interesting moments comes when the poet attempts to find a voice for his confession of new religious conviction.

The allegory of *Absalom and Achitophel* is a triumph of wit. The idea of such historical allegory was not, of course, original with Dryden,[24] but no one had played this particular game with such verve. Here is poetry with a key done to the hilt. Fitting the politicians to the portraits was a puzzle that Dryden's contemporaries solved with apparent pleasure. First editions are covered with names, and keys were quickly produced in manuscript and printed form.[25] There could not have been much doubt about the identity of the main characters, and even the minor figures, Amnon excepted, were easily unveiled. But the allegory of *The Hind and the Panther* is another story. Instead of keys, Dryden's contemporaries published imitations ridiculing the poem. Of course, Dryden's conversion had made him an obvious target for such attack, but the imitations not only struck at the poet, they also took literary issue with his invention. They thought the poem was vulnerable as a poem; it was for them long and ridiculous.[26] It violated the proprieties of the beast fable; it was too complicated; it was difficult and preposterous to pursue the niceties of theology when beasts discoursed on Arianism and the authority of the oral tradition. *The Hind and the Panther* suggested Aesop, but where was the moral of this fable? Who was the Buzzard? Whom should the swallows fear? How are the chickens and the pigeons like the Goths and Vandals who demolished Rome? Small wonder that in the California *Dryden*, the text should occupy sixty pages and the notes should run to one hundred thirty-two pages. And even after such labor, some issues defy historical reconstruction. We still have not decided so fundamental a question as the identity of the Buzzard. Is this Bishop Burnet or William, prince of Orange? It is as if we couldn't decide whether Achitophel were meant to depict Monmouth or Shaftesbury. Such confusion is unthinkable in *Absalom and Achitophel*, but it is fundamental to *The Hind and the Panther*. The obscurity is deliberate; the intricacies of the poem were an effort to complicate issues that for most men were very clear indeed. By the time that this poem was published in May of 1687, most Englishmen were quite clear about James's identity: he was the Pope's lieutenant in the subjugation of the English nation; he intended, by all legal and illegal means, to exterminate the northern heresy; and the Declaration of Indulgence was but his latest trick to defy the law, to ignore custom and privilege, to enslave the nation to Rome. These were not obscure issues, and there can be little wonder that Dryden chose either to ignore them or to imbed them in the most intricate folds of this allegorical poem whose every line Dryden knew would be parsed with malice and care.

And where the poem takes the offensive through direct satire, the poet argues that he aims only at the refractory few, and then denies satiric intention altogether. "There are in it two *Episodes*, or *Fables*, which are interwoven with the main Design; so that they are properly parts of it. . . . In both of these I have made use of the Common Places of *Satyr*, whether true or false, which are urg'd by the Members of the one Church against the other. At which I hope no *Reader* of either Party will be scandaliz'd; because they are not of my Invention: but as old, to my knowledge, as the Times of *Boccace* and *Chawcer* on the one side, and as those of the Reformation on the other" (II, 469-470, 100-107). How clever and how familiar. Dryden cannot attest to the truth of his satiric topoi nor can he even claim to have invented them; these are just some ancient saws that have conveniently come his way. We are reminded of the modesty of the *Essay of Dramatic Poesy*, of the distance of the historian at a number of junctures in the career, and of the disguise of translation that would increasingly become Dryden's own in the years that followed James's demise. The pose of translator and the art of translation were, in fact, a convenience and a passion that would determine most of his literary work in the last decade of the century when he assumed the stance and topoi of Juvenal and Persius, Chaucer and Boccaccio, Ovid and Virgil.

But the strategies of the preface to *The Hind and the Panther* are more complex than simple disclaimer, for Dryden was not quite ready to retire into his final guise. "The Nation is in too high a Ferment, for me to expect either fair War, or even so much as fair Quarter from a Reader of the opposite Party" (II, 467, 1-2). Here is the same account of a politicized readership that we meet in *Absalom and Achitophel*; indeed the opening sentences of these two prefaces are remarkably similar. In both, Dryden claims that political crisis denies him the possibility of a fair hearing, and while he attributes sharp partisanship to the nation, his own posture is a familiar composite of humility and moderation, the man caught between parties, not the poet laureate striking from a position of authority and political commitment. "He who draws his Pen for one Party, must expect to make Enemies of the other. For, *Wit* and *Fool*, are Consequents of *Whig* and *Tory*: And every man is a Knave or an Ass to the contrary side" (*Absalom and Achitophel*, "To the Reader," I, 215, 3-5). "All Men are engag'd either on this side or that: and tho' Conscience is the common *Word*, which is given by both, yet if a Writer fall among Enemies, and cannot give the Marks of *Their* Conscience, he is knock'd down before the Reasons of his own are heard" (*The Hind and the Panther*, "To the Reader," II, 467, 2-6). The positioning at the beginning of the two prefaces is remarkably similar, even to the extent of denying the efficacy of preface altogether; in such an atmosphere and among such readers, apology is quite useless. As in the earlier prefaces, the point from which Dryden begins to argue is weakness, or impotence—a candid admission of defeat. Having displayed such candor, the poet then defines his own position as the middle ground. As in the prefaces to *Absalom and Achitophel* and *Religio Laici*, the opening tactic leads to an argumentative swath cut between extremes. Dryden's appeal is always to the moderate center, the still point of honesty and tolerance. That still point is not, of course, always to be found in the same place. In the *Preface* to *Religio Laici*, the Anglican Church occupied the vulnerable territory between dangerous extremes; now it is the Catholic Church to be found cowering between rapacious Anglicans and refractory dissenters. In 1682, the dissenters were poised for rebellion, a ruthless community of strife.

In 1687, the Anglican Church strikes the same dangerous pos-
ture. My point in raising the inconsistencies is not to discover
that Dryden's perception of religion was determined by polit-
ical allegiance—we have been tutored in that issue long
enough—but rather to show how the rhetorical strategies that
Dryden chose ought to be considered as vehicles of argument
and persuasion rather than as principles. The "middle way"
was not a philosophical issue for Dryden but a polemical sit-
uation; it was the ground to occupy because it permitted the
poet to portray whomever he perceived as his enemies as men
who ran to extremes. And extremes were points on the polit-
ical and religious spectrum studiously to be avoided. The
"middle way" was a rhetorical strategy, and its repeated in-
vocation in quite contradictory circumstances ought to sug-
gest the degree to which it was gesture rather than belief.

The preface to *The Hind and the Panther* argues that the
king's Declaration was an act of piety and generosity. Dry-
den's aim is to depict policy as personality in an effort to deny
the Anglican attack on the Declaration as a political maneuver.
Anglicans were convinced that the Declaration was a way of
driving Catholics and dissenters into convenient alliance against
the Church of England and a method for the staffing of army
and government posts with Catholics, a strategy that the king
could not legally pursue so long as the Test Act was in place.
The effort to turn the Declaration into an expression of the
king's character is reminiscent of the use of generosity in *Ab-
salom and Achitophel*, and generosity and tolerance are also linked
to the Roman Catholic Church itself. In *The Hind and the
Panther*, Dryden's strategy is to depict the Catholic Church as
victim of Anglican rapacity, and the preface is an opening
move in that strategy. Indeed, the notion of the Church as
victim and the Anglican party as the brutal and rapacious en-
emy is both a general argument and a piece of self-presenta-
tion, nowhere more obvious than in Dryden's conflation of
sovereign, savior, and poet (II, 511, 298-305).

Why, then, Dryden's effort to disclaim any knowledge of
the Declaration? "If I had so soon expected [it], I might have
spar'd my self the labour of writing many things which are

contain'd in the third part of it" (II, 468, 61-62). Perhaps this was true, but I suspect that the argument is also part of the poet's efforts to distance himself from what he and a number of other Catholics perceived as a ruinous court policy.[27] The poem "was neither impos'd on me, nor so much as the Subject given me by any man" (II, 468, 57). If the poet wanted *The Hind and the Panther* to be read as personal testimony, if he were anxious to put some distance between himself and the policies of Father Petre—and I think that the fables in part 3 are strong evidence of such an effort—then the point of the disclaimer comes into focus. That he had undertaken an unpopular cause and an implausible client in *The Hind and the Panther*, I suspect Dryden was acutely and unhappily aware.

Indeed, it might be argued that the demise of James II came as a relief to Dryden. Personally, of course, it was a disaster. The letters from the 1690s show the poet in a constant state of anxiety over money and in frequent political fright. But there is a way of seeing the Glorious Revolution as a stroke of luck for Dryden. Of course, it is hardly fair to argue that from the glories of his old age we have ample evidence of how well the Revolution prompted Dryden's poetry. The Revolution forced Dryden back to the stage and to the writing of one of his finest plays, *Don Sebastian*; financial exigency argued the wisdom of a subscription *Virgil*, the great literary monument of the 1690s. But there is another way in which we might hear in the poetry that Dryden wrote after the Revolution a sigh of relief. For in those fables and translations Dryden now might act a more independent role than in the past. The Revolution freed him from the burdens of having to link political ideals with political figures. That he may not have seen his own circumstance in quite this way is, of course, not simply possible but likely. And yet political ideals could now be propounded in the realm of high fantasy rather than on the more obdurate soil of English political life. Less constrained by the particulars of domestic politics, fables and translations might touch, at telling and convenient points, on contemporary details. Heroes and heroines of ancient and modern fictions were more malleable figures than James Stuart and Mary of Modena. How much more graciously those two could be imagined as Pan and Syrinx than in the intractable character of their real historical presence.[28] And indeed there is something about the capaciousness of Dryden's writing in the years after the Revolution that argues such a spirit in general.

Even in the critical and prefatory writing there is an ease, at points a geniality, that expresses the same paradoxical effect of the Revolution on Dryden's literary temper. The *Preface* to the *Fables* is the masterpiece of that disposition, but even in *The Dedication of the Æneis*, Dryden's meditation on Roman history and English politics, the mood is no longer harsh and combative. That Dryden saw Virgil's poem of empire in a melancholy light is crucial to our understanding of both *Dedication* and translation, but that light is quite different from the brilliant and jittery effects that he had earlier achieved in the prefaces to *Absalom and Achitophel*, *Religio Laici*, or *The Hind and the Panther*. The gesture of casual disposition, of digression and laxity, is now both a mood and a strategy to cover the disparate proceedings of the essay with the name of digression. That the far-ranging subjects of the *Dedication* are in fact linked both by a consistent point of view and by a consistent political reading of Virgil is consummately true. But we can also hear in the insistence on disorder and digression an authentic note. Digression is at once anxiety and strategy. Dryden had reached so frequently for this particular cover that habit had become character. The same strategic purposes are still effected through digression, and indeed there is a startling moment of candor about the political meaning of digression in the *Dedication* (III, 1019-1020, 654-664), but what was once simply strategy was now a way of seeing the filaments of connection among disparate subjects and, in turn, a way of structuring an argument. In the prefatory and critical essays of Dryden's last years we witness a marvelous confluence of strategy, habitual manner, and the aesthetics of a late style.

Digression and association had become fundamental aesthetic principles for Dryden, and nowhere is this more obvious than in the composition of *Fables*, where juxtaposition is a mode of analysis and implications are seldom drawn into detailed argument. Both *Preface* and book mark the culmination of a poetic that had been in the making from Dryden's early years. In an obvious way, the Glorious Revolution forced Dryden into yet more cautious procedures; but it also released him from burdensome political obligations. Disenfranchised, Dryden was freed from political programs into beliefs and ideals. The poetic is more leisured, less combative, less programmatically urgent. Dryden was forced from office and power, but he seems to have come into a psychological dispensation that opened new aesthetic possibilities, and this whole complex of political, aesthetic, and psychological currents can be felt throughout the poetry of the 1690s. Of course, the disguise of fable and translation was not Dryden's alone. The last decade of the century saw a remarkable rise in the number of fables and translations that reached print. The Aesop publications are only the most visible of such evidence. How fitting and how likely for a Jacobite and a convicted plotter like Richard Graham, Viscount Preston, to turn from political conspiracy to translating Boethius's *Consolation of Philosophy*.[29] Translation was an ancient and honorable way to practice the art of writing in times of political turmoil.[30] But for many, uncertainty itself was a threat, and fable and translation provided a mediation between uncertainty and statement. There was, of course, a quite palpable reason for Dryden to emerge after the Revolution as translator and fabulist, but the number of publishing Catholic Jacobites was not, after all, very large. What Dryden came to out of need, others adopted as a shield against uncertainty. Nor can we underestimate Dryden's own sensitivity to change and contingency. The delicate and enigmatic lyrics of his last years hint at the perception of a flux darker than political revolution.

But I do not want to exaggerate the autumnal phase of Dryden's poetics to the exclusion of politics and polemical strategy as literary determinants in these years, and the *Dedication of the Æneis* is a powerful example of that nexus of political and literary strategies. The most obvious of the continuities between the *Dedication* and earlier works is Dryden's use of digression and poetics to cover political argument. The method of the essay is casual and disgressive; indeed, Dryden insists that this is an essay altogether without method. The poet seems frequently to lose control of his digressions; they appear without warning and often run to embarrassing length. Early on, Dryden apologizes for detaining his patron longer than he had intended, and yet we have hardly begun by this point (III, 1009, 249 f.). Dryden intends to counter those who have criticized Virgil, yet he seems not to have the necessary books at hand (III, 1009, 252). He relies on authorities to bolster his own arguments, but the defense is conducted in the most casual manner and citations are often but vaguely recalled (III, 1010, 298). His is a loose proceeding, and Dryden is tireless in calling our attention to that fact. He veers steadily away from his subject and then calls himself up short for digression. At one point he must return from his rambling; at another he has again "transgress'd his bounds." Twice he allows that he has spent longer than he intended on a particular subject, and then near the end of the *Dedication*, he suddenly realizes exactly how out of joint these proceedings have become. So much time has been spent in digression that scarcely any space remains for remarks on the translation itself (III, 1045, 1623 f.).

The gestures are of course reminiscent of a whole string of such remarks on the epistolary style, on the casual and discursive manner. As in the earlier essays, digression is partly imposture, allowing Dryden the claim of uncalculated address, while at the same time permitting him to raise a number of polemical issues that he would not want to pose in a "clear and exact method." And nowhere is this more true than in this *Dedication*. Indeed, I think the imperative to use digression in this manner was so deep that Dryden could not restrain himself from hinting exactly at such intent. "When I speak of your Lordship, 'tis never a digression, and therefore I need beg no pardon for it; but take up *Segrais* where I left him: And shall use him less often than I have occasion for him. For his Preface is a perfect piece of Criticism, full and clear, and digested into an exact Method; mine is loose, and, as I intended it, Epistolary. Yet I dwell on many things which he durst not touch: For 'tis dangerous to offend an Arbitrary Master: . . . In short, my Lord, I wou'd not Translate him, because I wou'd bring you somewhat of my own" (III, 1019-1020, 654-662). Dryden eschews Segrais because danger lies in clarity. Segrais could not raise dangerous subjects under an arbitrary master because his essay was full, clear, and digested into an exact method. Can there be any question that the arbitrary master whom Dryden had most on his mind was William III? What cannot be overtly stated might be raised under cover, raised in a dedication that seems devoid of method, structure, and argument. Digression allowed Dryden to explore the political implications of Roman history in a manner that Segrais would not have dared.

The complex analogy that Dryden creates between English and Roman political histories will be fully explored in the chapter on translation; here I want to suggest its center, for in that analogy lies the method of Dryden's digressive manner. The particular thrust of Dryden's reading of Roman history and his presentation of Virgil's motives and method of argument in the *Aeneid* is a conviction that Virgil had written a political poem in which Trojan history masked Roman imperatives. Dryden read the *Aeneid* as Virgil's warning and instructions to Augustus Caesar on the dangers of elective kingship. The center of the analogy was Virgil's portrait of Aeneas drawn to the measure of Caesar. Virgil instructs the emperor and flatters and counsels the nation. In the abandonment of Dido, Virgil permitted his contemporaries to see their own victory over Carthage, and in the piety and determination of Aeneas they will understand the virtues of their own emperor. But such virtues, Virgil warns Augustus, must not be transgressed. In the portraits of Mezentius and Tarquin, Virgil presents vivid images of tyranny and its consequences. What is taken by force or held at the pleasure of the people can be abruptly removed, and Augustus needs the lesson of this poem to avoid the errors of the past. Moreover, the whole of Roman politics in the century of the Caesars is presented as a series of public crimes, one revolution following another, and

65

all conducted for the worst of private motives, and always under the guise of the commonweal.

What brings such a reading into focus is the submerged element of the analogical argument. Dryden seems to be dealing with two halves of an analogy: the myth of Troy and the political history of imperial Rome. But in fact the analogy is threefold, and the hidden element is English political history of the later seventeenth century. The analogies that Dryden pursues are those among Trojan, Roman, and English histories; and Dryden's distortion of the Trojan past must be seen as his way of accommodating Virgil's circumstance to his own: "we are to consider him [Virgil] as writing his Poem in a time when the Old Form of Government was subverted, and a new one just Established by *Octavius Caesar*: In effect by force of Arms, but seemingly by the Consent of the *Roman* People" (III, 1012, 366-369). Dryden takes Roman history as his subject, but the language argues the Jacobite reading of the Glorious Revolution. Dryden uses Roman history to outline the course of politics in later seventeenth-century England: "Thus the *Roman* People were grosly gull'd; twice or thrice over: and as often enslav'd in one Century, and under the same pretence of Reformation" (III, 1013, 418-420). And such application animates Dryden's understanding of the whole of Roman history and informs his use of a series of intriguing details.

When Dryden writes of Tarquin, he strikes not at Virgil's Caesar but at William and Mary; when he discourses on Aeneas's office, he does so in order to force the issue of elective kingship to reflect on William III; and when he catalogues the complex and peculiar genealogy of Latinus, he does so to raise the issue of lineal descent, to argue the contingent character of Aeneas's claim to Latinus' throne, and of course to scorn the legitimacy of the "English" king:

> Our Author shews us another sort of Kingship in the Person of *Latinus*. He was descended from *Saturn*, and as I remember, in the Third Degree. He is describ'd a just and a gracious Prince; solicitous for the Welfare of his People;

always Consulting with his Senate to promote the common Good. We find him at the head of them, when he enters into the Council-Hall. Speaking first, but still demanding their Advice, and steering by it as far as the Iniquity of the Times wou'd suffer him. And this is the proper Character of a King by Inheritance, who is born a Father of his Country. *Æneas*, tho' he Married the Heiress of the Crown, yet claim'd no Title to it during the Life of his Father-in-Law. (III, 1017, 561-571)

Aeneas claimed no title during the life of Latinus, but William seized the throne while James was very much alive. The mode of the commentary is always covert, but the distance between overt and covert materials fluctuates through the historical digressions. In some places, the analogies are daringly open; the material does more than invite application, it seems to insist on contemporary meaning. But at other points, the historical analogy is pursued at more leisure and distance. Dryden did not aim in this preface to run an allegorical commentary on English politics under the cover of Roman terms simply to be discarded once the key had been discovered. He used the Roman past to contemplate English history, and he must have been struck by the deep parallels between the histories of these empires.

Of course, the *Dedication* does not announce itself as such a contemplation. The ostensible subject is heroic poetry. On that theme Dryden begins his essay, "A Heroick Poem, truly such, is undoubtedly the greatest Work which the Soul of Man is capable to perform" (III, 1003, 1-2); and on that theme he turns an appropriate and no doubt fully anticipated set of variations. The remarks on heroic poetry pay homage to the authorities whom Dryden quotes, paraphrases, and perhaps even plagiarizes. But these remarks are not the heart of his essay. They have been criticized as derivative and lifeless. And I suspect that Dryden knew this, that he performed in the manner of commentator because he knew that these remarks were not only appropriate but also requisite. The essay takes on point and rhetorical edge when Dryden begins the historical digression, the long central piece on Roman history. But he comes to that digression only after an engagement with the epic, and the digression itself does not begin as historical commentary. The meditation on Roman history begins with a defense of Virgil, that most esteemed of ancient poets. The point of entry to Roman history is Dryden's account of Virgil's own political circumstance, and what begins as a defense of poetic issues—the moral of the poem, its length, cavils raised against its grammar—becomes a set of reflections on Virgil's circumstances that seem remarkably like Dryden's own.

What Dryden wanders into as historical digression is, in fact, the center of the essay; the most revealing remarks that the translator has to make about his conception of epic come not in the opening reflections on genre and mode but in the apology for Virgil. The remarks on Virgil are a covert set of instructions on how to read this translation, cast in the very terms that Dryden sets in his preface. And on the subject of poetics, the *Dedication* again shares a central characteristic with Dryden's earlier prefatory works. For poetics is again a way of doing politics; indeed, if anything, the coupling of politics and poetics is more open in the *Dedication* than before. The dispensing powers, that constant sore point between the Stuarts and their parliaments, is raised under cover of the "rules of poetry." And Dryden mounts a sharp attack on fiscal policy under William III by contrasting the coinage of words and money. The literary and political arguments turn on the coincidence of this term, but Dryden means to attack more than the fiscal mismanagement evidenced by the coinage crisis.

> Words are not so easily Coyn'd as Money: And yet we see that the Credit not only of Banks, but of Exchequers cracks, when little comes in, and much goes out. *Virgil* call'd upon me in every line for some new word: And I paid so long, that I was almost Banckrupt. . . . What had become of me, if *Virgil* had tax'd me with another Book? I had certainly been reduc'd to pay the Publick in hammer'd Money for want of Mill'd; . . . I carry not out the Treasure of the Nation, which is never to return: but what I bring from *Italy*,

I spend in *England*: Here it remains, and here it circulates; for if the Coyn be good, it will pass from one hand to another. I Trade both with the Living and the Dead, for the enrichment of our Native Language. We have enough in *England* to supply our necessity; but if we will have things of Magnificence and Splendour, we must get them by Commerce. (III, 1058-1059, 2105-2174)

Dryden begins by contrasting the debased currency of the 1690s with his own coining for this translation, and I suspect that he knew this coining to be good, that what he had created would be valued and would endure. But the contrast at which he aims through poetics is not wholly contained by the coining metaphor. What Dryden wants to juxtapose finally is king and poet, warfare and translation. This poem will reverse the history of luxury and decline; Dryden's trade with the ancients and moderns has enriched England. William's wars end in waste and destruction. Not only is Dryden making a defense of style, but through poetics he raises a wide range of economic, political, and cultural issues. As in the past, he uses poetics to argue a specific point about the meaning of stylistic choice, but he now has an eye to eternity: "if the Coyn be good, it will pass from one hand to another." Dryden dares to argue the permanence of his own work and in so doing to defy a regime that has debased not only the English currency but a political tradition which Dryden had so often defended and celebrated.

The argument is subtly worked, and it is not easy to insist on the exact shape and details of its contemporary political meaning; but the whole of the preface and such passages in particular are an education in the method of the translation. The critical essays prepare us for and enact the strategies of Dryden's poems; they are often subtle and masterful in such preparation, and a careful reading of these works not only underscores the preoccupations and methods of the poetry but also delineates the character and development of the poet's art.

3. Ambiguities and Uncertainties

THE STUDY of irony and disguise in Dryden's prefaces and critical essays reveals persistent and significant topoi and strategies, and suggests as well a steady growth in power and sophistication as Dryden cultivated the readers' response to his work. The habit of such preparation was one that Dryden exercised more persistently and more brilliantly than any other poet of his time. He provided directions for reading all but one of the major poems and translations, and these exercises were integral to the strategy of the poems, setting their terms and rhetorical conditions, complementing and instructing in their subtlety of design and statement. Indeed, it is often difficult to separate the techniques of the prose strategist from those of the poet, and such strategies are in evidence from the beginning of the poetic career, as well. They are, in fact, highly conspicuous in Dryden's first major poem, *Heroique Stanza's, Consecrated to the Glorious Memory of his most Serene and Renowned Highnesse Oliver Late Lord Protector.*

But while the strategies of the first prefatory exercises are not difficult to fix, the elegy on Cromwell has steadily refused to reveal a point of view. The poem has remained a puzzle not because we have failed to discover the political principles concealed by its rhetoric but because there are no such principles. The difference of manner between the poem on Cromwell and those that Dryden wrote on the return and restoration of Charles Stuart are best explained not by a sudden maturity, the growth of the poet's techniques as panegyrist, but rather by the presence of a point of view in *Astraea Redux* and *To His Sacred Majesty.* The Stuart panegyrics are not powerful examples of Dryden's art, but they are sharply defined in manner and bearing. They articulate conventional notions of monarchy and history, and nothing about them suggests uncertainty. In *Heroique Stanza's* there is neither fixity on the personal figure of Oliver Cromwell nor on the Lord Protector as historical force. And I suspect that this is so because Dryden had neither his own convictions on these subjects nor did he know where to turn for conventional wisdom. *Heroique Stanza's* displays the techniques of the ironist, but not the fixity of perception that so marks Dryden's later work.

The abrupt shift of loyalties from *Heroique Stanza's* to *Astraea Redux* was to haunt Dryden for the rest of his life.[1] Dr. Johnson and Dryden's modern apologists have noted that as Dryden turned, so did the nation.[2] But there is a deeper contextual issue to be understood about *Heroique Stanza's* and contemporary politics. Not only did Dryden share the sudden shift of loyalties with his countrymen—if indeed *Heroique Stanza's* expresses "loyalty"—he also shared a profound uncertainty about the present and future, about Cromwell's character, and about the meaning of the Protectorate. And this uncertainty is a more telling commentary on *Heroique Stanza's* than is the political realignment that took place between Cromwell's death and the return of the king. Perhaps Dryden was consciously hedging his bets, allowing a modicum of praise while maintaining a cool distance from his subject.[3] Whatever the future might hold, Dryden would be free to move. Such a notion recognizes the contradictions and paradoxes of the poem; but, of course, silence would have provided more mobility than speech. History was more complex and ambiguous than the prophetic schemes of Puritan millenarianism had allowed; and if history were to rescue the nation from its dark uncertainties, the principle of such rescue was hardly apparent in 1659.

The problem of assessing the meaning of Cromwell in 1659 was not, of course, Dryden's alone. There were those who took the occasion of Cromwell's death to deify or vilify, but most men were perplexed by the uncertainty of the succession, by the meaning of godly politics in the face of such demise, and by the private and civic personality of the Protector.[4] Indeed, perplexity had been a technique of political control that Cromwell exercised with consummate skill. The public speeches in the later part of the Protectorate were careful exercises in ambiguity, complex and baroque productions that demand close analysis; and men perceived in Cromwell's use of language the political meaning of obfuscation:

> His Speeches were for the most part ambiguous, especially in publike meetings; wherein he rather left others to pick out the meaning then did it himself. But when Offenders came under his own examination, then would he speak plain English, and declare his power unto them in a ranting stile.[5]

But it was not personality alone or the craft of ambiguity that argued this character for the Protector. The rule itself was a set of contradictions, and the political and religious paradoxes of the Protectorate were catalogued and repeatedly turned against Cromwell in the 1650s by enemies of his regime.[6] Those who claimed impartiality saw the interregnum as a series of alternating comic and tragic scenes; they understood the Protector as a composite of valor and craft, godly resolution and personal ambition.[7] But even the harshest condemnations acknowledged Cromwell's charismatic authority. Faced with such contradictions and such a political figure, it is hardly surprising that Dryden should have sought refuge from perplexity. In *Heroique Stanza's* Dryden found such refuge in paradox and irony; rather than simply delay or partially conceal a statement of personal or public conviction, these techniques allowed him to escape resolution.

The impact of Cromwell's death ought to help fix the tone and stance of *Heroique Stanza's*; the veering exaggerations of Marvell's elegy on Cromwell suggest the power of the event itself. And yet the death is coolly distanced from this poem, and it is not Marvell's elegy that provides the closest analogue to Dryden's poem. It is, rather, that poet's *Horatian Ode upon Cromwell's Return from Ireland*, which both in its similarities and quite striking differences best illuminates Dryden's method. The *Horatian Ode* was written at the height of Marvell's powers, its lapidary perfection obvious in the poem's every gesture. And *Heroique Stanza's*, though conducted with surprising assurance, is hardly evidence of Dryden's mature manner, in which irony is never used as a disinterested mode of inquiry. Marvell's poem uses paradox as a way of exploring the nature of politics; its manner is its point of view. Such is hardly the case with *Heroique Stanza's*, where ironies and paradoxes are used less to contemplate the ambiguities of history than to hide from them. And yet the two poems share a technique of ironic qualification that more steadily illuminates Dryden's efforts than the immediately contemporary verse of Waller and Sprat. Central to both *Heroique Stanza's* and the *Horatian Ode* is a technique of assertion and qualification, of concession and denial that refuses to concede a single perspective on Cromwell.

My argument about technique and meaning in *Heroique Stanza's* turns not on a particular line or crux in the poem but on a gathered sense of its puzzles and incongruities. That Dryden understood the requisite manner of elegy, there is no question. However else the poem on Lord Hastings might be faulted, it argues no ignorance of the tropes and structure of elegiac verse. But the same cannot be said for *Heroique Stanza's*. The exclusions of this poem are as powerful as its inclusions, and none more obvious than the failure of the elegy to turn from praise to apotheosis. It seems no matter of slight indifference that the poem closes not with Christian consolation, but with the person of Oliver Cromwell reduced to ashes and to the status of prodigious exemplar.[8] At the close of the poem there is neither Elysium nor Abraham's bosom, and this fact is especially surprising given the significance of Scripture to Protestant poetics and in particular to the rhetoric of Puritan millenarianism. Nor is it only the closing of the poem that avoids Scripture. The language of *Heroique Stanza's* is remarkably, indeed inexplicably, free of that vocabulary whose traces can be found in every important public and occasional poem that Dryden wrote.[9] The exclusion of Scripture is surprising, but it is hardly an oversight. Sacred history so powerfully conveyed a point of view, a conviction about the meaning of Elect Nation and its destiny, that its use would have forced Dryden into a position that he was either unwilling or unable to take.

Not only is there a failure of apotheosis at the end of the poem, but the death itself is rendered with strict impersonality. There is neither personal grief nor rhetorical apostrophe, and but the slightest reference to those prodigies of nature that were relentlessly worked by Cromwell's other elegists. The storm which Marvell describes for thirty lines and which occupies a crucial place in Waller's elegy merits barely a line in Dryden's poem. The death itself is distanced through historical analogy:

His latest Victories still thickest came
As, near the *Center*, *Motion* does increase;
Till he, pres'd down by his own weighty name,
Did, like the *Vestall*, under spoyles decease.

(I, 12, 133-136)

And the analogy itself could hardly be more peculiar.[10] The coupling of military heroism with vestal virginity is odd enough. But what could Dryden have had in mind by comparing Cromwell's fame to the rewards heaped on the vestal Tarpeia as thankless vengeance for her betrayal of Rome? The thrust of the whole analogy is to reduce Cromwell from conquering hero to servile betrayer, and this figure darkens the closing quatrain of the poem in which Cromwell's name stands to show "How strangely high endeavours may be blest" (I, 12, 147). The grammar is slightly unsettled; we cannot be sure whether it is endeavors or blessings that are so qualified; but in either case, the mood is less awe than strained uncertainty. And such qualification is strewn through the whole field of the poem.

If there is an ethos to which Cromwell is assimilated in *Heroique Stanza's*, it is imperial Britain. And about foreign politics, few sought to quibble with Cromwell's achievements. The recitation of heroic deeds in foreign conquest occupies a good deal of the middle and least hesitant parts of the poem: the conquest of Ireland and Scotland, the humiliation of Holland, France, and Spain. But Cromwell's domestic career was more difficult to think on than Cromwell as subduer of the continent. On the first subject there would have been something like a benign consensus, especially if Cromwell's person were assimilated to some abstraction like the British nation. Yet the poem is not a celebration of Cromwell as distant Graeco-Roman hero, an English Alexander; its praise is nervously hedged at crucial points, and the hesitant manner, the anxiety, is as powerful a determinant of its poetics as the heroic gesture of the poem's account of foreign conquest.

From the beginning, and at crucial points throughout, *Heroique Stanza's* works through a dialectic of assertion and qualification. Puns, contradictions, ambiguities, and paradoxes provide the verbal material of qualification,[11] but the basic structural unit, the quatrain, is also used in this dialectic. In *Annus Mirabilis* and in that most famous exemplar of the quatrain, Davenant's *Gondibert*, this stanza functions as a structure of progressive argument, such couplers as "and" and "therefore" providing the quatrain with a grammar and rhythm of assent. But in *Heroique Stanza's*, Dryden frequently qualifies and turns the stanza at midpoint so that both structure and language undercut initial and primary meanings with ambiguities that allow a steady rift of contradictions to erode initial assertions. The poem itself begins neither in grief nor in elegiac apostrophe, but in self-justification:

> And now 'tis time; for their Officious haste,
> Who would before have born him to the sky,
> Like *eager Romans* ere all Rites were past
> Did let too soon the *sacred Eagle* fly.   (I, 6, 1-4)

Not only is Cromwell's name absent from the opening lines— it is, in fact, never mentioned in the poem—but the failure of personal grief coupled with such absence renders Cromwell not an object of mystery but of impersonal speculation. But that absence is not the only peculiarity of the poem's opening. This must be one of the very few poems in English to begin with the coupler "and." The oddly placed word suggests that this beginning is only equivocally a beginning, that Dryden had had his eyes fixed as steadily on Cromwell's other elegists as on the Lord Protector, and though the line might be read as bold assertion, "And now 'tis time . . ." its insistence on self-distinction not only differentiates the elegy from those officious poems written in unseemly haste, from the loud applause of public voice, but also seems to differentiate its hero from the subject of those elegies. The stanza allows, but then seems to withdraw, the analogy of Caesar: those officious elegists and their hero, this timely poem and its subject.

The succeeding stanzas, however, set the more disturbing pattern:

> Though our best notes are treason to his fame
> Joyn'd with the loud applause of publique voice;
> Since Heav'n, what praise we offer to his name,
> Hath render'd too authentick by its choice.   (I, 7, 5-8)

In simplest paraphrase, the poem becomes elegy through an act of Heaven. But there is a peculiarity of construction here, since the initial conjunction seems to subordinate the first clause to a nonexistent independent clause. The "since" of line 7 attempts to function as a logical connective, but in effect the conjunction seems to deny the construction. The elegy does a disservice to the memory of Cromwell "since" heaven turns praise into elegy. "Since" is a false signal for the relation between the two parts of the quatrain, which is analogy rather than cause and effect. If Dryden had used "and" rather than "since" the stanza would have assumed a more comfortably parallel construction: joined with the public voice (those hasty and officious elegies) these words of praise cannot do justice to Cromwell's fame; and Heaven has rendered the elegiac element of panegyric authentic through death. It is in fact not praise that has betrayed Cromwell, but Heaven's choice.

The same peculiarly disembodied conjunction marks the next stanza:

> Though in his praise no Arts can liberall be,
> Since they whose muses have the highest flown
> Add not to his immortall Memorie,
> But do an act of friendship to their own.   (I, 7, 9-12)

Of course the pun on "liberall" is not difficult to rescue, and yet the line just allows the possibility that there is more than one reason that no arts can be liberal in praise of Cromwell. His amplitude denies the efforts of art; his achievement is unworthy of free and full praise. The second construction is unlikely, but it takes some strength from the parallel construction to the initial line of stanza 2. The negatives suggest a parallel perception as well as parallel structure; and the effect of both is to undercut the figure. The stanzas are also similar in their use of the subordinating conjunction not properly resolved until the next stanza collects the subordinations of stanzas 2 and 3 and explains them in a line marked by its own ambiguity:

Though our best notes are treason to his fame

Though in his praise no Arts can liberall be,

Yet 'tis our duty and our interest too
Such monuments as we can build to raise;
Lest all the World prevent what we should do
And claime a *Title* in him by their praise.

(I, 7, 5; 7; 13-16)

The force of lines 5 through 15 turns on the meaning of "raise" which so obviously allows both a constructive and destructive sense that the effect of the pun is to unsettle the structure of the whole opening of the poem. The narrative denies the secondary meaning of the word, and yet as pun it remains fixed somewhere in the verbal texture of this poem which seems both to build and raze its own monuments of praise. Whether or not the pun was fully "intended"—there is not sufficient evidence or sense of strategy here to argue such a placement—the effect is to undermine the panegyric gesture, and though we may be dealing with ambiguity and error in a psychological sense rather than with intentional irony, the fact that the pun is an "error" certainly does not deny the ambivalence.

But the poem also works with more open and more self-conscious qualification. In stanza 6, Dryden maintains the familiar distinction between personal greatness and the grandeur of heaven:

His *Grandeur* he deriv'd from Heav'n alone,
For he was great e're Fortune made him so;
And Warr's like mists that rise against the Sunne
Made him but greater seem, not greater grow.

(I, 7, 21-24)

The opening lines of the stanza offer the most conventional statement of the trope,[12] a trope practiced by none more obviously than the Lord Protector himself, who both assigned his greatness to God and justified his grandeur in exactly those terms. And indeed the trope is familiar from condemnation as well as praise:

> But when the world shall see that those *Felicities* of his Sword and Brain were *derived* from, and *accountable* solely to the just *Judgement* of God, who gave us up a deserved *prey* to the *Spoiler*; and there was nothing *Extraordinary* in him but in the *Sins* and *vengeance* of the Times, he being the *Scourge* of our *Iniquity*, they will convert *their admiration* into a *reverence* of that *Supreme* overruling *power*.[13]

The distinction that Dryden suggests between Heaven and fortune seems to strengthen the hand of panegyric—though Dryden qualifies its meaning in stanza 8—but there is a peculiarity in the turning of the trope in stanza 6 that seems wholly to undermine the initial praise. In the second half of the stanza Dryden uses the favor of Heaven in order to deny greatness altogether:

> And Warr's like mists that rise against the Sunne
> Made him but greater seem, not greater grow.
>
> (I, 7, 23-24)

Military greatness was, in effect, an optical illusion. For Cromwell to assign his own greatness solely to heaven was one thing; it was quite another for his elegist to argue that military authority was a chimera.

And the following stanza does nothing to rescue such damaging ambiguity:

> No borrow'd Bay's his *Temples* did adorne,
> But to our *Crown* he did fresh *Jewells* bring,
> Nor was his Vertue poyson'd soon as born
> With the too early thoughts of being King.   (I, 7, 25-28)

There is a slight peculiarity in the first two lines of the stanza; the oddly placed reference to the "Crown" has an unsettling effect. But the thoughts of kingship in line 28 give a definitive shape to the earlier reference. The stanza seems less concerned with borrowed bays and conquest than it does with personal ambition and the kingship question that had been raised so forcefully in 1657 and had produced so profound an ambivalence in the Protector himself.[14] Cromwell's position on this question was extremely ambiguous; there were many contemporaries who thought that he leaned toward accepting the Humble Petition. In the context of that debate, Dryden seems to suggest that if the career had not begun in personal ambition, such ambition certainly drove the Protector at this point in his career. The phrase "too early thoughts" allows ample scope for Cromwell's ambitions, and the direct reference to kingship and crown leave no doubt that the subject of the stanza is the ambition for dynasty and crown. What Dryden's own opinion on that subject was remains entirely unclear; and ambivalence unsettles the subject without revealing the conviction.

Nor is this the sole reference to crown and kingship. Stanza 7 provides something of a context for the two other allusions to kingship, the reference in line 48 to Cromwell's "breathing of the vein,"[15] and that in line 76 to "Beds where Sov'raign Gold doth grow." The poem does not offer a systematic account of the problem of kingship within the context of Protectorate politics, and I suspect that Dryden would not have known, at this point, how to conduct such an account, since the intention of the poem seems neither consistently to deny nor affirm the grandeur of the Lord Protector. And yet the reference to the debate over the crown is unflattering, and reminiscences of the language and imagery of Stuart kingship are unsettling in this context. Was it only the malice of Dryden's calumniators who read line 48 as a reference to the execution of Charles I, "He fought to end our fighting, and assaid / To stanch the blood by breathing of the vein"? And might some have seen in the emblem of the palms a contrast between Cromwell's precipitate rise to greatness and the sufferings and martyrdom of Charles I:[16]

His *Palmes* though under weights they did not stand,
Still thriv'd; no *Winter* could his *Laurells* fade.

(I, 9, 57-58)

It is both difficult and, I think, wrong to see a specific refer-
ence as a crucial demonstration of ambiguity in the poem, and
yet the steady multiplication of meanings in *Heroique Stanza's*
seems to deny the possibility of altogether accidental refer-
ence.

Moreover, the reference to sovereign gold, even if we do
not read the martyred king in these lines, argues that Crom-
well's arts and ambitions should be construed in the peculiar
light of divination:

'Tis true, his Count'nance did imprint an awe,
And naturally all souls to his did bow;
As *Wands of Divination* downward draw
And point to Beds where Sov'raign Gold doth grow.

(I, 9, 73-76)

Not only does the suggestion of idolatry disturb these lines,
but the stanza seems to imply that Cromwell's political arts
bore more than a faint resemblance to divination. As *"Confi-
dent of Nature"* (I, 10, 99) he practiced "deep secrets" beyond
policy. Such a language is not peculiar to this account of
Cromwell's political arts. Indeed, it was a common perception
of Cromwell that he was a politician who rose to power and
maintained his station by craft and by an uncanny understand-
ing of other men's weaknesses.[17] And the language of *Her-
oique Stanza's* suggests just such a grudging admiration:

Successefull Councells did him soon approve
As fit for close *Intrigues*, as open field.   (I, 10, 79-80)

For from all tempers he could service draw,
The worth of each with its alloy he knew;
And as the *Confident* of *Nature* saw
How she Complexions did divide and brew.

(I, 10, 97-100)

But witchcraft and divination argue more than policy; not
only does Cromwell display political cunning, he seems to

exercise a power beyond human politics. The association of witchcraft and divination with political art allows a play of admiration against fear that sets much of the peculiar tone of this poem.

If the ambiguities of the opening and middle stanzas deny fixity of perception, the conclusion, as we have seen, is disturbed by what are at the very least mistakes and miscalculations. Cromwell's death is greeted by the sighting of the Leviathan, his own demise analogized with the death of the vestal Tarpeia. Perhaps the sighting of the Leviathan, an ominous portent and one much remarked in the contemporary literature on Cromwell's death, is an attempt to turn an unfavorable sign into a tribute. But one wonders what principle of selection argued the inclusion of the Leviathan and the exclusion of apotheosis. Such ambiguities do not of course explain the vestal virgin. The use of Tarpeia's history argues that the weight of Cromwell's astonishing victories lay as crushingly on him as the bucklers and swords hurled on Tarpeia. The analogy begins with neutral assertion, but the rational tone of the first lines is undercut by the extended analogy. By what logic does the poet move from victory to the betrayal of Rome?

Nor does the manner come to resolution in the final stanza where there is both ambiguity of language and argument.

> His Ashes in a peacefull Urne shall rest,
> His Name a great example stands to show
> How strangely high endeavours may be blest,
> Where *Piety* and *valour* joyntly goe.   (I, 12, 145-148)

The emblem that excites this response is the "peacefull Urne" containing the remnants of the body. Is death the reward of this high endeavor? Is Cromwell's end a blessing or a warning? The close of Dryden's poem has the same unsettling ambiguity as Marvell's *Horatian Ode*, an ambiguity that not only undercuts the meaning of the figure but one that seems, as well, to undercut the meaning of history. There is here neither the blessing nor the vengeance of heaven, but the tow of irony against history: "How strangely high endeavours may be blest."

To point out such ironies and incongruities, to add those other oblique references—lines that are simply puzzling rather than corrosive—and to represent these puzzles and ironies as the whole is, however, to distort the procedure of *Heroique Stanza's*. Unlike the *Horatian Ode*, there is no method here. The poem does not offer the order of steady irony. Not only are there simpler ways of construing some of these passages, there are also passages that do not allow any ironic perspective; and there is the reading of the foreign career, which begins with the analogy of Alexander and then traces the whole of the triumphant career abroad:

> Swift and resistlesse through the Land he past
> Like that bold *Greek* who did the East subdue;
> And made to battails such Heroick haste
> As if on wings of victory he flew.
> . . . .
> He made us *Freemen* of the *Continent*
> Whom Nature did like Captives treat before,
> To nobler prey's the *English Lyon* sent,
> And taught him first in *Belgian walks* to rore.
>
> (I, 8, 49-53; 11, 113-116)

The heroism of the man is national triumph. The subjugation of Ireland, the taming of Scotland, the humiliation of Holland, the suit of France and Spain for Cromwell's love: these topics are rendered without irony. And the stanzas in the middle of the poem take on their own restless pace. The movement of argument through the verse in these stanzas is quite different from the opening hesitations or the closing paradoxes. On the subject of foreign conquest, Dryden had touched a common chord; the contemporary histories are uniform in their treatment of the themes of foreign victory.[18] Dryden shared with his contemporaries this untroubled imperialism. The humbling of proud Rome is a longstanding theme in an English and aggressively Protestant foreign policy; it looks back to Elizabethan themes and remained an almost continuous trope in foreign policy throughout the century. It is, of course, one of the cruxes on which Marvell turned his celebration of the first year of Cromwell's rule in 1653, and Dryden would have been well aware of this theme's wide and uniform resonance. Moreover, it is in the passages that depict Cromwell in his European context that Dryden finally suggests the community of elegy:

He made us *Freemen* of the *Continent*
Whom Nature did like Captives treat before.

(I, 11, 113-114)

If this poem were confined to those passages in which Cromwell is depicted as hero of European conquest—if not the millenarian knight of Marvell's *First Anniversary*—we would have no difficulty in imagining his apotheosis at the end of the poem, an assumption to the pantheon of military gods.

But, in fact, the modes of this poem exist side by side. The example of the *Horatian Ode* is again instructive. In Marvell's poem, history acts as a screen against which we might read the inscrutable will of providence; we are thus brought to understand all aspects of Cromwell, the nakedly ambitious and the selflessly heroic. The multiple perspectives of Marvell's ode allow us to understand and assimilate the poem's ironies as the full meaning of the events which it reviews. *Heroique Stanza's* offers no such philosophical perspective. Dryden's Cromwell is outside of history, an anomaly that cannot be accounted for, a prodigy like the Leviathan that washes ashore to proclaim his death. The result is a poem in which praise and blame are arranged indifferently in relation to one another, a poem on a conquering hero that fails to provide either an historical scheme in which those acts of conquest might be understood, or an ironic assessment of the politician whose temporary grasp of fortune is defeated, as all policy is finally defeated, at God's hands in the fullness of time.

That the sense of a future, of a time after Cromwell's death in which England might reap the benefits of his heroic deeds and in which the victor himself might collect his permanent rewards, is so fully denied in this poem explains its failure of closure, its failure to come together to form a specific and identifiable point of view. But like others awaiting the outcome of events after Cromwell's death and Richard's unsteady assumption of the Protectorate, Dryden did not know what the future would bring. That he failed to order the poem according to a vision of that future does not imply that he was calculating the odds either in favor of or against a Stuart restoration. He simply did not know, and chose neither deification nor vilification because he had little capacity to imagine a future in the terms that either point of view implied. The poem is stuck at its conclusion in the unknowing present. And it is a mark of the lack of calculation at this point in his career that Dryden did not force his understanding into false resolution.

Heroique Stanza's was published together with poems by Waller and Sprat; it would have been easy enough for Dryden to have written in their mode. The high panegyric model that Marvell had already provided in *The First Anniversary* suggested an appropriate drift of both language and opinion, and Dryden would have had no reason to distrust Marvell's sense of the Protector, whether or not he knew the poem that Marvell had contributed to the originally scheduled *Three poems to the happy memory of the most renowned Oliver*.[19] But perhaps it is to put too high a value on the failure of resolution in *Heroique Stanza's* to argue that Dryden's honesty denied this poem a simpler mode than the one he achieved. The lack of steady perspective in *Heroique Stanza's* derives from Dryden's own failure to achieve an understanding of Cromwell and of the meaning of his history. The failure is not, I think, a loss of literary control, for the same lack of resolution marks a number of the contemporary histories. *Heroique Stanza's* contains open praise, praise qualified by ironies, and something like troubled disenchantment. In abstract statement, such a scheme ought to render the poem evenhanded and disinterested. But in the reading, evenhandedness is experienced more as confusion than design. *Heroique Stanza's* is Dryden's only poem troubled in this particular way. And though some of the complication looks like moderation and disinterestedness, when Dryden later adopted such a pose and turned again to the techniques of irony and ambiguity, the results were neither indifferent nor confused. With the Restoration he began a long and brilliant career of advocacy and disguise.

4. Politics and Religion

THE "MIDDLE WAY"

Absalom and Achitophel

ABSALOM and Achitophel and Religio Laici are Dryden's great poems of the "middle way." Moderation is the warp of their metaphors, the engine of their dialectic; at all costs, they argue their convictions and prescriptions, they soften their satiric edge and unsparing condemnations, in the name of beloved moderation. This language was taught by the bitter experience of civil war and it was adopted in Exclusion by all men, regardless of conviction.[1] So powerful and so artful are the claims for moderation in Absalom and Achitophel that students of the poem have come to see language as belief, to see the political intelligence of this poem as indifferent to, indeed contemptuous of, the "party color'd mind."[2]

Generalities about Dryden's temper, the poet as philosophical skeptic, as disinterested critic of extremes,[3] together with the seemingly ingenuous and repeated claims of moderation and balance in the preface, have led a number of critics to understand the narrator's espoused moderation as Dryden's political conviction.[4] Such a judgment Dryden's contemporaries would hardly have allowed. The anonymous publication of the poem was followed in a matter of weeks by a torrent of political outrage and personal abuse.[5] What indeed were Dryden's contemporaries responding to if the political argument of the poem, like much of its language, was conciliatory? If rhetoric is understood as intent, never has a poem been so misread by contemporaries. Men who spoke the language of politics as Dryden must have heard it spoken perceived in his use of that language neither mildness nor moderation. Absalom and Achitophel is a sophisticated compound of memories and adaptations of Virgil, Shakespeare, and Milton; yet it is also persuasive speech. And as persuasive speech, it entered the fray of political debate, was perceived as part of that debate, and in important ways behaved like other such contributions. Understood as a poem of brilliant rhetorical strategies and read in the context of a political crisis that demanded the appearance of moderation regardless of belief, the poem emerges not as a plea for toleration but as a warning that the court could mount and might well act on the bold and vindictive claim for executive vengeance that appears as the climax of David's speech. As prophecy, the argument for executive vengeance was remarkably prescient.

The reasons why moderation has come to be regarded as the political theme of *Absalom and Achitophel* are not, of course, difficult to understand. Such a reading takes those elements of David's lengthy final speech appealing to the supremacy of the law and asserting its applicability to all, king and rebellious subjects alike, as the keynote of the poem. Backed by assorted *obiter dicta* of the narrator, by veiled and at times daring criticism of a promiscuous king, and by praise of Achitophel the judge,[6] a case can be made for the poem as manifesto of evenhandedness and reasoned moderation. The poet, identified as the narrator, is thus seen as the classic seventeenth-century moderate, fully in the mainstream of near-universal appeals to an "ancient constitution." The overwhelming majority of the political nation would have agreed with the narrator's assertion that "Innovation is the Blow of Fate," that "To change Foundations" is tantamount to rebellion. To remove old landmarks, even the most unsightly and insignificant, was to risk running the body politic into chaos and the wilderness.[7] Yet to identify the conventional character of such opinions is neither to describe the politics of the poem as a whole nor to account for their presence in this text of sharply partisan argument.

Of course, not all claims of moderation were specious. The nearest to a truly moderate response to Exclusion was Halifax's advocacy of limitations on a future Catholic king and reconciliation with those who had supported Exclusion, a policy that Charles appeared to follow in the early months of the crisis. But as the crisis lengthened and deepened, the voice of true moderation grew fainter. Cries were heard from the Cornish gentry vowing to confirm in a "red" letter their declarations of devotion, and while such explicitness was hardly typical, the advice to unsheathe the sword was not unusual in the later months of 1681.[8] It is, furthermore, advice that David himself is shown soberly to contemplate near the end of Dryden's poem. But the diversity of the poet's audience—unhappy moderates shading in both directions toward extremists with arms—as well as the complexity of the poet's aims explain why the poem's final recognition of the necessity of the sword could only emerge after the reasoned exposition of political alternatives in the midst of crisis.

In addressing an audience of diverse and at points contradictory political interests, Dryden was forced to adopt the camouflage of conventional rhetoric; he was political everyman preaching moderation and balance, disinterested historian, poet before and above partisan. Where Dryden claims such a guise in the preface to *Annus Mirabilis*, there is not much reason to credit nor has there been much accession to the self-portrait. But the same posturing in the materials of *Absalom and Achitophel* has inspired wide assent among modern students of this poem. The self-portrait in the preface depicts the poet as honest broker, judicious advocate of the middle way. But why, we might wonder, in the midst of the most serious and damaging political crisis that the nation had endured since the civil wars, should the poet laureate and historiographer royal have wanted to report accurately and disinterestedly, when not one among his contemporaries had gone into the business of contributing to the literature of this crisis with truly disinterested accounts? Why, in the face of the preposterous and yet powerful and damaging "confessions" of Titus Oates, confessions that had once again brought to the boiling point the anti-Catholic hysteria of the nation and linked the king's brother and the king's Catholic wife in a conspiracy to murder Charles and reduce the nation to papal slavery, would the poet laureate conceive it to have been his business to give an evenhanded account of the faults that lay both on the king's side and on the side of republicans and king-killers? Why, indeed, would the nation's most brilliant man of letters, who had perfected the techniques of dissembling and propagandizing, now, in the face of constitutional crisis, be interested in turning from persuasion to representation?

Of course, this way of posing questions suggests their answer. Perhaps a more fair-minded proposal would be to ask why Dryden might have been interested in appearing fairminded and judicious, evenhanded and disinterested in the midst of the Exclusion Crisis? And that question has, I think, a real answer. Dryden sought such cover because he intended to persuade, because all those who entered public debate also covered themselves with the garb of moderation, because the language of the ancient constitution, of rights and liberties, of balance and moderation, was the accepted language of political discourse. Dryden was a clever rhetorician, and he behaved as clever rhetoricians behave on such occasions; he was also a poet, and these conditions did not deny one another. Indeed, in Dryden's case, they enhanced each other, and perhaps our current willingness to believe in the rhetoric of moderation because it was proposed in a poem of balance and judicious appearances is itself testimony to the success of the poet as rhetorician.

But polemic and disguise are not tied only to the ostensibly political elements of the poem. The very issue of poetic kind in *Absalom and Achitophel* is a masterstroke of illusion: "*Absalom and Achitophel*, A Poem." If we label the work satire, we are already in violation of generic conditions because the poem explicitly denies the label: " 'Tis not my intention to make an Apology for my *Poem*." Why, if Dryden has satiric, historical, epic, mock-heroic, and political business to conduct, does he not do so forthrightly under one of these rubrics? Nor has this seemed a question with so obvious an answer for students of the poem. The debate over literary kind is extensive and serious.[9] But to conclude from the contradictory evidence of the preface—at one point the poet claims the mantle of history, at another he is satirist; at the opening he is unwilling partisan, pushed against his own intention into the unfortunate label of party man; but by the end of the preface we see

him ironically allowing party—that there is real generic con-
fusion here is wrong.

Dryden is the willing source of such confusion because his
conception of genre was politically motivated. In this poem,
genre is not a category that identifies and reveals meaning and
intention, but a condition to be avoided. The poem has an
array of satiric, political, quasi-historical, and epic intentions,
but it will not realize them under limiting conditions. The
poem is all the various kinds, as Dryden well knew—indeed
as he makes sure that we understand, by direction, by gesture,
by Virgilian and Miltonic allusion—but it is not any one of
them; it is a poem, finally, of no genre at all, not because
Dryden was confused by the conflicting claims he wanted to
make for the poem but because he knew how delicately bal-
anced they were, often one against the other: satire redeeming
prophecy; prophecy allowing a perspective that satire could
not claim; history strengthening the hand of veracity; epic
enlarging the dimensions and significance of history. This is a
complicated balancing act; here is a set of overlapping and, at
moments, conflicting agendas best accommodated by generic
mixture, even by a carefully induced generic confusion that
refuses to identify kind, enlarging the claims of the poem by
eluding the fixity of generic prescription and using indeter-
minacy as a dodge. As history *Absalom and Achitophel* might
be corrected; as satire, it could be answered; as prophecy it
might be denied. *Annus Mirabilis* is such a history and has
essentially one function. But Dryden's arts and ambitions were
much fuller in 1681 than in that year of wonders. And those
arts are in evidence from the moment we examine the title, in
every line of the preface, and through the complex maneuver-
ing of the poem that follows.

In delineating his audience, Dryden recognized that there
were indeed committed Whigs and Tories, but claimed that
they were few. The poem's reference to the need for the Plot
to stampede men behind Shaftesbury's banner accurately re-
flects the lack of any widespread and deeply held antimon-
archism; similarly, the difficulties Charles faced in dealing with
a parliament of erstwhile Cavaliers in the 1670s, and the slow-

ness of the evolution of a Tory party in the crisis are the po-
litical realities suggested by the poem's "virtuous few." As
Dryden acknowledges, the king had very few allies at the height
of the crisis; the tardy alignment of the center, the bulk of the
political nation, suggested that here lay the largest political
audience of the poem, and that their reclamation ought to be
the poem's central polemical aim. But it is not the poem's only
political address; despite Dryden's apparent dismissal in the
preface of partisan Whigs and Tories as an audience, there is
a message for them, and it is contained in David's concluding
oration, where the emphasis on blood must have seemed a
gratifying rallying cry to those high-flying Tories who by late
1681 were openly declaring their readiness to go to war in
the name of the crown and succession. On the other hand,
the speech also served as a warning to the malcontent Whigs
of their impending fate. But, of course, there is far more to
the poem than the poet's maneuvering in the preface or Dav-
id's speech.

The narrator's constitutional address, harping as it does on
the inevitability of absolutism once the continuity of the im-
memorial constitution has been broken, is clearly pitched to
those estranged from Charles by the specter of absolutism they
had seen in the king's domestic and foreign policies in the
decade before the crisis. On the one hand, a case is being
argued to constitutionalist readers that stern and perhaps star-
tling measures are imperative if the absolutism they had feared
was to be averted. On the other hand, in the handling of the
Absalom and Achitophel legend, with its clear emphasis on
questions of legitimacy, primogeniture, and title, Dryden ad-
dresses himself to fallen but redeemable Whigs. These may be
shown that legitimacy, because of its implications for property
and the laws (doubly sacred because God-given to an England
identified as Old Testament Israel) as well as for the crown, is
infinitely more important than the personal characteristics of
the king, whether they be the sexual proclivities of David or
the significantly undefined propensities of his brother. More-
over, the very conflation of England and Israel plays to a Prot-
estant certainty of national election, and thus serves to preempt

the contention that the accession of James spells the death of Protestantism. James is as much a part of Israel as are the self-proclaimed Protestant guardians of true religion; furthermore the English Catholics, so carefully identified as mere Jebusites, are not Egyptian slaves. The detailed portrait of these Jebusites, Dryden's careful separation of native from Egyptian rites, the vulgar jibing at French Roman Catholic tastes, like the insistent claim that native Catholics are submissive and powerless, all contrive to combat the Exclusionist charge that a French invasion is imminent and will find the welcome and support of a native Catholic fifth column. But Dryden's subject here is not only Jebusite impotence. He must also take on the knowledge of Charles's alliance to Louis XIV and the telling and accurate rumors of French sympathizers at court, disastrously confirmed by the disclosure that James's secretary Coleman had been in treasonous correspondence with France. His only resort in this case is a desperate joking at the gullibility of a nation more fit for conversion than conquest, a joking that belittles the Catholic threat by exposing the folly of all converts, even their chief. How else are we to understand the peculiar coupling of "Court and Stews" (I, 220, 127)?

Although Dryden is appealing to disparate groups, the poem is not constructed as a series of clearly defined addresses to easily identifiable segments of its audience; its mode of address is both more complex and covert. The narrator is one of the instruments of this complexity, for he adopts a stance that is variously ingenuous, disinterested, and evenhanded. This rhetorical complexity is set in a structure that reveals the poem's bold endorsement of a Tory solution only after the studied and apparently impartial weighing and discarding of alternatives. Dryden's preface to *Absalom and Achitophel* serves as an example of this rhetorical mode and as a model for the poem as a whole, moving as it does from an elaborate show of moderation and impartiality to an advocacy of the block. What Dryden stresses at the opening of the preface are his aims as poet rather than as party instrument: honesty of design and the sweetness of good verse. His stance is the independence of satire: to laugh at folly, commend virtue, and tax crime without prejudice. Steering the middle course, aiming disinterestedly at the amendment of vice, he is physician to the patient, historian and not inventor, moderate poised between the violent of both sides. The strategy is both elaborate and subtle, and nowhere more so than in the poet's engagingly open acknowledgment of vulnerability. Dryden aims to capture the moderates of both parties by making allowance for their reluctance to proceed to extremes: satire is abated, and at the same time commendation is balanced by the taxing of crimes. Dryden is aware that such attempts at moderation may be specious devices, as in the case of his calumniators, those Commonwealthsmen who cry "King and Country." But there is an implicit distinction between such wholesale fraudulence and the narrator's acknowledged softening of divisive truths. He claims the middle ground not, as opponents might suggest, to cover vindictive aims; he rebates the satire not as a ploy but as a genuine effort to gain the support of the moderate sort, the honest party, with the ultimate intention of healing the body politic. But the strategy is a double bluff: covering vindictiveness with moderation while disarming the attack by confessing vulnerability to it.

The harsh political warning begins to emerge in the final paragraph. The true end of satire is the exposure and correction of folly through laughter; the aim of this poet is to suggest the possibility, perhaps even the propriety, of an *Ense rescindendum*, an excision of a diseased limb from the body politic. Dryden observes that in a case of serious illness amputation can only be avoided by the prescription of harsh remedies. He then deploys a variant of the traditional analogy between the natural body and body politic. In conventional imagery, the king is the head, and thus a part of the body. Here, in the implied analogy with the surgeon (I, 216, 60), he stands outside the nation ministering to its need. The tactic here, as throughout the poem, is subtly but thoroughly to distance the king from the illness and corruption of the nation. The satirist as physician (I, 216, 58-59) would avert amputation by prescribing harsh measures, not opiates, in a fever.

What the king ought to have done in 1660, the metaphor seems to argue, is a bit of judicious bleeding, for how else might a fever be controlled? But an opiate had been given to the body politic in 1660 in the form of an Act of Oblivion (I, 216, 63). Now the fever rages; poets must turn satirists and the surgeon's knife—the king's sword of justice—becomes a necessity. The harsh remedy (I, 216, 59) that this poem prescribes is the block for Whig leaders; only such action could avert the wholesale proscription then being advocated by some of the king's more vengeful supporters, a proscription ominously paralleled by Louis XIV's persecution of Calvinist dissenters in France. The narrator's protestation that he would not urge the knife even for his enemies ought to be put in the same category as his equally pious hope that the devil will be saved.

The poem itself begins with a witty and daring portrait of the king; the narrator admits the king's sexual indulgence, but answers the criticism by asserting that in David sexual excess is evidence of God's creative bounty. In so doing, he averts the moralist charge that the king's indulgence in private pleasures has been the source of the constitutional crisis. Further, by dwelling on a peccadillo, on sexual excess as prime example of the king's indulgence, and conveniently ignoring other, more serious charges—financial extravagance and the political implications of a Catholic successor—Dryden can deftly argue that the failure to beget a legitimate heir and thus, ultimately, the creation of political crisis, is a result of Michal's ingratitude rather than David's tillage (I, 217, 12). The isolation of political error as sexual excess allows Dryden to address the king's critics on the one issue he can most conveniently refute. The critique of the king's behavior usually discovered in these lines is hardly evidence of evenhandedness; it is, in fact, rhetorical bluff, for Dryden criticizes here only what he can excuse. While raising the issue of sexual excess and answering the charge in his own terms Dryden introduces his real theme: ingratitude.

Michal's ingratitude implies the political argument of the poem as a whole.[10] David the man is characterized by indulgence, a failing (if it is such) after God's own heart (I, 217, 7). David the king is also indulgent, and the endeavors of both man and king are met with ingratitude. In the bedchamber ingratitude is infertility and perhaps even frigidity; in the state it is godless rebellion. And ingratitude forms the subject of Dryden's lengthy portrait of the Jews, a portrait which begins with epithets, insults, and sneers (I, 218, 45-47). But the argument that ingratitude not only names the Jews but reveals their political and theological characteristics is conducted not simply as slander. Ingratitude is a history that begins with the Fall, marks the nation in desert exile, and concludes in this passage with the inconstancy of Israel under both Ishbosheth and David, protector and king (I, 218, 57-60). As impartial rhetorician, Dryden defines ingratitude not as a party issue but as the permanent and lamentable condition of graceless man. And yet, Dryden's stress on political ingratitude can only be aimed in one direction. Shortly before the poem was written, the extremely influential Tory propagandist Roger L'Estrange had provided the original and seminal definition of a Whig: a man who "must never Remember Benefits."[11]

Ingratitude is common not just to the governed, the collective nation, but also to the best, for men like Shaftesbury, Holles, and Delamere, elevated and given place by Charles at the Restoration, showed themselves incapable of gratitude:

> Some by their Monarch's fatal mercy grown,
> From Pardon'd Rebels, Kinsmen to the Throne;
> Were rais'd in Power and publick Office high:
> Strong Bands, if Bands ungratefull men could tye.
>
> (I, 220, 146-149)

Moreover, defined as niggardliness, meanness, and closeness, the term ingratitude covers a whole range of disloyal political behavior (I, 232-233, 587-589, 591-592, 596, 599, 613-622). The strong and suggestive undertow of greed links Achitophel with the lowest of the rebels; and against their parsimony stands the generosity of allies.[12] Barzillai, Zadock, and Hushai are not only bound by loyalty but linked through generosity (I, 238-240, 826, 867, 892-893). The counterpointing of rebel

and ally is particularly marked in the cases of Zimri and Bar-
zillai, where Zimri's indiscriminate squandering is contrasted
with Barzillai's judicious use of wealth; the contrast begins as
verbal echo:

> In squandring Wealth was his peculiar Art:
> Nothing went unrewarded, but Desert. (I, 231, 559-560)

> The Court he practis'd, not the Courtier's art:
> Large was his Wealth, but larger was his Heart:
> Which, well the Noblest Objects knew to choose.
> (I, 238, 825-827)

But the juxtaposition serves ends larger than personal praise
and blame; it underscores the civic meaning of patronage, for
it was on the proper distribution and reception of favors that
the health of the early-modern body politic depended. Greed
and ambition are thus political traits linked with rebellion; all
are subsumed in the common theme of ingratitude. And the
particular genius of Dryden's large metaphor—England as Is-
rael—is to allow the suggestion, by recording English political
ingratitude as Israelite murmuring, that the execution of Charles
I recapitulates the supreme ingratitude of Jewish deicide, and
to imply that Charles II's generosity to the nation—conven-
iently not itemized—expresses God's munificence. The confla-
tion of God's bounty and the king's largesse is argued at length
and variously in the poem, but its political point in the por-
trait of the Jews is identical to the blaming of Michal: the
king is sinless. The charges laid against the nation and the
majority of its leaders recover and give particular point to the
seemingly innocuous aside in the opening description of Ab-
salom: "In him alone, 'twas Natural to please" (I, 217, 28).

The political consequence of Jewish ingratitude is recurrent
upheaval. Rebellion threatens when the king persists in ex-
tending fatherly love to a graceless nation that recognizes only
Achitophel's law of self-preservation (I, 228, 458). But the
criticism of the king's mildness as political impotence, often
construed as the narrator's opinion,[13] is in fact voiced not by
the narrator but by Achitophel as he attempts the first corrup-

tion of Absalom. Here alone is mildness causally linked with rebellion. David as a weak and friendless figure inviting coercion—indeed, in terms of Achitophel's final analogy (I, 229, 471-474), covertly demanding it—is a case in which credibility is obviously strained by the identity and persuasive intent of the proponent. Yet Achitophel, like all clever rhetoricians, bases his pleas upon a semblance of reality, one that David himself wearily acknowledges in his review of "native mercy":

> But now so far my Clemency they slight,
> Th' Offenders question my Forgiving Right.
> . . . .
> They call my tenderness of Blood, my Fear:
> Though Manly tempers can the longest bear.
>
> (I, 241, 943-944; 947-948)

At the end of the poem, David regretfully allows that the nation has understood mildness not as generosity and political sagacity, but as weakness and indecision. Mildness can, however, be interpreted in other ways. For the narrator, judicious mildness had managed to keep a semblance of peace in an unruly state (I, 219, 77-78). And Absalom eloquently rehearses the extent and implications of David's mildness and generosity in the speech that begins, "And what Pretence have I / To take up Arms for Publick Liberty?" Absalom details at length the king's unstinting generosity and the signs of mercy and mildness that have characterized his father's reign (I, 225, 315-330).

> His Favour leaves me nothing to require;
> Prevents my Wishes, and outruns Desire.
>
> (I, 225, 343-344)

Such mildness and generosity ought to entail gratitude, and this the son realizes:

> Why then shoud I, Encouraging the Bad,
> Turn Rebell, and run Popularly Mad?
> Were he a Tyrant who, by Lawless Might,
> Opprest the *Jews*, and Rais'd the *Jebusite*,

Well might I Mourn; but Natures Holy Bands
Woud Curb my Spirits, and Restrain my Hands.
(I, 225, 335-340)

The image of hands restrained from rebellion by gratitude and
obligation looks ominously forward to the figure of Esau the
hunter in David's final speech (I, 242, 982). Perhaps the king
now realizes, and certainly the poet is aware, that such hands,
unbound by gratitude, can only be restrained through fear.

It is in the latter context—politics in a remorseless and sin-
ful nation—that we must understand David's reluctant turn
from mercy to rigorous justice and the poem's eventual rec-
ommendation of the sword. Both David and the narrator come
to an acceptance of this necessary and bloody conclusion only
after the poem's studied exposition of the meaning and extent
of David's mercy. As in the preface, the rhetorical strategy of
the poem as a whole is progressive revelation: a lengthy re-
view of the narrator's impartiality, the nation's repeated
ingratitude, the king's fatherly indulgence, the debate over the
meaning of mercy, and the final unsheathing of the sword.
Now the image of the surgeon's knife in Dryden's preface
comes into full resolution; since David's reign has favored mercy
over the prescription of harsh remedies for that inveterate dis-
ease of rebellion, since forgetfulness was chosen over a few
judicious acts of bloodletting, the sword of justice must now
be drawn. The delay in unsheathing that sword is neither
weakness nor indecision, for it is delay itself that reveals the
true nature of David's kingship (I, 241-242, 940-950; 1002-
1005). Acting the merciful father to Israel is eventually under-
stood to be inappropriate in a fallen world, but such conduct,
the poem stresses, is God's beloved attribute. Once again the
criticism falls clear of the king.

The ill-advisedness of mercy as political behavior is most
pointedly seen in the poem's handling of Oblivion. Oblivion
is an issue that specifically identifies David's general mercy
with a major policy of Charles II, and in so doing firmly re-
veals Dryden's political bias. The attack on Oblivion as a po-
litical course, conducted through allusion and word play, be-

gins in the preface with the unflattering comparison between
acts of oblivion and opiates administered in raging fevers. An
Act of Oblivion grants pardon to all except those individuals
named in the Act. Dryden's condemnation of Oblivion looks
both forward and back; when desperate Whigs are now plead-
ing for indemnity,[14] it becomes a prescription for Charles's
actions toward the likes of Nadab and Corah, who, by being
named, are thereby excluded from the safety of anonymity.

And Canting *Nadab* let Oblivion damn,   (I, 231, 575)

Yet, *Corah*, thou shalt from Oblivion pass.   (I, 233, 632)

In the preface, Dryden implies criticism of the near universal
forgiveness granted in the Act of Oblivion in 1660, and in
the poem underscores that criticism by the suggestion of in-
credulity recorded in Absalom's lines, "What Millions has he
Pardon'd of his Foes, / Whom Just Revenge did to his Wrath
expose?" (I, 225, 323-324). The effects of Oblivion are ob-
vious in the bitter reflections on those pardoned rebels who
battened on the king's "fatal mercy," and turned rebel anew
(I, 220, 146-149). The conflation of king and Christ sug-
gested in the phrase "fatal mercy" is an allusion to David as
image of the godhead (I, 237, 792) and serves here to sepa-
rate the spiritual from the political realm. On the one hand,
as political policy Oblivion has been a fatal error; but in terms
of the poem's insistent identification of David's indulgence
with God's bounty and Christ's mercy, the account of David's
kingship balances the criticism of indulgence with an insist-
ence on its spiritual meaning. That Christ's mercy was impol-
itic is no sharper an observation than the poem's discovery
that indulgence is inappropriate in fallen Israel. The political
conclusion that mildness ill suits the stubborn, and can pro-
vide no hope of balance and stability, is clear.

David's speech reveals his final appreciation that stability
and balance can only be secured through fear, a conclusion
that had been foreshadowed in the narrator's ominous cou-
plet, "Thus, in a Pageant Show, a Plot is made; / And Peace
it self is War in Masquerade" (I, 236, 751-752). The Whigs

made protestations of loyalty, but they also indulged in a daring show of arms and retinues at the Oxford parliament, and when men appeared in arms they altered the rules of the legal game. If the Whigs wanted war, then the king also had a sword. There are two separate audiences to whom that message is delivered in the king's closing speech: the fallen, to whom the king speaks in the only language that they will understand; and those zealous Tories, finally gratified by his promise of the bloodletting which they, unlike the narrator, have eagerly urged. For the former, the language should induce not just fear, the natural response of those who believed that self-preservation is nature's eldest law, but also, and importantly, a sense of sin. There is an apparent paradox in writing a poem ostensibly aimed at reasoned persuasion and pitching that poem to a nation blackened as endemically corrupt. Perhaps Dryden's awareness of this dilemma helps to explain the repeated emphasis laid on near-universal sin, a tactic that neatly exploits the Calvinist convictions of the king's dissenter opponents. For it was the central tenet of Protestant casuistry that regeneration could begin only after the individual acknowledged the extent of his own corruption. Both the scriptural metaphor and the rhetoric of moderation provided Dryden with a language that might allow a Tory case to be heard and understood by the fallen nation; only thus could "willing Nations [know] their Lawfull Lord."

That David draws the sword of justice as the last resort is hardly a novel observation. What needs to be remarked is the play of contradictory elements in this scene: the abruptness and harshness of David's language, the steady elevation and, indeed, mystification of the king, the sentiments of high-minded regretfulness, the not so thinly veiled threats of judicial murder, and finally the relish with which David contemplates and Dryden rehearses the bloodletting as witness turns against witness. From lines 1000 and following, David reveals the power of the law:

Must I at length the Sword of Justice draw?
Oh curst Effects of necessary Law!

How ill my Fear they by my Mercy scan,
Beware the Fury of a Patient Man.
Law they require, let Law then shew her Face;
They coud not be content to look on Grace,
Her hinder parts, but with a daring Eye
To tempt the terror of her Front, and Dye.

(I, 242-243, 1002-1009)

The language manages neatly to combine threat and elevation. While the sword is drawn, the hand wielding that sword emerges emblematically from the heavens, heavens of a distinctly Old Testament character. Furthermore, there is an interesting and strategic gap between Dryden's presentation of David as divine justiciar, and the actual bloodletting. At line 1010, as Dryden turns the figure from scriptural analogue to contemporary politics, the deaths imagined issue not from the sword of justice but from the self-inflicted wounds of deceit, betrayal, and rage. This suggestive narrative gap enables the king to hold erect the sword of justice, yet to have the blame for blood fall clear of his hand. As so often in the poem, Dryden's strategy is to acknowledge harsh realities while by sleight of hand to distance the king from blame. The *Ense rescindendum* of the preface is recalled by the vivid imagery of this passage, whose bloody particulars release vindictiveness under the auspices of moderation and evenhandedness.

By their own arts 'tis Righteously decreed,
Those dire Artificers of Death shall bleed.
Against themselves their Witnesses will Swear,
Till Viper-like their Mother Plot they tear:
And suck for Nutriment that bloody gore
Which was their Principle of Life before.

(I, 243, 1010-1015)

In this context, the tone of regret with which the narrator contemplates the absence of stern measures in 1660 is especially striking.

Indeed, that tone of regret is the key to Dryden's political position at this juncture. It was tactically impossible to proclaim a reactionary creed while writing for an audience that passionately believed in stability. Yet the phrases David uses in his final speech ("A King's at least a part of Government. . . . What then is left but with a Jealous Eye / To guard the Small remains of Royalty?") indicate a commitment to an undiminished monarchy, a commitment that can be seen in the repeated and almost Jacobean stress on the divinity of kingship. What then of the narrator's central assertion of the necessity of balanced government, an assertion often understood as a statement of Dryden's political convictions?

There is, as we have seen, a critical problem in assuming that any one passage isolated from the thrust of the whole of the poem serves explicitly to voice Dryden's real beliefs. We ought to be open to the possibility that the persona of the narrator may be as much a fiction—and as deliberately so—as any other character in the poem. To take one speech verbatim as an expression of Dryden's real belief violates the rhetorical integrity of the poem. The high degree to which the narrator functions doubly, as covert tactician as well as overt spokesman, is surely obvious in the preface, and we ought to be similarly alert to rhetorical motives in the narrator's lengthy constitutional address. The overt rhetorical function of this avowedly traditionalist speech is to preface David's decisive intervention, and by so doing to define his course as moderation. But the speech is more complex in its purpose than mere definition; its covert function is to put in polar opposition the preservation of the status quo and the Exclusionist cause with its inevitably absolutist consequences. By so doing it rules out any course other than commitment to the king. The studied and reasoned review of constitutional alternatives espouses moderation and paradoxically denies the possibility of treading a middle course.

While we can allow as sincere Dryden's hostility to innovation and his acceptance of the balance which the narrator lauds, it does seem clear that he was convinced such balance could not be achieved by allowing the good intentions of moderate men free rein, an assumption implicit in the current notion that *Absalom and Achitophel* is an intellectual persuasion to moderation and as such will heal the nation. The poem's insistence on near-universal corruption and the narrator's acknowledgment that David's mildness can bring but temporary relief (I, 219, 77-80) cast doubt from the first on the narrator's moderation as political prescription and on the efficacy of intellectual persuasion as political remedy. The poem's conclusion is that a government of balance can only be achieved by the most rigorous policing. The predominant political motives ascribed to most men in this poem are not natural obligation and gratitude but self-interest and self-preservation. If balance is to be preserved, then the free actions of such men are inadequate to that task; the politics of consensus in a fallen nation can only lead to recurrent crises.

The events of the years after 1681 showed what an exact sense of politics Dryden possessed. The rhetoric may seem backward-looking and the recommendations have come to seem reactionary in light of a Whiggishness almost universal since the acceptance of Locke after 1700, but neither the language nor the politics was anachronistic. The typology of kingship enjoyed a surprising vogue well into the last decades of the century. Not only had the Restoration itself been welcomed in unabashedly christic and prophetic schemes, but such schemes were again deployed in the propaganda efforts mounted by the court in 1666, and in tracts and sermons condemning Exclusion in the 1680s. Moreover, the Tory resurgence late in the 1690s was accompanied by a remarkable revival of interest in the *Eikon Basilike* and obvious attention to such doctrines as divine right, passive obedience, and hereditary succession.[15] That quintessential Anglican Tory, John Evelyn, contemplated James II as a new Herod, and Tillotson privately hailed the unlikely William and Mary as "two angels in human shape sent down to pluck a whole nation out of Sodom."[16] Dryden's practical politics were equally congruent with contemporary *realpolitik*; his plea for refurbishment of monarchy was echoed by the response of a purged, now Tory, political nation to Charles's reassertion of authority. An important segment of the political nation rallied eagerly to the monarchy when Charles bid for augmented power; corporations enthusiastically surrendered their borough charters in the early 1680s; and James II's first parliament made a generous grant of supply. Recent historical scholarship has indicated not only the real potential for a restored Stuart absolutism in the 1680s but also its parallels to widespread and fashionable European development.[17]

Identifying Dryden's political commitment and demonstrating the significance of specific political issues like Oblivion serve to point a distinction between the rhetoric of moderation which recurs as a political language in *Absalom and Achitophel* and the political meaning of the poem. Such a reading aims not to disengage political particulars from mythic and figural schemes, but to demonstrate the integral relation between the political and mythic levels of argument in the poem.[18] The irrefutably absolute moral and political implications of II Samuel cannot be realized in a reading of the poem as reasoned moderation. If the politics of this poem are moderate, the point of view balanced, if the poet is a disinterested critic of extremes, then the thrust of Scripture in *Absalom and Achitophel* is hard to perceive.[19] We are left with the paradox of metaphors that imply the case for anointed absolutism and a rhetoric that proclaims balance and moderation. What, we might wonder, are the practical political implications of the choice of a scriptural fable whose figural meaning is to type rebellion as primal disobedience and the king as Christlike healer and Godlike lawgiver? This poem emerges not from moderate truisms but from vigorously held partisan positions and reactionary politics whose advocacy in the fall of 1681 demanded care.[20]

Religio Laici

Four months after the publication of *Absalom and Achitophel*, Dryden issued another anonymous poem;[21] but if anonymity in *Absalom and Achitophel* were part of an effort to deflect and subvert partisan response, such caution was superfluous for *The Medall*. In the "Satyre Against Sedition" anonymity was a ruse; Dryden meant to engage, indeed to inflame, the opposition in his prefatory "Epistle To the Whigs." And in the poem itself, there is not the slightest gesture of conciliation. *The Medall* is a harsh and brilliant and momentary lapse into a flagrancy that the poet could not or would not long sustain. In November of the same year, eight months after publication of *The Medall*, came another poem of political argument; this one, however, bore the poet's name and declared itself: *Religio Laici or A Laymans Faith. A Poem.*[22]

But *Religio Laici* does not begin with political definition. It begins in nocturnal calm and spiritual uncertainty. The opening motif is religious pilgrimage; the mode is confessional, the manner epistolary. Yet neither spiritual quest nor generic and stylistic claims goes very far in describing the poem's rhetoric or its structural and argumentative properties. Dryden guides the religious pilgrim on a path to salvation; he narrates a history of philosophical and religious beliefs. Yet at the poem's close we discover that "common quiet" and not salvation is mankind's concern. This is an odd discovery for a confession of faith, though I suspect that for its original audience, men steeped in the language and strategies of political and religious controversy, such a conclusion was not surprising. An audience familiar with the poet laureate's controversial and brilliant poems on Exclusion would not only have understood the logic that drew this poem from confession to politics; they might have anticipated such a conclusion, and would have been attentive to the kind of political statement that the poet laureate was making late in 1682, at the beginning of what we have come to know as the Tory revenge.

Of course, Dryden's enemies were bound to find politics lurking under Dryden's cover of religious confession. His collaboration on *The Duke of Guise* was denounced as partisan hackwork.[23] But it was not an enemy who thought that the religious poem was fundamentally about politics, an analogue to *Absalom and Achitophel*. Charles Blount, friend and admirer of Dryden, read *Religio Laici* in the context of Exclusion, and proposed his own continuation of the poem as public defense now that "the Name of Christ is made use of to palliate so great Villanies and Treasons under the Pretext of God's cause, against both king and government."[24] Of course, Anglican monarchists had long combatted irreligion and civic disorder in such terms; James I's "no bishop, no king" was only the most obvious and most concise statement of that conflation. And an understanding of the extent to which the languages of religion and politics were interconnected, even interchangeable, in the later seventeenth century ought to dispel some perplexity over Dryden's motives in choosing religious confession as an occasion for political statement.[25] But even the general understanding, so ably argued by E. N. Hooker,[26] does not resolve all of the paradoxes and problems in *Religio Laici*, nor does it very precisely locate either Dryden's religious or political stance in the poem or, more specifically, the bearing that the statement of religious charity has on his political argument. Religion and politics were inextricably bound in this age—and the political meaning of religious frenzy had once again come fully into view with the Popish Plot and Exclusion—but Dryden nevertheless chose theology and not politics as his initial ground in *Religio Laici*.

While it might be clear that "common quiet" is a tenet of Anglican monarchism, it is not at all clear why Dryden should repeatedly stress the private and confessional character of *Religio Laici* in light of that conclusion. But this is only the most obvious of the poem's paradoxes. Despite Dryden's claim in *Preface* and poem that Father Simon's *Critical History of the Old Testament* "bred" his charity, the role of that history in the poem is not obvious. The *History* is an attack on the textual integrity of the Old Testament, and Dryden dismisses the whole subject of textual criticism as irrelevant to salvation. Recent scholarship suggests that Dryden had, in fact, only a cursory knowledge of Father Simon's work.[27] *The Critical History* had, however, some slight controversial interest in 1682, the year of its English translation.[28] The same cannot be said for the Athanasian creed. And to that subject Dryden devotes considerable attention in both *Preface* and poem. He combats Athanasius's harshness toward heathens, and uses the Egyptian bishop to stress his own charity in matters of conscience. Yet the meaning of that much-vaunted charity is puzzling in the context of Dryden's splenetic handling of the sectaries. Indeed, the distance between Dryden's charity for the heathens and his harshness toward dissenters is not only puzzling; by the end of the poem it has taken on the appearance of a calculated disturbance.

Such opposition is at once reminiscent of the play between generosity and political harshness in *Absalom and Achitophel* and in Charles II's attitude toward religion and politics by the time of Exclusion. The invocation of religious charity against a backdrop of political uniformity began to emerge as early as the Declaration of Breda, and it is certainly a policy that the king had hoped to adopt in the pursuit of a Tory revenge which would come to political climax in the judicial murders of Russell and Sidney and to religious climax after Charles's death with James's Declaration of Indulgence of 1687.[29] But the Tory revenge was not entirely Charles's to wield; in the religious aspects of the Tory revenge, the king was captive rather than architect of policy.[30]

Religio Laici claims to be a defense of the Anglican confession against enemies of piety, but it is a defense of a specific shade of that confession. The Anglicanism of *Religio Laici* which Dryden claims as personal and private was, in fact, a public conviction of some importance. The poet laureate and historiographer royal was moved to personal confession in 1682 in order to articulate the king's position at a time when the king's own expression of that position would have been difficult, given his reliance on the bishops and Anglican squirearchy in the parliamentary defeat of Exclusion.[31] The High Church party called not only for political revenge, which Charles realized in the remodeling of charters,[32] but also for a harsh repression of dissenting religion, a call that the king had never favored. A confession of conscience by the poet laureate would permit the public reiteration of the king's belief in liberty of tender conscience while insisting on the primacy of political order.

From the time Charles assumed the crown, he favored a measure of public conformity to the Church of England; but he also insisted on a liberty of conscience. However genuine his belief in religious toleration, the king steadily aimed at

such toleration, no doubt both to ease the political circum-
stance of English Catholics and to promote civic quiet among
his Protestant citizenry. This is the position of the Declaration
of Breda, and it is the language of the king's Indulgences of
1662 and 1672. In these public statements, Charles combined
resolute support for the Anglican doctrine, discipline, and
governance as the standard for "the general public worship of
God" with an express and contradictory approval of "liberty
of tender conscience." What the king advocated was some-
thing like theological indifference and civic order, and such I
believe is what Dryden advocates in *Religio Laici*. But the poem
also draws a very marked distinction between spiritual toler-
ation and the obligations of private reason in matters of state.
The narrator's charity allows a wide latitude on matters per-
taining to salvation; on that question the poem seems to ad-
mit not only heathens but a number of other souls, Catholic
and Protestant alike, to heaven. Liberty of conscience was not,
however, to be confused with political disorder or with polit-
ical weakness. When liberty of conscience is abused as political
license, *Religio Laici* harshly and splenetically condemns that
liberty. The theologian in this poem is willing to tolerate a
wide margin of dissent, but the politician is not. The poem
shares a political stance and a technique of argument with
Absalom and Achitophel, and nowhere is this more obvious than
in both poems' strategic celebration of the middle way.

But it is not only to *Absalom and Achitophel* that the tech-
niques of *Religio Laici* point. There are connections to the
earlier poetry and refinements of the position that Dryden
adopted in *Absalom and Achitophel* which reflect the particu-
larly delicate circumstance in which the king found himself
after the defeat of Exclusion. The language and argument of
Religio Laici must be understood both as a reflection of the
poet's general practices and in terms of those specific political
accommodations. From the title through the *Preface* to the
concluding lines of the poem, Dryden depicts himself as the-
ological amateur. Perhaps the role of amateur had become
something of a reflex, but there is more to this narration than
a familiar argumentative trope. Of course, there are similari-

ties among all of Dryden's works in their use of humility and incapacity as argumentative techniques; and the confessions of humility and incapacity are also part of a stylistic claim especially important in *Religio Laici*, where humility and honesty are linked as narrative stance and stylistic definition. But the humility of *Religio Laici* is not only personality; it is also a technical position in relation to the Anglican clergy on matters of doctrine and worship. Dryden's position as a layman is a self-conscious assertion of distance from the Anglican clergy. In part, Dryden uses this posture in order to range broadly over topics that the professional might not dare assemble; he also argues that the disinterested layman may be able to penetrate moral and theological problems more deeply than the cleric. Moreover, the whole treatment of Athanasius depends on the self-conscious amateurism that Dryden adopts in the *Preface*. The denial of Athanasius is at the center of Dryden's claims for charity, claims that this poet might not have made had he "prudently" followed the advice of his judicious clerical friend.

But the aim of this poem is not to establish the Anglican confession as stated by the Anglican clergy. It is to establish a confession of that faith not in defiance of but in distinction to the repressive position on dissenting theology that the Anglican clergy now loudly proclaimed after the defeat of Exclusion and the exposure of the Popish Plot. The position that this artless theological amateur would like to occupy is that familiar territory midway between extremes, that honest ground threatened on both sides. By identifying theological charity and political order with the true *via media*, Dryden's poem implicitly defines the king's religion and politics as those most conformable to the true spirit of the Anglican confession.

The device of the innocent narrator is, of course, only part of this strategy of the middle way. Not only does Dryden self-consciously identify his position as that endangered and embattled midpoint in the *Preface* (I, 305-306, 146-160), but the systems of argument in the poem render the same conclusion. The narrator conducts his search for the middle ground along a chronological continuum, through a structure of progressively more difficult and strident refutations, and between spiritual and intellectual extremes.[33] The narrative moves over time and ascends in argumentative power, and the cumulative force is the poem's final discovery that common quiet is mankind's most urgent concern. The rhetorical and dialectical thrust of argument and structure reach their climax in the penultimate stanza, where the narrator recoils from his tangle to ask, "What then remains, but, waving each Extreme, / The Tides of Ignorance, and Pride to stem?" (I, 322, 427-428). Dryden releases a spring that he has carefully wound for the preceding four hundred lines. The question suggests a fit of exasperation, but the drama has been prepared from the opening calm, and to such calm, now purged of doubts and perplexities, the poem returns. What this poem discovers is that theological precision does not determine salvation, which is a gift of God and is apparently dispensed to heathens and Christians alike. What is more difficult to obtain is common quiet and, to that end, even theological convictions must be sacrificed. Common quiet is the *summum bonum* of theological inquiry.

The central moral principle of *Religio Laici* is charity; this is a motif steadily adumbrated in the *Preface*, a theme that acts as an argumentative crux in the poem; it is part of Dryden's posture as layman, it guides the discussion of pre-Christian religions and textual authority in Scripture. Charity links spirit and intellect; it is at once personality and argumentative technique. And it is, of course, a stance crucially reminiscent of Charles II's public statements on theological matters. As such, Dryden's treatment and invocation of charity deserve close attention, particularly for the ways in which Dryden articulates that theme, for where he chooses to make his stand is not on the much contested ground of salvational authority in the late seventeenth century, but on questions of spiritual authority in the third century.

What precisely suggested the propriety of the Athanasian controversy as ground for a discussion of charity is difficult to determine; yet that distant ground is where the poet begins. Dryden claims that a judicious and learned friend censured his discussion of the Egyptian bishop;[34] yet he chose, in the face of that criticism, to make Athanasius his stalking horse for charity; and I suspect that Dryden made this choice partly because the problems that Athanasius poses are so distant from the religious pressures of the 1680s. In matters of a purely spiritual character, Dryden wants to clear the space between theology and politics as fully as possible. Dryden's suggestion that his clerical friend found his stance on Athanasius troubling and dangerous is part of this strategy, for Dryden wants to insist that *Religio Laici* is personal confession rather than clerical authority. And in his charity, he runs counter to the spirit of the Anglican clergy in 1682. He is willing to call on the stock of historical treatises of the Anglican Church, for the distance that Dryden desired was not from the historical spirit of the Church—not from Hooker—but from the contemporary spirit of that Church, from a stance less charitable than his own in matters of salvation.

And we hear of that charity in both *Preface* and poem. Dryden's errors in the *Preface* are those of charity; the Athanasian Creed on the question of condemnation is "of too hard a digestion" for Dryden's charity; and it is this same charity that confronts the Egyptian bishop in the poem. The subject in both *Preface* and poem is heathen salvation, "It has always been my *thought*, that Heathens, who never did, nor without Miracle cou'd hear of the name of Christ were yet in a possibility of Salvation" (I, 303, 38-40). For all those who lived before the incarnation, Dryden reserves the possibility of salvation in Christ. And for those generations between revealed religion in Israel and the incarnation, the possibility of salvation was first the fading light of revelation, and then the "light of Nature" (I, 303, 63). What remained of revealed religion was the notion of one deity, and that notion itself, without benefit of purer forms of worship, was sufficient for the posterity of Noah. Not only could the progeny of Cham and Japhet claim salvation, but those who lived wholly without the possibility of revelation might also be saved. Nor does Dryden, while criticizing the Deists and those who would "prove Religion by Reason" celebrating reason over revelation (I, 304, 89), at any point deny them the possibility of salvation. He reproves the false application of reason in matters of the spirit, but that reproval is not damnation.

Whatever the extent of Dryden's interest in the question of salvation for heathens—and there is, of course, the evidence of religious debate in *The Indian Emperor* and *Tyrannic Love*, which suggests a longstanding interest in that question[35]—the conclusions that he reaches on such issues as the knowledge necessary for salvation, the role of Scripture, and the function of forms of worship were meant to apply not only to the posterity of Noah but also to Dryden's exact contemporaries: to Anglicans, to sectaries, to Deists, and to Roman Catholics. Dryden nowhere argues directly that the form of worship within or without the Anglican confession is wholly indifferent to salvation, but such a conclusion would be justified by applying the debate over heathen salvation to contemporary religion. The application is most directly invited in Dryden's refutation of the Preface to the Athanasian Creed. To apply that Preface to heathens, Dryden argues, is to ignore its partisan context. Athanasius's Preface was developed not to exclude heathens from salvation, but as "a kind of Test, which whosoever took, was look'd on as an Orthodox Believer. 'Tis manifest from hence, that the Heathen part of the Empire was not concerned in it: for its business was not to distinguish betwixt Pagans and Christians, but betwixt Hereticks and true Believers. This, well consider'd, takes off the heavy weight of Censure, which I wou'd willingly avoid. . . . the Anathema, reaches not the Heathens, who had never heard of Christ, and were nothing interested in that dispute" (I, 305, 114-124). The most telling suggestion is Dryden's casual remark that the Preface was drawn up as "a kind of Test" to distinguish one sort of Christian from another. The Preface derives from third-century polemics, but such tests have a contemporary meaning. They might be appropriate among Protestants, but should they be applied to Catholics who are not "interested in that dispute"? On the propriety of the Test the court had been abundantly clear as Charles attempted to brush aside such tests in 1662 and 1672. Moreover, the Test Act had a particular political character: it was prompted "if not invented by the Earl of Shaftesbury who resolved to strike directly at the Duke of York and his friends."

But it was not simply the Test that Dryden raised in this discussion; Dryden attacks Athanasius because the poet would pursue, under cover of patristics, an advocacy of charity, of kindness, of "mollified Interpretation" of Scripture toward all Christians (I, 305, 110). *Religio Laici* was branded by Dryden's contemporaries as atheistical,[36] and it is not difficult to understand why. Dryden criticizes the elevation of reason by the Deists; he is scornful of ancient philosophy, but he damns neither heathen nor Deist. The thrust of his whole discussion of theology is that what is necessary for salvation is simple, clear, and accessible, because of God's grace, to heathen and Christian alike, lettered and unlettered. Of course, the knowledge of Scripture made it easier for the Christian to achieve salvation because Scripture points a broad path. Yet it was more likely that Socrates and those who followed "*Reasons* Dictates right; / Liv'd up, and lifted high their *Natural Light*" would find salvation than a "Thousand *Rubrick-Martyrs*" (I, 316, 208-211). Dryden jokes at the expense of Roman Catholic ceremony, but he is also making an important theological point: ceremony itself is quite indifferent to salvation. And of that, the poet is so powerfully convinced that he is willing to confront Church authority:

> Nor does it baulk my *Charity*, to find
> Th' *Egyptian* Bishop of another mind:
> For, though his *Creed Eternal Truth* contains,
> 'Tis hard for *Man* to doom to *endless pains*
> All who believ'd not all, his Zeal requir'd;
> Unless he first cou'd prove he was inspir'd.
> Then let us either think he meant to say
> *This Faith*, where *publish'd*, was the onely way;
> Or else conclude that, *Arius* to confute,
> The good old Man, too eager in dispute,
> Flew high; and as his *Christian* Fury rose
> Damn'd all for *Hereticks* who durst *oppose*.
>   (I, 316-317, 212-223)

Not only does Dryden assert his own charity against Athanasius, he argues that such authority is not divine, that Athanasius is guilty of the false inspiration and zeal that characterizes the piety and fanaticism of dissenting Protestants. Athanasius emerges from this passage as an ethusiast who mistook polemic for inspiration, who damned with *"Christian* Fury" all who opposed him. The attack is softer than the portrait of Corah as Titus Oates; Athanasius was a fool rather than a villain ("The good old Man, too eager in dispute, / Flew high"). But the categories of criticism are familiar and damaging: false prophecy, zeal, and fanaticism. It is exactly these terms that Dryden uses to strike against the spirit of Calvin in the second half of *Preface* and poem, and the link is not fortuitous. Athanasius's false zeal is a foil to the poet's charity, to the charity of the true Anglican spirit; it also links Catholicism and Calvinism in their advocacy of extremes. Moreover, the play on "high flying" suggests the similarity of the Egyptian bishop to those Anglican "high flyers" who would deny salvation to all but those conforming to their tenets and ceremonies. Dryden's Anglican confession offers charity and affirms spiritual and temperamental moderation. That moderation, the midpoint between extremes, is the key to the second half of the poem, which turns from spiritual to civic behavior.

What acts as a structural link between theology and politics is the digression on Father Simon's *Critical History of the Old Testament* (I, 317, 224-251). Phillip Harth has suggested that the digression is the core of this poem—originally, he speculates, a piece of complimentary verse intended to preface Henry Dickinson's translation of the *History*.[37] If this were so, the publisher bought himself a rather strange commendation. The thirty lines that compose the "digression" playfully compliment the translator, but they are also a sarcastic denial of the *History* itself. And how could it have been otherwise? It is a central premise of *Religio Laici* that in things necessary for salvation, the Scriptures are ample, plain, and clear; this premise is used to deny the institutional arrogance of the Roman Catholic Church and the impudence of dissenting "inspiration." In light of the polemical importance of Scripture plain

and clear, it would be odd indeed to find Dryden compli-
menting a book that discovered the textual corruption of
Scripture and argued against any certainty of its divine au-
thorship and authority. Dryden found a way of using Father
Simon's *History* against Rome, but that is a secondary issue
based on the theory of corrupt transmission. Of the central
premise of the *History*, Dryden is scornful.

The attack on Father Simon is not a direct refutation of his
History. Of Father Simon's discoveries, Dryden suggests he is
not competent to judge. And the digression on the *History*
begins with an assertion of technical incompetence and a link-
ing of charity and laity:

> Thus far my Charity this path has try'd;
> (A much unskilfull, but well meaning guide:)
> Yet what they are, ev'n these crude thoughts were bred
> By reading that, which better thou hast read,
> Thy Matchless Author's work: which thou, my Friend,
> By well translating better dost commend.
>
> (I, 317, 224-229)

Henry Dickinson has read Father Simon "better" than Dry-
den, and can commend *The Critical History* "better" than the
poet because he has translated it. What Dryden can commend
in this author is very little indeed; and when he turns from
translator to author, the mode changes from innuendo to sar-
casm:

> Witness this weighty Book, in which appears
> The crabbed Toil of many thoughtfull years,
> Spent by thy Authour, in the Sifting Care
> Of *Rabbins* old Sophisticated Ware
> From Gold Divine; which he who well can sort
> May afterwards make *Algebra* a Sport.
> A Treasure, which if *Country-Curates* buy,
> They *Junius*, and *Tremellius* may defy:
> Save pains in various readings, and Translations;
> And without *Hebrew* make most learn'd quotations.
> A Work so full with various Learning fraught,

So nicely pondred, yet so strongly wrought,
As Natures height and Arts last hand requir'd:
As much as Man cou'd compass, uninspir'd.

(I, 317, 234-247)

The *History* is a trot for country curates; ponderous, crabbed, and uninspired, it is "fraught" with learning.[38] Of Simon's great discovery, that the text of Scripture is corrupt, Dryden argues that rather than deny the sanctity of the holy writ, it undermines Rome:

If *written words* from time are not secur'd,
How can we think have *oral Sounds* endur'd?
Which *thus* transmitted, if *one* Mouth has fail'd,
Immortal Lyes on *Ages* are intail'd:
And that some such have been, is prov'd too plain;
If we consider *Interest, Church,* and *Gain.*

(I, 318, 270-275)

Intended to cast the authority of all Protestantism in doubt, in fact the "secret meaning" (I, 317, 252) of the *History* argues more sharply against Roman Catholicism than Protestantism. Scriptures are "not *every where* Free from Corruption," but they are uncorrupt, sufficient, clear, and entire "In *all* things which our needfull *Faith* require." In affirming this conclusion, the compliment which Dryden pays to Father Simon's *History* at the opening of the digression comes clear: "Yet what they are, ev'n these crude thoughts were bred / By reading that, which better thou hast read, / Thy Matchless Author's work." Dickinson has read Father Simon more carefully than Dryden; this the poet allows. But what Dryden has discovered is that his charity based on a broad reading of Scripture is not only untouched by Roman Catholic apologetics, it is reaffirmed by this confrontation.

And now the poet asserts his convictions with a new boldness:

Shall I speak plain, and in a Nation free
Assume an honest *Layman's Liberty*?
I think (according to my little Skill,

115

To my own Mother-Church submitting still:)
That many have been sav'd, and many may,
Who never heard this Question brought in play.
Th' *unletter'd* Christian, who believes in *gross*,
Plods on to *Heaven*; and ne'er is at a loss:
For the *Streight-gate* wou'd be made *streighter* yet,
Were *none* admitted there but men of *Wit*.
The few, by Nature form'd, with Learning fraught,
Born to instruct, as others to be taught,
Must Study well the Sacred Page; and see
Which Doctrine, this, or that, does best agree
With the whole Tenour of the Work Divine:
And plainlyest points to Heaven's reveal'd Design:
Which Exposition flows from *genuine Sense*;
And which is *forc'd* by *Wit* and *Eloquence*.

(I, 319, 316-333)

The gate to heaven is not so straight as some would like to make it, and the path that guides the Christian pilgrim to that gate is broad and unlettered. The sophistication of *The Critical History* is irrelevant to salvation. The passage reiterates and links a doctrinal and stylistic issue by conflating plainness and liberty, charity and laity. The style of heaven is limpid, plain, and clear; and the conflation of theology and style points back to the opening assertions of humility and forward to the invocation of Sternhold and Shadwell. Style is the man, and heaven is to be won not by wit but by charity and plainness. But salvation is not the only business of this poem; it is in a way not even its central, and certainly not its most pressing concern.

That business, the politics of public conformity and civic quiet, forms Dryden's subject in the second part of *Preface* and poem, and both pursue the subject through a technique of dialectical analysis. The technique is a staple in Dryden's repertoire; its structure of the middle and the extremes is crucial to Dryden's efforts to assert moderation, allowing the poet the political geography of the middle ground and preparing the portrayal of the opposition through caricature of extremes. In *Absalom and Achitophel*, the middle way enabled Dryden to jeer at Catholic ceremony and to harass the sectaries; and the same is true of *Religio Laici*, where Dryden derides both Roman Catholics and fanatics, though the wit exercised on the Catholics has a noticeably softer edge than that practiced on the sectaries. Both king and poet laureate maintained a show of moderation and balance in their handling of the sectaries, but there is no question that the royal memory of benefits from the civil wars repeatedly sought for ways in which to ease the conditions of English Roman Catholics. And both king and poet laureate linked a general theological charity with the harsh condemnation of Protestant sectarian politics. Such a connection leads the poet from a discussion of Scripture to politics in 1682:

> The Scripture is a Rule; that in all things needfull to Salvation, it is clear, sufficient, and ordain'd by God Almighty for that purpose, . . . But, by asserting the Scripture to be the Canon of our Faith, I have unavoidably created to my self two sorts of Enemies: The Papists indeed, more directly, because they have kept the Scripture from us, what they cou'd; and have reserv'd to themselves a right of Interpreting what they have deliver'd under the pretence of Infalibility: and the Fanaticks more collaterally, because they have assum'd what amounts to an Infalibility, in the private Spirit: and have detorted those Texts of Scripture, which are not necessary to Salvation, to the damnable uses of Sedition, disturbance and destruction of the Civil Government. (I, 305-306, 140-154)

The discovery of "two sorts of Enemies" is the crux of political dialectic in the poem. As in *Absalom and Achitophel* and *The Hind and the Panther*, the middle way is neither philosophical conviction nor temperament, but political strategy. Regardless of real political geography, where the king stood was the middle ground. In *Religio Laici*, the charitable layman, whose opinions exactly mirror those of the king, distinguishes himself from the theological rigidity of the Anglican clergy and discovers a middle way between the arrogance of papal infallibility and the "rigid opinions and imperious discipline of *Calvin*" (I, 308, 247).

It was not, of course, difficult to make a case for the Anglican confession as the *via media*. Hooker's great invocation had made this a standard rhetorical trope for Anglicanism, and Dryden invokes the "venerable Hooker" more than once in condemning the Presbyterian discipline. But Dryden's *via media* is not a middle ground in theological terms; it is an attempt to portray and to justify the king's political position in relation to Roman Catholics and dissenters. By linking devotion and politics, Dryden would link spiritual toleration and political exigency, exactly the king's own position after the defeat of Exclusion. In *Religio Laici*, the position is not developed topically, though there is a glancing reference to the Test Act in the *Preface*, a suggestion of Catholic innocence in the Popish Plot, and a memory of loyalty to Charles; but the cast of Dryden's whole discussion of Catholicism and sectarianism bears the imprint of the political position that the king himself had developed over the previous twenty years. It reflects as well Dryden's position in *Absalom and Achitophel*, where the criticism of Jebusites is noticeably more oblique than the handling of the sectaries. Of the spiritual implications of Roman Catholicism, we hear nothing at all; indeed, the papists are "*part* / Of that vast Frame, the Church" (I, 320, 360). They falsely arrogate authority in the interpretation of Scripture, but such institutional arrogance is not as dangerous as the private impudence of dissenting Protestants. What springs from the reform of Roman Catholic clerical arrogance is private zeal and political destruction.

And to that subject Dryden turns with a harshness that seems to contradict the spirit of religious charity so often invoked in *Preface* and poem. But charity is sharply limited to theology. The poem is divided, analytically and rhetorically, between theology and politics. The humble layman at the opening of the *Preface* and the anxious pilgrim at the opening of the poem are both postures, preparations for spiritual inquiry. The politician hardly needed such humility, and when Dryden turns to politics, he reaches a familiar stride:

Thus Sectaries, we may see, were born with teeth, foul-mouth'd and scurrilous from their Infancy: and if Spiritual Pride, Venome, Violence, Contempt of Superiours and Slander had been the marks of Orthodox Belief; the Pres-bytery and the rest of our Schismaticks, which are their Spawn, were always the most visible Church in the Chris-tian World. (I, 309, 275-280)

Here is no trace of the diffident pilgrim, no inquiring spirit, no philosophical skepticism, but the familiar rhythms and ironies of contempt. The language is sharp and splenetic, the syntax is broken into short, harsh expletives; this is the rhetorical culmination of a movement that had begun in suspension and careful qualification at the opening of the *Preface*. The con-demnation of sectaries forms the explosive climax of both *Preface* and poem, the point at which Dryden had aimed from the beginning.

The movement from qualification to condemnation in the *Preface* is exactly mirrored in the poem, which begins with a masterful invocation of rhetorical diffidence. The hushed sus-pension of the opening lines creates a delicately unsettled mood. Imagery and language suggest uncertainty; the rhythms are unsteady; the syntax is inverted; the opening altogether denies certitude:[39]

Dim, as the borrow'd beams of Moon and Stars
To *lonely, weary, wandring* Travellers,
Is *Reason* to the *Soul*: And as on high,
Those rowling Fires *discover* but the Sky
Not light us *here*; So *Reason*'s glimmering Ray
Was lent, not to *assure* our *doubtfull* way,
But *guide* us upward to a *better Day*.   (I, 311, 1-7)

At the poem's close, Dryden claims to have written in verse fittest for discourse, nearest prose, and yet the effects at the opening are achieved not by conformity to the syntax and rhythms of prose but by a careful departure from those norms. The subject of the first independent clause is suspended until the third line; and in the second and third clauses, negation

119

and compound verbs attenuate the sense. The grammatical and syntactical extensions suspend the movement of argument; the language and syntax suggest hesitation, and the verse rhythms echo that hesitation. The poem begins in unusual metrical inversion, and that rhythmic trepidation is reflected in the carefully deliberated rhythms of the second line. The argument itself is steadily carried past the line endings so that verse and syntax contradict rather than compel assent. The effect of the whole is similar to the claims of spiritual and intellectual diffidence at the beginning of the *Preface*; but while those prose rhythms suggest uncertainty, the verse here orchestrates an even subtler hesitation, hardly the rugged measures of the Sternhold psalter. This is verse aiming not at discourse but at persuasion. The design of the poem as a whole is to begin in uncertainty and to conclude in condemnation. In a gradually ascending line of assurance, the narrator moves through the false steps of ancient philosophy, the errors of Deism and natural religion, toward popery and fanaticism. The climax to this rhythm of rational inquiry comes at line 400, when the disinterested philosopher weighs the consequence of religious reformation:

> 'Tis true, my Friend, (and far be Flattery hence)
> This good had full as bad a Consequence:
> The Book thus put in every vulgar hand,
> Which each presum'd he best cou'd understand,
> The *Common Rule* was made the *common Prey*;
> And at the mercy of the *Rabble* lay.
> The tender Page with horney Fists was gaul'd;
> And he was gifted most that loudest baul'd:
> The *Spirit* gave the *Doctoral Degree*:
> And every member of a *Company*
> Was of *his Trade*, and of the *Bible free*.
> Plain *Truths* enough for needfull *use* they found;
> But men wou'd still be itching to *expound*:
> . . . .
> While Crouds unlearn'd, with rude Devotion warm,
> About the Sacred Viands buz and swarm,

The *Fly-blown Text* creates a *crawling Brood*;
And turns to *Maggots* what was meant for *Food.*
A Thousand daily Sects rise up, and dye;
A Thousand more the perish'd Race supply.
So all we make of Heavens discover'd Will
Is, not to have it, or to use it ill.   (I, 321-322, 398-424)

Now we are on familiar ground; the hesitation, the slanted
rhymes and oblique rhythms of the opening all have disap-
peared. This is the manner not of spiritual quest but political
condemnation, and the evocation of *Absalom and Achitophel* is
neither surprising nor accidental. Not only are the epithets
familiar, not only is there a similarity of argument and im-
agery, but the voicing of the argument is strikingly reminis-
cent of the overt political poem. Here is the lock step of rhythm
and rhyme that Dryden had made his own in *Absalom and
Achitophel.*

The verse paragraph begins by suggesting balanced inquiry,
the guileless search for truth. But the claims of disinterested-
ness and balance quickly give way to argument by juxtaposi-
tion of extremes: the book / the vulgar hand; the common
rule / the common prey; the tender page / the horny fist. The
dissenting pretense to spiritual inspiration is undercut by im-
ages and epithets that turn spiritual yearning into physiology:
the hand and voice—oddly disembodied and disjointed figures
themselves—become maggots and swarming insects. Sectarian
inspiration transforms the sacred text into garbage. Dryden
claims that he has chosen the epistolary manner, the style nearest
prose; he intends discovery, not persuasion, but discovery is
not among the aims of this passage.

While offering wide latitude in matters of the spirit, this
poem swiftly and harshly condemns sectarian politics, and the
spirit of the condemnation is not disinterested inquiry. Dry-
den's aim in this poem is to argue the king's case in religion
and politics; like the king he is cautiously lenient toward
Catholics, and like the king he is willing to tolerate a wide
spectrum of religious beliefs. But such toleration, the poem
argues, should not be construed as political indifference or

political weakness. The king had the task of moving forcefully against political dissent, and he did so in no uncertain terms following the dissolution of the Oxford parliament. But he did not wish, as did members of the High Church party, to condemn religious dissent in spiritual terms. So long as religious dissent remained wholly a spiritual matter, the king's message was toleration; he did not aim to impose a uniformity in these matters. What he had advocated through his reign was religious toleration and political discipline; *Religio Laici* is an attempt to give the authority of verse to a policy now under siege. What the king could no longer advocate, the poet laureate might expound in the freedom of poetry and laity.

5. Fables, Allegories, and Enigmas

The Hind and the Panther

DRYDEN turned once more to poetry and "laicy" in defense of religious faith; but the circumstances in which he wrote and published *The Hind and the Panther* were very different from those in which he conceived his Anglican confession—and not least because Dryden now had the formidable task of reversing those opinions on religion and politics to which he had given such definitive edge in *Religio Laici*.[1] In the earlier poem Dryden had stressed laity in order to define an Anglican toleration distinct from repressive clericalism; in light of that distinction, he used the poem to articulate the king's position on toleration at a time when the king could not do so himself. *Religio Laici* was written at a moment of high tide in the political and literary fortunes of Charles Stuart and his poet laureate. It followed closely on the enormous success of *Absalom and Achitophel*; and the assurance and brusqueness of the political elements of the *Preface* to *Religio Laici* suggest the confidence with which Dryden undertook, among other things, religious "confession." Much had changed by the spring of 1687. James had come to the throne with a remarkably solid financial and political base, but from the moment of his accession he had conducted a zealous and implacable campaign to achieve toleration for English Catholics and a free hand in staffing the army and public offices with his coreligionists.[2] By the spring of 1687, in the face of resistance and defeat, James switched tactics from persuasion, from an attempt to court Anglican compliance with his political aims, to open confrontation by issuing a Declaration of Indulgence.[3]

It was at such a moment, following the Declaration, that *The Hind and the Panther* was published. The poet took seriously the obligation to defend the Declaration, a political tactic consistent, of course, with Charles II's own use of prerogative in attempting to achieve similar indulgence in 1662 and

1672. But Dryden did not share James's missionary zeal or the political aims of the "forward party" at James's court.[4] Moreover, the need for personal confession, a need that Dryden claims but hardly fulfills in *Religio Laici*, had now become a necessity. The poet had been under steady and scurrilous attack since his conversion to Rome, and the pressure of such attack can be felt in the poem's confessional elements.

The task of defending both the Declaration and his own conversion spurred the exploration of fable; the mode had a long and distinguished tradition in political application, a tradition that Dryden himself invokes in the opening lines of part 3. But the complexity, the daring, even the copiousness of invention suggest that Dryden found more here than convenience. Fable was a way of achieving distance and protection, of invoking the tradition of veiled meaning,[5] of putting at arm's length the uncomfortable facts of 1687. But fable also touched an imaginative chord that would repeatedly draw the poet. It was an extension of earlier efforts to achieve a strategic rhetoric, and the fulfillment of an aesthetic that had been practiced as early as *Annus Mirabilis* and had reached one kind of perfection in *Absalom and Achitophel*. But in effecting that allegory, Dryden intended translucency; he had no final need for obscurity and enigma. The mask of biblical parable and the distance of allegory were part of a political campaign and part of an aesthetic of wit. The reach toward obscurity and the use of enigmas suggest a different political motive—fear rather than persuasion—and a fuller exploration of digression, association, and indirection as expressive modes. In the later poetry, fable and translation allowed the poet to find a voice in which to meditate rather than argue, to disclose principles and ideals rather than hew to the political aims of the court.

The Glorious Revolution was of course the catalyst in this change, but *The Hind and the Panther* can be seen as something of a turning point, sharply and brilliantly polemical as in the past—indeed if anything more resourceful since more territory needed defense—but also newly concerned with mysteries and enigmas, with the difficulties and uncertainties of interpretation and application, and with the multivalence of

124

language itself. But it was with defense and attack that Dryden was still principally concerned, and there can be little doubt that in these terms Dryden knew exactly what he wanted to effect in turning to fable to exercise a new religious vocation and a long-mastered rhetorical art.[6] But the meanings of fable and enigma are not disclosed in the overt remarks on style and mode in the preface (II, 469, 91-107). There Dryden calls the first part of the poem "Heroick," the second "plain and perspicuous," and part 3, the complex and obscure set of fables, is described as a "Domestick Conversation [which] is, or ought to be more free and familiar than the two former." Of course, there is some slyness in the qualifying "is, or ought to be," and some play in describing beast fables as the "Domestick Conversation" of beasts. But these stylistic remarks are oblique in their relation to the poem itself,[7] and what Dryden has to say about the fables is intentionally misleading. "There are in it two *Episodes*, or *Fables*, which are interwoven with the main Design. . . . In both of these I have made use of the Common Places of *Satyr*, whether true or false, which are urg'd by the Members of the one Church against the other. At which I hope no *Reader* of either Party will be scandaliz'd; because they are not of my Invention" (II, 469, 100-105).

The topos is familiar indeed; Dryden attempts to distance the materials of his poem by claiming that they are not of his invention, by dismissing the satire as convention. This is a variant of an earlier trope—"were I the Inventour, who am only the Historian"—but now history has turned to adaptation. Could Dryden have assumed that anyone reading his attack on the Anglican Church would have mistaken the nasty and topical barbs for ancient satiric commonplaces, or that he might have thus escaped notice and censure? What Dryden does establish is the authority of the fable tradition and the impersonality and conventions of the mode, topoi that he repeats in the poem itself. However, the real meaning of fable and enigma and their antithesis to malice and wit emerge in the discourse on language in part 2, where the obscurity of prophetic writ, the difficulty of interpretation, the unsteadi-

125

ness of language itself, provide a new coloration for the political poet.

Perhaps Dryden anticipated the ridicule and censure to which *The Hind and the Panther* would be subject. He could hardly have assumed otherwise. Not only had he long been a target for such censure—and the florid self-display in this poem takes as its subject the sufferings of the poet at the hands of his enemies—but he must have known that he had provided instruments for his detractors. He could not have enjoyed the ridicule to which the poem was in fact subject, but the very complexity and the daring of the beast portraits and the fable elements may themselves have been an invitation, perhaps a target to draw immediate fire away from the poem's more difficult and embattled theological and political materials. And Dryden all but anticipates the tenor of the criticisms that he was to receive:

> Much malice mingl'd with a little wit
> Perhaps may censure this mysterious writ,
> Because the Muse has peopl'd *Caledon*
> With *Panthers, Bears,* and *Wolves,* and Beasts unknown,
> As if we were not stock'd with monsters of our own.
> Let *Æsop* answer, who has set to view,
> Such kinds as *Greece* and *Phrygia* never knew;
> And mother *Hubbard* in her homely dress
> Has sharply blam'd a *British Lioness,*
> . . . .
> Led by those great examples, may not I
> The wanted organs of their words supply?
> If men transact like brutes 'tis equal then
> For brutes to claim the privilege of men.
>
> (II, 503-504, 1-15)

The defense is poetic tradition; Dryden does what other poets have done before him. But it is more than political fable that Dryden suggests here. The poem is an example of "mysterious writ," and the term has been carefully pondered and prepared. By it Dryden argues the connections among beast fable, scriptural prophecy, and religious mystery. "Mysterious writ" not only links the materials of fable and prophecy but argues their connection through style and prepares the ground for distinguishing inspired texts from malicious fables. And it is this distinction between true and false prophecy, between the clarity of malice and the inevitable ambiguities of the Word that Dryden invokes in delineating the character and meaning of the fables in part 3. There is yet a further significance of mysterious writ which Sanford Budick has persuasively demonstrated, the relation of the apocalyptic materials in the poem to Scripture and to the tradition of Protestant apocalyptic.[8] The material from Daniel that Dryden integrated with his bestiary and concluding fables forms part of the poet's efforts to reverse the tradition and charges of Protestant apocalyptic against Roman Catholicism.[9] And here Budick sees a connection between such a use of mysterious writ and the place of mystery in Roman Catholic spiritual exercise.[10] Dryden at once reverses the claims of *Religio Laici* that in things needful for salvation, Scripture is plain, simple, and clear, and demonstrates his new religious and spiritual mode. The central position of mystery in Roman Catholicism is argued in the passages on transubstantiation in parts 1 and 2, and the contrasting styles of *Religio Laici* and *The Hind and the Panther* are evidence of the way in which Dryden linked poetic style and spiritual identity.[11]

Although it is true that there are continuities of imagery between *Religio Laici* and *The Hind and the Panther*,[12] those continuities are slight in the context of the vastly different styles and modes of the two poems, and especially so, given the sharp divergence of political and religious opinions that these poems articulate. Of course, the conversion demanded a new profession of faith, but had *Religio Laici* concerned itself solely with matters of faith, then the business of *The Hind and the Panther* would have been much simpler to conduct. *Religio Laici* is a harsh condemnation of popery and fanaticism; it attempts to claim for the Anglican confession the middle ground as exclusive domain; and it links charity with the spirit of the king's religion. All these issues would now have to be redressed. Not only did Dryden need to refute charges that he

127

himself had leveled at the Catholic Church, but he must also have felt some need for rapprochement with the dissenters.

James had issued the Declaration of Indulgence as part of a program to drive dissenters into political alliance with Roman Catholics. The king had abandoned efforts at a parliamentary repeal of the Test Act and Penal Laws; the Church of England men who sat in parliament and the Anglican bishops steadfastly repelled such an effort. Through alliance with the dissenters, James hoped eventually to challenge the political hegemony of the Anglican party in parliament; and his use of *quo warranto* to remodel municipal charters and eventually to achieve, through rigged elections, a new power base in parliament suggests the direction of his political program.[13] It is this program and James's tactic of prerogative that Dryden now had to face in *The Hind and the Panther*, and it is his discomfort with both the tactic of prerogative and with the ultimate direction of James's political program that explains the peculiar insistence in the preface that the motive for the poem and the time of its composition have no relation to the Declaration of Indulgence:

> As for the Poem in general, I will only thus far satisfie the *Reader*: That it was neither impos'd on me, nor so much as the Subject given me by any man. It was written during the last Winter and the beginning of this Spring; though with long interruptions of ill health, and other hindrances. About a Fortnight before I had finish'd it, His Majesties Declaration for Liberty of Conscience came abroad: which, if I had so soon expected, I might have spar'd my self the labour of writing many things which are contain'd in the third part of it. But I was always in some hope, that the Church of *England* might have been perswaded to have taken off the *Penal Lawes* and the *Test*, which was one Design of the Poem when I propos'd to my self the writing of it. (II, 468, 56-65)

There are several interesting and puzzling things here. Three times in the space of these few sentences, Dryden insists that subject and form are solely his. And yet paradoxically he also allows a public and political purpose for his poem, to persuade the Church of England to "have taken off the *Penal Lawes* and the *Test*." The confession of political intention is especially interesting in light of the timing of the Indulgence. What Dryden means to establish here is his own position, not in favor of abrogation of parliamentary laws through prerogative, but of the safer course of attempting to achieve a parliamentary repeal of those laws. *The Hind and the Panther* does the best it can with the Declaration, but such a declaration was not this poet's aim. Indeed, he claims that the poem was written in complete ignorance of the imminence of the Declaration.[14] But rumors of such a declaration were abroad from the beginning of James's reign, and its issuance after the failure of the "closeting" efforts and after the February 12, 1687 Scottish Declaration of Indulgence,[15] could not have taken the poet by surprise. The disclaimer was intended to distance the poet from the court and to distinguish this poem of Roman Catholic apologetics from the policies that James now seemed bent on enacting. It is a strategy to define territory, and the territory that Dryden would have liked to occupy in the spring of 1687 was not in the immediate environs of Whitehall.[16]

And yet in coming to terms with the Declaration which, disclaimers aside, he clearly had to do in *The Hind and the Panther*, Dryden had also to come to terms with the dissenters. It was one thing for James to declare that his liberty of tender conscience applied to all, Catholics and dissenters alike, but it was another matter for Dryden to figure out a rapprochement with the sects. Nothing is more forceful in *Religio Laici* than the splenetic condemnation of the sectaries as agents of political disorder. Whatever spiritual quarrels the Anglican poet of *Religio Laici* may have had with Baptists and Presbyterians—and the spiritual differences seem slight given the theological indifference of the poem—it is the political threat of fanaticism that drives the poem's satire. Charles II had no reason to seek political support among the dissenters; his political alliance with the vindictive and repressive High Church party had been sealed in the Exclusion Crisis. But for James, the dissenting sects were a political hope.

Not, of course, that the portraits of the dissenters in part 1 form a particularly charming gallery. Yet the quarrel with the sects in *The Hind and the Panther* is not initially political. In the preface, Dryden turns to his familiar strategy of claiming the middle ground. Roman Catholicism stands in the embattled center; and the Anglican Church, which in 1682 had suffered from fanaticism of the left and right, has been moved to the side. The enemies of the Roman Church are grouped as the vast majority of voracious Anglicans and those sectaries not properly thankful and grateful to the king. But the strategy of the defenseless middle flanked by hostile and rigid fanatics has been given a new turn in *The Hind and the Panther*. For here the center is not so much flanked by extremes as ringed by enemies, and the function of the initial portraits is not to raise political argument with the sects or to distinguish between two opposing evils but rather to conjure a specter of dissenting theologues, to suggest through the taint of association, through a constellation of images and metaphors, and finally through the structure of the gallery itself that the Anglican Church is nothing so much as one of the dissenting sects. When the political themes of dissenting Protestantism are raised—riot, disorder, destruction, and instability—they are attached to the Anglican Church; by transferring familiar satiric topics to a new target Dryden can tar the enemies of the king and his poet laureate, and correctly align the poem with James's political aims in 1687.

On the contemporary politics of English dissent, both the preface and the poem are surprisingly mild. There is, for example, no mention of sectarian support for Monmouth's rebellion. The bestiary in part 1 of the poem is an important element in Dryden's efforts to depict the Catholic Church as an embattled and nearly defenseless institution in a world dense with religious terrors and political dangers. And, of course, it is the beast fable that enables Dryden to render such danger through the satiric tradition of the animal portraits. But the effect of these portraits is not the same as the harsh authorial condemnation of *Religio Laici*.

The portraits themselves are initially turned in a manner to raise theological and not political issues. What had been a matter of almost total indifference in *Religio Laici* is now given first importance. Athanasius had been censured in the Anglican poem for his lack of charity; but in *The Hind and the Panther* he is one of the heroes who chased the beast of Socinianism (II, 471, 54-56). The attack on heresy is part of the poem's general effort to undermine Protestant claims for the authority of private reason—an argument conducted at much greater length in part 2—but what is most striking in the initial portraits is the sudden attention to particulars of faith. The satiric sharpness of the portraits cuts against ceremonial and spiritual indifference: Independents are ridiculed for negligence of forms; Quakers for their religious aversion to swearing; Atheists for their aping the forms of other religions; Baptists for their "first rebellion," the rebellion of Luther against the Roman Catholic Church; Socinians for their blasphemy against the godhood of the infant Christ. These are new subjects for Dryden as religious poet. The psychology of conversion emphasizes faith, and if Dryden wished to authenticate such conversion—and the apostrophe that follows the first portraits makes the experience of conversion an important subject of this spiritual autobiography—then the careful attention to the failure of sectarian Protestanism in formal and theological terms is almost a matter of compulsion.

But the initial encounter with sectarianism in *The Hind and the Panther* is dictated by other motives as well. If the king's Declaration were both a promise to respect tenderness of conscience and an invitation to the sectaries to form a political alliance, it would hardly do to conduct the polemic of this poem as a harsh denunciation of sectarian political disorder. It is impossible to say whether the poet, like the king, saw the alliance with the sectaries as a necessary weapon in the fight against the Anglican monopoly on place. And perhaps the question of personal conviction is somewhat beside the point. Nothing could have been more obvious to Dryden's contem-

131

poraries than the public character of *The Hind and the Panther*; whatever the personal belief, Dryden could not have turned against so central a strategy as James's efforts to achieve the new alliance:

> This Indulgence being granted to all the Sects, it ought in reason to be expected, that they should both receive it, and receive it thankfully. For at this time of day to refuse the Benefit, and adhere to those whom they have esteem'd their Persecutors, what is it else, but publickly to own that they suffer'd not before for Conscience sake. . . . Of the receiving this Toleration thankfully, I shall say no more, than that they ought, and I doubt not they will consider from what hands they receiv'd it. 'Tis not from a *Cyrus*, a Heathen Prince, and a Foreigner, but from a Christian King, their Native Sovereign: who expects a Return in *Specie* from them; that the Kindness which He has Graciously shown them, may be retaliated on those of his own perswasion. (II, 468, 40-55)

This passage from the preface to *The Hind and the Panther* is a clear indication of policy. The king expects compliance and thankfulness, "a Return in *Specie* from them." And such return he got. The addresses of thanks that poured into London from the dissenters argue the correctness of the strategy.[17] That it was late for the strategy to have any real chances for success was also a fact. But Dryden rather carefully suggests the political dimensions of the Declaration in these veiled demands.

Dryden could afford to raise theological problems with the sects, because the effect of the Indulgence was finally to argue that theological problems were indifferent to a king who had "*restor'd God to his Empire over Conscience.*" The poem suggests that the Roman Catholic Church will convert by the comeliness of her appearance, but the poem does not strenuously aim at conversion. The Hind herself abandons such efforts by the end of the poem; she is perfectly ready to tolerate theological error. That is an essential argument of the Declaration. This Roman Catholic Church is not interested in persecution—an instrument of the Anglicans, not of tolerant Rome.

To suggest that the portraits attend solely to matters of religious form and faith is, however, to simplify the texture and argument of part 1. The initial portraits are so concerned, but the portraits to which Dryden turns after the personal confession are more sharply drawn and argue more carefully the political disorder consequent on religious reform. But the problem of such disorder is not raised in a contemporary English context, only in distant lands and distant times. Hence the concern for Socinianism in Poland, Presbyterianism in ancient Wales, heresies in the fourteenth century, Zwinglianism in Switzerland, the origins of Calvinism in the Jewish Sanhedrin. The historical reach of the bestiary touches the Flood, but Dryden is silent on the 1680s. The geographical range is equally extensive, but Dryden comes no closer to home than Holland and Scotland. The contemporary English experience of sectarian violence is barely alluded to. Nothing is heard of the role of sectarianism in Exclusion. But one could hardly have issued an invitation to join the king in political alliance and then covered that invitation with political abuse.

Moreover, the dissenters are only one of Dryden's targets. Dryden had business to conduct not only with the errors of dissenting theology but also with the Anglican Church. And on the subject of Anglican politics, Dryden has a good deal to say. With the sectaries he had been content to raise theological issues and the sins of the past; it is with the Anglican party that he means to do his most serious political business. On this issue Dryden appears in *The Hind and the Panther* to be at one with his king. The Church of England men posed what James perceived as the most serious threat to his religious and political goals. The persecution of the Seven Bishops and the case against Magdalen College showed how very seriously James himself undertook political warfare with the Anglicans.[18] That Dryden was unwilling to follow the king in some aspects of this policy I think he dares to suggest in part 3, although the complex fable mode of the last section makes it difficult to determine Dryden's own politics. But on the question of political subversion, there is no doubt that the most serious civic issues are not to be raised with sectaries but with that former bastion of monarchical loyalty, the Anglican Church.

That James was absolutely wrong to turn his staunchest natural allies into political opponents, Dryden may or may not have realized. He was, however, quite willing in the spring of 1687 to conduct a campaign against the Anglican establishment. There is an implicit continuity between Dryden's efforts in *Religio Laici* to distinguish his own religious confession from that of the Anglican establishment, to argue a theologically tolerant line against the Church of England's support for the Test Act. But there is more to the portrait of the Anglican party in *The Hind and the Panther* than their complicity in or even use of that piece of legislation. *The Hind and the Panther* argues that the spiritual authority of the Anglican Church is at every point compromised by self-interest, a trait that emerges variously as greed, opportunism, and complicity in parliamentary inquisition; and the charges remain steady throughout. They are the foundation of the opening portrait of the Panther, which aims at once to discredit Anglican politics in 1687 and the whole of the Church of England from its inception.

Not, of course, that Dryden begins in full fury. That was hardly his way; the habit of appearances, the claims of impartiality and evenhandedness, demanded otherwise, and Dryden was true to those demands:

> The *Panther* sure the noblest, next the *Hind*,
> And fairest creature of the spotted kind;
> Oh, could her in-born stains be wash'd away,
> She were too good to be a beast of Prey!
> How can I praise, or blame, and not offend,
> Or how divide the frailty from the friend!
> Her faults and vertues lye so mix'd, that she
> Nor wholly stands condemn'd, nor wholly free.
> Then, like her injur'd *Lyon*, let me speak,
> He can not bend her, and he would not break.
>
> (II, 478, 327-336)

And yet from such invitation and solicitude, from the balance of praise and blame, comes a torrent of abuse. The portrait of the Panther is turned far more carefully and is modulated over a wider range of issues than the portraits that open the bestiary, for Dryden aims at more than a condemnation of Anglican politics in 1687. He wants to argue the taint of political interest from the beginning. The theme of self-interest dominates the portrait of the Panther and is crucial to the handling of the Anglican Church throughout. The initial portrait of the Panther takes full advantage of the modes of the poem, mixing bestiary and allegory in a manner that first suggests but then transforms the distinguished literary models that Dryden claims for his own in this portrait:

A *Lyon* old, obscene, and furious made
By lust, compress'd her mother in a shade.
Then, by a left-hand marr'age weds the Dame,
Cov'ring adult'ry with a specious name:
So schism begot; and sacrilege and she,
A well-match'd pair, got graceless heresie.
God's and kings rebels have the same good cause,
To trample down divine and humane laws:
Both would be call'd Reformers, and their hate,
Alike destructive both to church and state:
The fruit proclaims the plant; a lawless Prince
By luxury reform'd incontinence,
By ruins, charity; by riots, abstinence.
Confessions, fasts and penance set aside;
Oh with what ease we follow such a guide!
Where souls are starv'd, and senses gratify'd.
Where marr'age pleasures, midnight pray'r supply,
And mattin bells (a melancholy cry)
Are tun'd to merrier notes, *encrease* and *multiply*.
Religion shows a Rosie colour'd face;
Not hatter'd out with drudging works of grace;
A down-hill Reformation rolls apace.
What flesh and bloud wou'd croud the narrow gate,
Or, till they waste their pamper'd paunches, wait?
All wou'd be happy at the cheapest rate.

(II, 479, 351-375)

The evocations of Spenser and Milton are converted into the satiric rhymes of Dryden's mature style. The choice of fable allowed the portraits to be conducted in a manner that already offered a vehicle for caricature. The charges of libidinous rage are neatly contained in the materials of the bestiary and then argued as a subliminal theme in the whole of the passage. But Dryden's use of fable is not limited to the satiric topicality of *Mother Hubbard*. From bestiary, Dryden turns to the allegory of Sin and Death, compounding the satiric effects of the first mode with the moral resonance of Milton's allegorical fantasy.[19] And though the literary allusions are very clear, the effect of the whole is not a combination of Spenser and Milton. Language and mode suggest the earlier models, but the coupling of satire and allegory creates a new idiom; the rhythms, the diction, and the wit are very much Dryden's own. The harsh ironic edge to these couplets, the swift and relentless thrust of condemnation, the abstractions that function as images and reduce complex arguments to irrefutable antitheses—these are the lessons that Dryden had mastered in *Absalom and Achitophel*, and they are applied with absolute authority in this poem. But the manner of this passage, with its complex system of allusion and irony, is not sustained in the poem as a whole. The wide range of problems which Dryden had to face in *The Hind and the Panther* could not have been solved through the strict impersonality and brilliance of satiric portraiture, though if Dryden's own religious position and the politics of James's Declaration had been easier to defend, more of *The Hind and the Panther* might have been cast in this subtle but sharply aggressive manner.

It is, of course, difficult to argue from the evidence of the best passages in *The Hind and the Panther*—those that use the resources of mode and suggest the poet's deepest strengths as satirist—that the more strictly Dryden obeyed his impulses as political strategist, or the more artfully he masked his own convictions or used the stance of those convictions as a cover for political argument, the more successfully he engaged his audience. And yet there is support for such a thesis in the peculiar and embarrassing moment in part 3 when the masks seem inadvertently to drop and the poet emerges in an unfamiliar voice to claim "That suff'ring from ill tongues he bears no more / Than what his Sovereign bears, and what his Saviour bore"[20] (II, 511, 304-305). This is the climax to the Hind's discipline of her son, a poet who needs to be reminded that vengeance is the Lord's. The whole passage rehearses the poet's earlier confessional prayer (II, 471-472, 68-99) but renders that material more sharply aggressive, hinting that what we have seen thus far of mildness and probity could well, and perhaps may at any moment, give way to unchecked fury. This much is familiar, the poet suggesting untold reserves of anger. There is, as well, throughout the Hind's discourse, a political argument, an alignment of poet and monarch, a suggestion of protection from above. What is new is the climactic declaration, the bold assimilation of poet to savior. The couplet argues that in his scandal and suffering the poet bears no more contumely than James and Christ. The conflation with James does not disturb at this distance, and probably did not disturb Dryden's contemporaries, some of whom had heaped a good deal of clever and nasty abuse on the duke of York and would have been perfectly willing to couple the king and his poet laureate—though perhaps not in the way that the Hind is about to offer. What is strange here is the oddly weighted assimilation of the poet to the savior—a surprising move, for the passage is something other than an imitation of Christ with analogy through mortification. It is, in fact, an assertion that the poet suffers as much as the savior, that the savior bore no greater contumely than the poet. The analogies seem correctly to ascend from poet laureate to sovereign to savior, but the crux of the comparison—"bears no more than"—allows us to reverse the analogy. If the poet suffers no more than what his savior bore, then it must also be allowed that the savior suffered no more than the poet; and the couplet structure emphasizes analogy rather than ascending comparison. The rhyme linkage of "more" and "bore," poet and savior, argues not an ascending order of suffering but an equality of contumely. The claim is peculiar and grandiose, and we can gauge something of its inadvertancy by comparing this presentation with the earlier confessional prayer, that familiar rehearsal of humility and reverence, the admission of error, the recounting of the sins of youth. Those materials can be wholly and easily assimilated to the poet's steady insistence in the prefaces and critical essays on the reserved and digressive self. This couplet suggests a lapse into a deeper and perhaps more primitive version of the self, at once fearful and grandiose. Here is the poet touched to the quick by insult and abuse, emerging in a frightened and utterly unguarded sense of person and place. There are, finally, no clients in this passage other than the self, and I think that what we see is at once a failure and a revelation. Beneath the dense artifice of the political poet lay no untold reserves of power and vengeance, but an uncharted depth of fear and injury.

The problems with which this poem deals are not, however, those of uncontrolled confession, but of religious and political strategy. The lapse is momentary and Dryden quickly regains control through accusation, a mode that he sustains for long stretches of part 3 and a mode that, through the dialogue of the Hind and the Panther, allows him to achieve the artfully arranged balance of charge and countercharge. Even in the most damaging sections of part 3, Dryden is less interested in diatribe than in dialogue; it is through the rhythm of turn and counterturn that he is able to place the most strategic blows against the arrogance and self-interest of the Panther.

The bestiary of part 1 and the beast fables of part 3 are separated by an extensive doctrinal debate that forms the second part of the poem. Dryden claims some aesthetic discomfort with such materials; they allowed neither the occasion for the sharpness of the initial portraits nor the invention and evasion of fable. The preface indicates a degree of self-consciousness over such stylistic issues, "The *second* [part], being Matter of Dispute, and chiefly concerning Church Authority, I was oblig'd to make as plain and perspicuous as possibly I cou'd: yet not wholly neglecting the Numbers, though I had not frequent occasions for the Magnificence of Verse" (II, 469, 94-97). Yet there are crucial personal, doctrinal, and aesthetic problems that he poses and solves in part 2; and the claim of

"plain" and "perspicuous" ought not to make us oblivious either
to the fact that the "matter of church dispute" is rendered in
a very carefully devised conversation between the Hind and
the Panther or that church dispute is not the only subject of
part 2. The riddling and difficult questions of textual ambi-
guity and linguistic multivalence—questions that the Hind
places at the center of the problem of ecclesiastical authority
and that Dryden ponders at considerable length, exploring their
implications for language in new ways—are centrally impor-
tant not only to the mysterious writ he is about to indulge
but for the whole fable mode to whose ambiguities and rich-
ness he would return in the fables, adaptations, and transla-
tions of the 1690s.

Part 2 begins not with the central question of ecclesiastical
authority but with an exchange of accusations. The Panther
raises the issue of cowardice, and the lines evoke the plight
and behavior of English Catholics during the Popish Plot:[21]

> While you their carefull mother wisely fled
> Not trusting destiny to save your head.
> For, what e'er promises you have apply'd
> To your unfailing church, the surer side
> Is four fair leggs in danger to provide.   (II, 485, 10-14)

Dryden has the Panther raise this and other problems so that
he can vent and deny some of the common charges leveled
against the Catholics. Here the Hind returns malice and in-
nuendo in kind:

>   As I remember, said the sober *Hind*,
> Those toils were for your own dear self design'd,
> As well as me; and, with the self same throw,
> To catch the quarry, and the vermin too,
> (Forgive the sland'rous tongues that call'd you so.)
>   (II, 485, 18-22)

Her strategy is not, however, to answer accusations of fear
and flight, but to launch a counteroffensive, an attack on the
Panther's advocacy of the Test Act. The central provision of
that act, one that barred Roman Catholics from subscription,

Test act

was a denial of transubstantiation.[22] But it is not the theological question that is now debated; it is rather the shifting positions of the Anglican Church on this question:

> There chang'd your faith, and what may change may fall.
> Who can believe what varies every day,
> Nor ever was, nor will be at a stay?   (II, 486, 35-37)

And again, a few lines later,

> Then said the *Hind*, as you the matter state
> Not onely *Jesuits* can equivocate;
> For *real*, as you now the word expound,
> From solid substance dwindles to a sound.
> Methinks an *Æsop*'s fable you repeat,
> You know who took the shadow for the meat:
> Your churches substance thus you change at will,
> And yet retain your former figure still.
> I freely grant you spoke to save your life,
> For then you lay beneath the butcher's knife.
> Long time you fought, redoubl'd batt'ry bore,
> But, after all, against your self you swore;
> Your former self, for ev'ry hour your form
> Is chop'd and chang'd, like winds before a storm.
> Thus fear and int'rest will prevail with some,
> For all have not the gift of martyrdome.   (II, 486, 44-59)

Of the many issues the Catholics took up with Anglicans, and of the serious charges of greed and self-interest that Dryden raises throughout the poem, the accusations in this passage are neither the most serious nor cast in the most immediate and telling form. Indeed, what is the theological issue behind these charges of fickleness and equivocation? I suspect that what lies behind this passage is Dryden's perception that here was a chance to combine polemical attack with personal defense. In part the passage argues that Anglican theology is contaminated by politics, that the church is guilty of a moment-by-moment pursuit of interest—devoid of belief, principle, or ideal. But fickleness and equivocation were also charges now leveled at the poet himself. And what motivates the Hind is also the personal interests of the poet, who had, after all, changed with the wind, who had been repeatedly accused of self-interest and fickleness in such change, and who could hardly have denied such charges in the face of their accuracy. Of course, there is a considerable effort made to deflect them in part 3, but here, instead of denying their accuracy, Dryden takes a different approach. He raises the very charges leveled at his own person and turns them against the Anglicans: "Who can believe what varies every day, / Nor ever was, nor will be at a stay?" If Dryden felt implicated by such charges, he does his best here to spread the discomfort. Moreover, the Panther does not deny their accuracy; indeed, she seems to admit to them, and she turns them away in a manner that defends both the changeable church and the changeable poet: "That men may err was never yet deny'd" (II, 486, 61). So the poet himself had admitted, and with considerable art, in part 1:

> My thoughtless youth was wing'd with vain desires,
> My manhood, long misled by wandring fires,
> Follow'd false lights; and when their glimps was gone,
> My pride struck out new sparkles of her own.
> Such was I, such by nature still I am,
> Be thine the glory, and be mine and the shame.
>
> (II, 472, 72-77)

In a clever tactical move, Dryden has the Panther raise in her own defense exactly the same admission of change and the same defense of fallibility that the poet himself had earlier rehearsed.

The central theological issue in part 2 is not, however, change and fallibility. The Hind makes considerable capital out of the Panther's implicit denial of ultimate certainty, but the most pressing concern is the source and character of ecclesiastical authority. And here the Hind and the Panther take very clear and distinctive lines. For the Anglican Church, the ultimate authority is Scripture; for the Catholic Church, that ultimate authority, according to Dryden, is Pope and council. Where the two traditions come into explicit conflict is over the interpretation and character of Scripture. In embracing its final

authority, Anglicans insist that in points necessary for salva-
tion Scripture is plain and clear. This is exactly Dryden's po-
sition in *Religio Laici*, but for Dryden as Roman Catholic
apologist, the interpretation of Scripture can no longer be the
individual conscience in its encounter with these passages, plain
and clear, but the oral tradition mediated by Pope and coun-
cil:

> Suppose we on things traditive divide,
> And both appeal to Scripture to decide;
> By various texts we both uphold our claim,
> Nay, often ground our titles on the same:
> After long labour lost, and times expence,
> Both grant the words, and quarrel for the sense.
>
> (II, 490, 196-201)

And again,

> He cou'd have writ himself, but well foresaw
> Th' event would be like that of *Moyses* law;
> Some difference wou'd arise, some doubts remain,
> Like those, which yet the jarring *Jews* maintain.
> No written laws can be so plain, so pure,
> But wit may gloss, and malice may obscure,
> Not those indited by his first command,
> A Prophet grav'd the text, an Angel held his hand.
> Thus faith was e'er the written word appear'd,
> And men believ'd, not what they read, but heard.
> . . . .
> And what one Saint has said of holy *Paul*,
> *He darkly writ*, is true apply'd to all.
> . . . .
> The sense is intricate, 'tis onely clear
> What vowels and what consonants are there.
>
> (II, 493-495, 314-386)

Not only does *The Hind and the Panther* record the poet's
change on theological issues—issues such as transubstantia-
tion or the character of ecclesiastical authority—but it also
records a quite remarkable and important change in the poet's

attitude toward language. Although the controversial impli- *Levy*
cations of these passages are quite clear in the context of part
2 of the poem—if the authority of the Scripture cannot ulti-
mately be settled, then the faithful believer must look to a
guide for solution to such issues, and that guide is the un-
changing and ancient Mother Church—those ecclesiastical im-
plications are only part of the significance of this change. No
longer is it simply brash and rebellious sectaries who will de-
tort Scripture to their own purposes; we must carefully watch
the meaning and uses of all words; ambiguity inheres in the
nature of language. Even if we can grant the textual authority
of a particular passage, the sense of that passage can never be
plain and clear: "*He darkly writ*, is true apply'd to all."

Nor is it Scripture alone that will not sustain single and
unambiguous meaning; language itself cannot be reduced from
multiplicity.[23] While it clearly serves the interest of the "oral"
tradition to claim that written language, irreducibly multiple
and ambiguous, can never be its own interpretive authority,
such ambiguity and multivalence is a condition toward which
the whole enterprise of disguise had driven the poet and which,
for aesthetic as well as polemical reasons, he now found en-
tirely to his liking. For in the poem's capaciousness we find
not a struggle against ambiguity and enigma but its embrace.
In parts 1 and 3, Dryden argues that the central emotional
and psychological experience of Roman Catholicism is the
embrace of mystery. Nor does he suggest this experience only
through the traditional paradoxes and tropes. Mystery is a
linguistic and literary issue, and the exegetical stance in part 2
makes explicit the implications of the embrace advocated in
the opening passages:[24]

(What more could fright my faith, than Three in One?)
Can I believe eternal God could lye
Disguis'd in mortal mold and infancy?
That the great maker of the world could dye?
And after that, trust my imperfect sense
Which calls in question his omnipotence?
Can I my reason to my faith compell,

And shall my sight, and touch, and taste rebell?
. . . .

Then let the moon usurp the rule of day,
And winking tapers shew the sun his way.

(II, 472, 79-86, 89-90)

There is surely an effort in these lines to embrace the "mysterious things of faith," to "launch into the deep." And there is a corollary between such an embrace of theological mystery and the Hind's conviction that language is essentially and irreducibly ambiguous, multiple, perhaps even mysterious in character. And that mystery will be explored in the fables in part 3.

But the multiplicity of language, even in the plain and perspicuous style of part 2, is made to sustain one further argument. Dryden claims in the preface that part 2 is chiefly concerned with church authority; his position on the question of church authority is rendered in a language that not only outlines an ecclesiastical stance but also implies a political one.

On the question of Roman Catholic authority and infallibility, Dryden develops a position that has distinct and crucial political implications. Such infallibility resides not in the Pope alone, but in the combined wisdom of Pope and council:

I then affirm that this unfailing guide
In Pope and gen'ral councils must reside;
Both lawfull, both combin'd, what one decrees
By numerous votes, the other ratifies:
On this undoubted sense the church relies.
'Tis true, some Doctours in a scantier space,
I mean in each apart, contract the place.
Some, who to greater length extend the line,
The churches after acceptation join.
This last circumference appears too wide,
The church diffus'd is by the council ty'd;
As members by their representatives
Oblig'd to laws which Prince and Senate gives.

(II, 487, 80-92)

The analysis of infallibility is conducted in a language and results in a position crucially reminiscent of the balanced constitution of English legal tradition. Dryden's position is again the "middle way," the embrace of the mean between extremes, an embrace that extends, through the implications and resonance of the language, beyond Roman Catholic ecclesiastical matters to English constitutional issues. No charge was more frequently leveled at James II than his intention to reduce the nation to slavery, as the arbitrary and tyrannous Louis XIV had done in France. Popery and arbitrary government were synonyms in the political literature of James's reign.[25] Dryden's aim here, as elsewhere in part 2, is to outline a Catholic approach to the question of authority that would imply a distinctly English and hence balanced position, a position that this Roman Catholic, John Dryden, might openly and publicly embrace. Nor is the argument about ecclesiastics left implicit. By the close of the passage, the political implications are drawn forth with exactness:

> As members by their representatives
> Oblig'd to laws which Prince and Senate gives.
>
> (II, 487, 91-92)

The analogy is complete and unmistakable: civic authority resides in the combination of king and parliament, ecclesiastical authority resides in Pope and council. Some "Doctours" would contract the locus of authority, but not this Catholic layman, who makes very clear and very explicit the political overtones of the language in which he casts this discussion of papal infallibility.

Nor are all the political overtones defensive. The sanctity of lineal succession links the apostolic tradition of Roman Catholicism with the successive rights of English monarchy:

> Despair at our foundations then to strike
> Till you can prove your faith Apostolick;
> A limpid stream drawn from the native source;
> Succession lawfull in a lineal course.   (II, 500, 612-615)

145

And the attack on Protestant individualism is used to imply a connection between spiritual reform and political anarchy:

> But mark how sandy is your own pretence,
> Who setting Councils, Pope, and Church aside,
> Are ev'ry man his own presuming guide.
>
> (II, 487, 105-107)

Once interpretive authority is placed in the individual conscience, then "gospell-liberty" becomes the excuse for political rebellion. The Anglican rejection of Roman Catholic authority not only implies but embraces such rebellion. Of course, it is exactly Dryden's manner to drive an opponent by reduction and exaggeration into an untenable position, but we should hardly expect evenhandedness from this poet and at this moment: "The Nation is in too high a Ferment, for me to expect either fair War, or even so much as fair Quarter from a Reader of the opposite Party" (II, 467, 1-2). And a reader of the opposite party would have been foolish to expect fair quarter from the author of *The Hind and the Panther*.

What exactly he might expect from part 3 of this poem is not altogether clear. Wit and malice would censure the mode; but the poet, like the Hind, is willing to endure criticism. Dryden embraces the mysteries of fable and the tradition of Aesop; the Hind means to entertain a dangerous guest by night. But the Hind is not defenseless in her encounter with the Panther, nor is Dryden in his embrace of mysterious writ. The entertainment that the Hind is about to offer is a nasty account of the Panther's motives in supporting the Test Act and clinging to legal ploys and maneuvers in order to bar Roman Catholics from office.[26] Through the fables, Dryden is about to exercise his own defense of a new religious and literary identity.

Part 3 of *The Hind and the Panther* consists of two literary actions, a direct attack on the politics of Anglican monopoly and a pair of fables, one narrated by the Panther and the other by the Hind. The charges that the Hind and the Panther exchange in the first section of part 3 elaborate issues that have appeared earlier in the poem, though the Hind's critique of self-interest, and especially the attack on latitude,[27] have a redoubled energy for this, the final direct assault on the morality of Anglican politics. The fables extend these charges and add a new prophetic dimension to the topical issues, but they do so by indirection. The fables are, however, fully integrated with the political issues explicitly raised in the first half of part 3, and it is difficult to pin down exactly what Dryden had in mind when he says in the preface, "if I had so soon expected [the Declaration for Liberty of Conscience], I might have spar'd my self the labour of writing many things which are contain'd in the third part of it" (II, 468, 61-62).[28] I suspect that this is again part of Dryden's efforts to distinguish the position of this poem from the politics of James's Declaration which was, after all, an abrogation of parliamentary law. This poem, Dryden claims, is an effort at persuasion. And yet persuasion is a little difficult to credit when it is couched in abusive and threatening terms.

Part 3 begins, however, not in abuse but in a final invitation by the Hind to have the Panther join in friendship and communion; and to such an end the Hind rehearses topics of mutual sympathy, "To common dangers past, a sadly pleasing theam; / Remembring ev'ry storm which toss'd the state, / When both were objects of the publick hate" (II, 504, 35-37). But this theme is sadly pleasing only to the Hind; the Panther rejects commonality, "The *Panther* nodded when her speech was done, / And thank'd her coldly in a hollow tone. / But said her gratitude had gone too far / For common offices of Christian care. / If to the lawfull Heir she had been true, / She paid but *Caesar* what was *Caesar*'s due" (II, 505, 55-60). Grudging acknowledgment rather than affection is the most that the Panther will allow of their common past, and on the crucial subject of obedience to the crown, Dryden gives the Panther a nicely ambiguous scriptural quotation: "She paid but *Caesar* what was *Caesar*'s due." The Panther's remark is correct, but suggests a cool and indifferent obedience; and the placement of the modifier "but" in line 60 argues more than indifference, it suggests hostility. The Panther will offer Caesar what is his due by law, and that alone. The scriptural allusion underscores the hostility of this grudging admission, for while these are Christ's words in confuting the Herodians, Christ distinguished the secular realm of a pagan society, Caesar's polity, from the divine realm that belonged to God alone. But James was no heathen monarch (II, 468, 50-54), and the force of Scripture in this passage is to undercut the Anglican pledge of loyalty.

The central charges against the Anglican Church in part 3 are greed, self-interest, and envy. The broad church, all efforts at Anglican comprehension, are dismissed as opportunism, and the vocabulary of Dryden's analysis repeats such words as envy, malice, and ambition, interest, pride, jealousy, and revenge. But the effect of this language is surprising, for the sweeping condemnation of Anglican greed and opportunism is daringly close to the charges brought against the poet laureate himself:

Your sons of breadth at home, are much like these,
Their soft and yielding metals run with ease,
They melt, and take the figure of the mould:
But harden, and preserve it best in gold.

(II, 508, 187-190)

Dryden did not naively raise such issues nor cast them in such language out of folly. He counted the best defense as attack; as in part 2, he courted his opponents with their own language, and he attacked them with their own barbs. The degree of self-consciousness in this strategy is revealed by the Panther's remark:

Your *Delphick* Sword, the *Panther* then reply'd,
Is double edg'd, and cuts on either side.

(II, 508, 191-192)

Of course, it was easy enough for Dryden to supply the Panther with such an admission; yet what he seems to achieve here is not only an admission that the Hind's charges of greed and envy in the maintenance of the Test Act are true, but that the broad tarring of Anglicans and Catholics alike with such motives had some credibility.

The orchestration of such charges is extremely careful, and

by it Dryden achieves something like a disinterested application of the charges of greed and self-interest; both sides might be accused of such motives, and both, the poet suggests, are to some degree vulnerable to, if not guilty of, such charges. Dryden's strategy is, again, not to deny the accuracy of charges that were made after his conversion, but to spread them as widely as he could, to suggest that those who accused him of base motives in following the king in his religion had better look closely to their own religious politics. Of course, Dryden does not in the end allow his own guilt. What he argues on his own behalf is that the appearance of self-interest does not convict, that such charges are hearsay and slander:

> Now for my converts, who you say unfed
> Have follow'd me for miracles of bread,
> Judge not by hear-say, but observe at least,
> If since their change, their loaves have been increast.
> The *Lyon* buyes no Converts, if he did,
> Beasts wou'd be sold as fast as he cou'd bid.
>
> (II, 509, 221-226)

Dryden's admission that the king was indeed thankless for the poet laureate's conversion could not have been an easy defense; but of course it argues that faith alone was the motive for this or any other conversion to Rome during James's reign. Perhaps there is as well a note of ruefulness here. If the "*Lyon*" were not buying converts, there could not have been many beasts in England foolish enough to put themselves on the market.

It seems particularly revealing that the passages of most open religious confession, the moments of broadest autobiography—though voiced by the Hind—should occur directly following this high-minded defense of the conversion:

> Mean-time my sons accus'd, by fames report
> Pay small attendance at the *Lyon*'s court,
> Nor rise with early crowds, nor flatter late,
> (For silently they beg who daily wait.)
> Preferment is bestow'd that comes unsought,
> Attendance is a bribe, and then 'tis bought.

How they shou'd speed, their fortune is untry'd,
For not to ask, is not to be deny'd.
For what they have, their *God* and *King* they bless,
And hope they shou'd not murmur, had they less.

(II, 509-510, 235-244)

What sons might Dryden have had in mind? Here and for the next seventy lines the son that he has most directly on his mind is John Dryden, and the defense of faith is simultaneously an effort to distinguish himself from the court party (II, 509, 236-238) and to rise above calumny by embracing it:

Then welcome infamy and publick shame,
And, last, a long farwell to worldly fame.
'Tis said with ease, but oh, how hardly try'd
By haughty souls to humane honour ty'd!

(II, 511, 283-286)

The accusations of ambition and self-interest are turned to proof of faith. Earlier, the poet had defended himself through attack. In these passages he embraces martyrdom, and the failure of control suggests that the charges must have injured Dryden, that the conversion itself resulted in some doubts.

But the strategies of this poem have not yet been played out in this moment of high religious melodrama. Dryden now turns to the pair of fables with which the poem closes. The fables bear some resemblance to one another, but they spring from different motives and stand as contrasting models. These fables illustrate allegory and enigma; they show fable as revelation of character and as prophetic mystery; and they demonstrate the political functions of mysterious writ.

The Panther's fable is in some ways the more interesting, for it serves a complex set of motives. It is, first of all, a device to frighten the Hind, to suggest that if Catholics take advantage of the false spring of James's reign, they will end up dead in the snow. The transparent moral is, fly while the weather permits. But the Hind rejects such counsel; she sees through the Panther's false prophecies and sham exegesis, and she exposes the fable not as mysterious writ but as self-expression.

Moreover, the Hind's perception and judgment are not necessarily those of the poet. While the Catholic Church might well scorn the Anglican fable of Catholic demise, the poet himself might also be using this nasty tale as a way of indirectly criticizing James's submission to Father Petre, a character mercilessly ridiculed in the figure of the martin. Although the Panther counsels flight out of base motives—she would frighten the Catholics into exile in order to prey on their meager leavings—such counsel and such a perception of the circumstance and fate of English Catholics might not itself be wrong, from Dryden's point of view.[29] The fable allows Dryden to voice criticism of Father Petre but to voice it from two removes: the natural malice of the Panther, and the distance of fable itself. Father Petre is depicted as a fearful and witless prophet counseling safety at any price; but this seemingly pious care is, in fact, cowardice. The truths that Dryden is able to project through the malicious fable are twofold. First, the truth of the portrait itself—and I think the wit of the character sketch suggests as much Dryden's perception as the Panther's malice; and second, and perhaps more importantly, the language of the Panther reveals a political truth: in the spring of 1687 there was widespread suspicion, envy, and hatred of the Roman Catholics in England. The specifics of the Panther's prophecy may not be true, but the motives revealed by that prophecy are.

This fable, as the Hind so sharply notes, reveals character; its language is an expression not of the future but of the teller's wishes for that future. The Hind is a sophisticated exegete, for she looks at words not as literal prophecy but as intention. Indeed, the whole problem of prophecy and augury is repeatedly explored in the Panther's fable. Early in the fable Dryden introduces two interpretive modes, instinct and prophecy (II, 515, 442), and it seems not by accident that the mode of instinctual response should be pitted against augury in a beast fable. Dryden would not have us forget that it is beasts who discourse on prophecy in this poem. The portrait of the martin is itself a brilliant exercise in abuse; and though the exercise is conducted by the Panther, the charges are not

with letter

motivated solely by malice. The martin is, in superstition, silly
to excess; he casts schemes, guesses by planets, reads the
weather, interprets omens, and trumps up false prophetic evi-
dence to support his dubious augury:

> To strengthen this, he told a boding dream,
> Of rising waters, and a troubl'd stream,
> Sure signs of anguish, dangers and distress,
> With something more not lawfull to express:
> By which he slyly seem'd to intimate
> Some secret revelation of their fate.
> For he concluded, once upon a time,
> He found a leaf inscrib'd with sacred rime,
> Whose antique characters did well denote
> The *Sibyl's* hand of the *Cumaean* Grott:
> The mad Divineress had plainly writ,
> A time shou'd come (but many ages yet,)
> In which, sinister destinies ordain,
> A *Dame* shou'd drown with all her feather'd train.
>
> (II, 516, 480-493)

Whatever the truth of this prophecy, the martin's motives are
thoroughly impugned; it is no accident that the concluding
couplet to this passage (II, 517, 521-522), "Not naming per-
sons, and confounding times, / One casual truth supports a
thousand lying rimes," should remind us so exactly of Titus
Oates and of Dryden's excoriation of that rabbinical exegete.
The uses of prophecy for personal gain, the fabrication of pro-
phetic signs, the false reading of prophetic texts—this is a fa-
miliar arsenal; and there is a rather neat fit between the Pan-
ther's amusing account of the martin and Dryden's own
contempt for self-made divination.

And yet, while suggesting contempt for the misuses of
prophecy, Dryden neither condemns the martin nor denies
the truly prophetic character of mysterious writ. The Panther
is Dryden's mask for such condemnation, and while she denies
the sanctity of divination to the martin, there is nothing in
the tale that denies mystery, neither the casual or accidental
coincidence of blind prophecy and history (II, 517, 543-544),

nor the brilliantly contemptuous prophetic function that the
martin serves at the end of the fable:[30]

> High on an Oak which never leaf shall bear,
> He breath'd his last, expos'd to open air,
> And there his corps, unbless'd, are hanging still,
> To show the change of winds with his prophetick bill.
>
> (II, 520, 635-638)

But Dryden is very careful to distance this contemptuous
portrait from his own person and, of course, from the Hind.
She counters that the fable is not prophetic but malicious; it
is fueled by malice, as the whole tradition of Protestant satire
against Roman Catholicism has been nurtured on malice:

> But most in *Martyn*'s character and fate,
> She saw her slander'd sons, the *Panther*'s hate,
> The people's rage, the persecuting state:
> Then said, I take th' advice in friendly part,
> You clear your conscience, or at least your heart.
>
> (II, 520, 644-648)

The Hind sees, through the language and the shape of the
parable, not a divination of the future but the cruelty of the
present. This fable allows Dryden both to criticize the direc-
tion of court politics and to stand clear himself of such criti-
cism. Dryden allows us to assent to the accuracy of the por-
trait and yet to understand that what the Hind says is also
true. Indeed, nothing the Hind says denies the accuracy of the
satire; it simply impugns the Panther's motives.

The Hind is not, however, only an exegete; she too has a
fable to tell, and her fable combines allegory and enigma. There
is, however, one additional fiction in this section of part 3:
the Panther's brief interpolation of the *Aeneid*. The allusion to
the *Aeneid* serves to bridge the two fables and it looks, though
inadvertently, toward the great project of the 1690s, the trans-
lation of Virgil, foreshadowing the major political theme of
that translation. Dryden could not have known at this point
what the Panther's reading of Virgil would come to mean,

but it serves its own interesting purpose in *The Hind and the Panther*.

> Methinks such terms of proferr'd peace you bring
> As once *Æneas* to th' *Italian* King:
> By long possession all the land is mine,
> You strangers come with your intruding line,
> To share my sceptre, which you call to join.
> You plead like him an ancient Pedigree,
> And claim a peacefull seat by fates decree.
> In ready pomp your Sacrificer stands,
> T' unite the *Trojan* and the *Latin* bands,
> And that the League more firmly may be ty'd,
> Demand the fair *Lavinia* for your bride.
> Thus plausibly you veil th' intended wrong,
> But still you bring your exil'd gods along;
> And will endeavour in succeeding space,
> Those household Poppits on our hearths to place.
>
> (II, 523, 766-780)

The Panther uses the *Aeneid* to raise issues of invasion and conquest, of property and propriety, of political deceit and political legitimacy.[31] It is exactly these issues that Dryden would raise again through the *Aeneid*, but then on behalf of the sovereignty now questioned by the Panther. It is an interesting commentary on Dryden's *Virgil* that he should already in 1687 have conceived its central action not as imperial destiny but as invasion and conquest. In *The Hind and the Panther*, of course, it is the Anglican Church that thrusts this implication against a Catholic monarch and his household gods, but the interpretive scheme is already well formulated. The events of 1688 would turn Dryden's mind to another application. Through the *Aeneid* the Panther raises the issues of possession and sovereignty by analogizing James's "entry" into kingship with Aeneas's invasion of Latium. She uses the *Aeneid* to question the legitimacy of James's possession, for invasion and conquest are terms that deny legitimacy, and the Hind answers those issues in her fable:

> A Plain good Man, whose Name is understood,
> (So few deserve the name of Plain and Good)
> Of three fair lineal Lordships stood possess'd,
> . . . .
> As Fortune wou'd (his fortune came tho' late)
> He took Possession of his just Estate.
>
> (II, 526-527, 906-916)

Dryden has the Panther raise questions of legitimacy and sovereignty through the *Aeneid* so that the final Catholic statement might begin by stressing those unquestioned and unquestionable strengths with which James had come to the throne. The allusion to the *Aeneid* is itself prefaced by the Hind's reminder of the Exclusion Crisis (II, 521, 705 ff.) and by direct application of Exclusion to the Anglicans:

> Suppose some great Oppressour had by slight
> Of law, disseis'd your brother of his right,
> Your common sire surrendring in a fright;
> Would you to that unrighteous title stand,
> Left by the villain's will to heir the land?
>
> (II, 522, 710-714)

As in *Absalom and Achitophel*, Dryden links property rights and the sanctity of lineal descent in the case of Stuart monarchy to the general case in English common law. Although the Panther attempts to turn aside the violation of property rights in the Exclusion Crisis by applying the history of Aeneas's "invasion" of Italy to the reintroduction of Catholicism into England, such application could not hold; James had succeeded to the throne in full and correct exercise of the rights of lineal descent and inheritance. The Hind's fable is set in the barnyard, with James as "Master of the Farm." By illustrating James's rights in such a circumstance, who could question the legitimacy of this king, his rightful claim to inheritance, the right of all property-owning Englishmen?[32]

The fable begins with fundamental political issues; not only is its application at the opening transparent but Dryden calls attention to that transparency: "A Plain good Man, whose

155

Name is understood, / (So few deserve the name of Plain and Good)." This tale need not name names, because its epithets are so exact that we cannot mistake the master of this farm. But what begins in transparency ends in obscurity and enigma, a strategy that, while it has proved a frustration to readers, is neither an inadvertency nor a failure of historical scholarship. Where Dryden means to be clear in this fable, he has not the slightest trouble indicating identity and meaning. James is master of the farm; the lineal estates are England, Scotland, and Ireland; the pigeons alias doves are Anglican clergy; and the domestic poultry are Roman Catholic clergy. The tale of avarice and gluttony that the Hind spins from her initial premise repeats, with subtle and clever variation, the charges that the Hind has made throughout the poem: greed and envy rather than conscience and religious principle are the real reasons for the Anglican refusal to yield to James's wish to remove the Test Act and Penal Laws. But where the Hind turns from present ills to future strife, the fable moves into a rather different mode.

Beginning with the "grave Consult" (II, 532, 1108), the Hind elaborates her tale as prophecy in a way that has long puzzled students of the poem.[33] The Anglican clergy invite a potent bird of prey either to frighten or devour the chickens; the Buzzard arrives, he assumes sovereignty—though whether sacred or secular rule is intended is not clear—he frightens the chickens, but in the end it is the confused and wrangling pigeons who fall victim to the scavenger. This action takes less than two hundred lines, but the annotations that accompany the poem's conclusion indicate an enormous amount of puzzling. And indeed puzzles abound, and none more central or more troubling than the identity of the Buzzard. In the elaborate portrait, Dryden has the Hind plant a number of important clues, but the clues reveal two quite distinct historical figures. There are details that clearly argue the Buzzard's identity as Gilbert Burnet, an Anglican churchman with whom Dryden had longstanding quarrels and some rather specific scores to settle contemporary with the publication of the poem.[34] Yet other details suggest William, Prince of Orange and intimate that Dryden was looking nervously toward the invasion.[35] So convincing are the details for both identities that the most recent scholarly edition of the poem argues not a single but a double historical identity for the figure. It is Earl Miner's thesis that the portrait began as a characterization of William, but at the last minute Dryden added material to complicate the characterization so that Gilbert Burnet as well as William might, at points, be alluded to.[36]

Miner himself points out that such a doubling of historical characters behind one figure is probably unique in Dryden's writing; certainly it is unique in this poem. This and similar hypotheses about the identity of the Buzzard either explicitly or implicitly argue that the portrait resulted from either inadvertent or last-minute additions. We know that Dryden often worked in haste, but this solution implies that the materials are out of control, that the characterization is, in the end, a confusion which Dryden did not or could not sort out. If Dryden intended to satirize Gilbert Burnet, why didn't he introduce another bird to carry William's identity? And if he had William clearly in mind, why did he compromise the figure with confusing details? We might solve this problem not by assuming that the Buzzard is a last-minute or inadvertent confusion, but that what we have is the finished text, a portrait which Dryden intended to read exactly as we have it. The contradictory identities represent a calculation rather than an error. The confusion renders the identity of the Buzzard uncertain in much the same way that the final prophecy of the poem is ambiguous, its details unclear. Not only is the Buzzard's identity uncertain, but we cannot be sure of the English referents for the pigeons' Rubicon, the two Czars, or the English identities of Shiloh and Dyonysius.[37] That the fable predicts a general Anglican demise is clear, but the details are not. Their meaning is difficult to fix, and the uncertainty turns the Hind's fable into a proper example of mysterious writ.

Dryden uses a pair of fables to explore the character of false and true prophecy, and to argue a connection between the language of secular prophecy and Scripture. He demonstrates that the nostradamus of the martin is an example of false prophecy, the clear and exact details of the Panther's fable are in fact easy to see through. He also shows that truly mysterious writ is not exact in particulars; like Scripture it is difficult to interpret; the sense is intricate and not easy to unfold. And what better example than the ending of the Hind's fable, whose general import is clear but whose details are obscure, difficult of exact interpretation?

The historical confusion is planted so that the Hind's prophecy might bear the marks of mysterious writ; it is a nice coincidence that such writ should also accommodate the poet's uncertainty about the future. The Hind and the Panther remove themselves for quiet rest after this debate. But I suspect that on the night of May 27, 1687, ten thousand angels with glorious visions of his future state did not wait on the poet.

Fables Ancient and Modern

Dryden could not have known in the spring of 1687 that less than a year hence James would have fled England and that he as poet laureate would be without place or pension, in disfavor and disrepute. He sensed impending political crisis; the anxious prophecies of both fables in *The Hind and the Panther* suggest as much. But there was no bloodletting after 1688; and Dryden not only survived, he triumphed over the Glorious Revolution. Of course, Dryden did not see displacement and penury as ideals of retirement; but the last years of his life were filled with remarkable projects. Fear and the imperative of political statement drove him to seek the cover of other men's fictions; but in so doing Dryden turned translation and adaptation to his own ends. He used Virgil for a long and beautifully sustained meditation on English politics; and he turned the scenes and narratives of Ovid and Boccaccio, Homer and Chaucer into a group of poems that reflected, in the various light of adaptation, the ideals and convictions of his last years.

Fables celebrates the virtues of charity and constancy, the sanctity of lineal descent, the integrity of estate; they extoll the rites of gratitude.[38] But Dryden also reminds us of the politics of waste and corruption; of conquest and tyranny; of the crimes of usurpation and ingratitude. These are not new themes, but their handling and coloration in the *Fables* seems more personal than before; the poems are less polemically charged and less argumentatively sustained than earlier political texts, but the weight and immediacy of Dryden's own sense of gratitude and displacement can often be felt, as can on occasion his reconciliation to such change. By the end of the century, Dryden was no longer defending political programs; there were, however, ideals to record and crimes that would not be forgotten.

The Hind and the Panther had been Dryden's most sustained effort at fable; it proved a fortunate exercise for the years to come. Dyrden's writing in the 1690s can be seen as the logical extension of the poet's impulses in *The Hind and the Panther*, the exercise in fable and allegory a preparation for the handling of the fables as political texts. But, in fact, the whole career might be understood from the perspective of the last work, the translations and fables of the 1690s absorbing and reflecting a life spent in the pursuit and use of strategy and disguise. Had William not come to the throne in 1688, the poet's last decade would have been different. But the impulse to reach toward disguise can be traced through the whole career, and this last phase is the culmination of a need that ran very deep. It was not, however, only personal and particular impulses that turned Dryden toward fable and translation. Anxiety and displacement suggested the need for more and more artful distance, but the revolution that drove this poet to cover did not leave other men's lives untouched.

Nor do I refer only to a small band of Jacobites. Uncertainty and volatility had persuaded men early in the Restoration to adopt masks; nothing in the years following Charles II's death had done much to invite them into the open. The stability of the crown's position and the political quiescence of Charles's last years were quickly destroyed by James II. He undermined his own authority and credibility, and convinced a nation all too willing to credit such intentions that he aimed to invade liberty and property. He had come to power with a wide margin of approval; within three years he fled over the channel, mindful of his father's fate. In such a time, it was not only those who dissented from the crown that sought comfort in disguise. Dryden's exploration of fable, though conducted with a breadth of political and lyric impulse unmatched by his contemporaries, shared with those contemporaries a powerful sense of the ways in which the pressures of revolution and the sense of contingency had altered their lives.

I have earlier suggested that the fictions of Dryden's last years provided both a cover for political argument and a relief from historical representation. The central political figures on whom Dryden had pinned his civic ideals had turned out to be disappointing, and Dryden occasionally hints at such disappointment. A man with Dryden's powers of observation, a poet with his gift for exploiting and exaggerating what was most vulnerable in the opposition, could not have been blind to the vulnerability of those he had praised. Such vulnerability is turned to polemical advantage in *Absalom and Achitophel*, perhaps even in *The Hind and the Panther*, where James's "plainness" is argued as evidence of his honesty. But James provided the poet with little more than plainness. The Glorious Revolution meant that Dryden might continue to explore the themes of loyalty and legitimacy without having to pin them on such political figures. Fable was for Dryden at once a disguise and a realm for the open-ended and idealized expression of civic themes.

But Dryden's *Fables* is not without history nor entirely void of names and families. The two original poems in the collection turn repeated variations on the meaning of name and family in history; and the *Dedication* to James Butler, duke of Ormond, is an elegant essay on these subjects. In the life of James Butler and in the history of the Ormonds, Dryden located the central themes of his collection: personal honor, the sanctity of line, the virtues of name, the integrity of estate. And their exploration begins in the dedicatory letter:

> Some Estates are held in *England*, by paying a Fine at the change of every Lord: I have enjoy'd the Patronage of your Family, from the time of your excellent Grandfather to this

present Day. I have dedicated the Lives of *Plutarch* to the first Duke; and have celebrated the Memory of your Heroick Father. Tho' I am very short of the Age of *Nestor*, yet I have liv'd to a third Generation of your House; and by your Grace's Favour am admitted still to hold from you by the same Tenure. . . . 'Tis true, that by delaying the Payment of my last Fine, when it was due by your Grace's Accession to the Titles, and Patrimonies of your House, I may seem in rigour of Law to have made a forfeiture of my Claim, yet my Heart has always been devoted to your Service: And since you have been graciously pleas'd, by your permission of this Address, to accept the tender of my Duty, 'tis not yet too late to lay these Poems at your Feet. (IV, 1439, 1-23)

Dryden casts the patronage relationship in the language of estate because tenancy allowed him to insist on the economy and greatness of the Ormond house: the rightful descent of line, the responsible exercise of lordship through the descent, the rewards reaped through proper cultivation. In the correct exercise of patronage and estate, the Ormonds stand preeminent; now that James and Mary had fled, the Ormonds remained the true locus of English civic virtues, and these virtues are explored through the text of the *Dedication*, in the verses to the duchess of Ormond, and throughout the *Fables*. With each restatement in the *Dedication*, Dryden turns the language variously to broaden compliment into ideological, political, and topical gesture. The praise of Ormond ancestry becomes a hymn to the sanctity of lineal descent, and the play of that ancestry against the Roman nobility is both a way of elevating a particular family and its virtues, and of contrasting them with a "stern, rigid Virtue, salvage, haughty, parcimonious and unpopular" (IV, 1440, 36). This family is distinguished by its ease of access and its exercise of charity—qualities now of special concern to Dryden.

The display of Ormond virtues against other tempers—"Oppression on one side, and Ambition on the other"—is a general contrast and a particular juxtaposition; it suggests,

without exact articulation, the contrast between the true exemplar of civic virtues and that ursurping and ambitious man
of iron, William III, the Theseus of *Palamon and Arcite*, the
Agamemnon of Dryden's translation of the *Iliad*, or the Tancred of Boccaccio's *Sigismonda and Guiscardo*.[39] By combining
a celebration of James Butler with praise for the family, by
alternating the individual and the estate, Dryden is able to
celebrate the present duke and the Ormond family, and explore the power of name and family in history. Their exaltation draws special meaning from the violation of lineage and
estate in the great example of 1688, and such exaltation also
takes on a personal resonance, for Dryden—now deprived of
pension and place—celebrates the honor that inheres in name
and family, honor quite independent of the vagaries of fortune. The theme is further explored in the *Dedication* (IV,
1442-1443, 150-181) and in *To my Honour'd Kinsman*.

Dryden's verse epistle to his cousin is a complex piece of
political writing with both overt and covert arguments.[40] It
uses fable as commentary on pastoral retreat and civic engagement, and through fable it renders a portrait of the independent politician aimed as praise and persuasion. The poem is also
an argument against the policies of William's government; it
attempts, by idealizing John Driden's independence and political responsibility, to turn this particular Whig, and those
independent country gentlemen who might see themselves
mirrored in its portrait, against William's policies. It is yet a
more personal statement which, through its discourse on name
and family, celebrates the poet and his namesake, as well as
the virtues of this particular line of Englishmen:

> O true Descendent of a Patriot Line,
> Who, while thou shar'st their Lustre, lend'st 'em thine,
> Vouchsafe this Picture of thy Soul to see;
> 'Tis so far Good, as it resembles thee:
> The Beauties to th' Original I owe;
> Which, when I miss, my own Defects I show:
> Nor think the Kindred-Muses thy Disgrace;
> A Poet is not born in ev'ry Race.

Two of a House, few Ages can afford;
One to perform, another to record.
Praise-worthy Actions are by thee embrac'd;
And 'tis my Praise, to make thy Praises last.
For ev'n when Death dissolves our Humane Frame,
The Soul returns to Heav'n, from whence it came;
Earth keeps the Body, Verse preserves the Fame.

(IV, 1534-1535, 195-209)

The center of this passage is lineage, which begins with the doubling of the cousins' names and argues connection and continuity in the two lives. The family is a patriot line, a "house" guaranteed the immortality of name through heroic action and political independence. And finally name, rather than estate, is the incorruptible portion of man. The cousins share name and function: they are both makers, one acting the ideal life and the other recording it. Line itself might expire, but name will never dissappear, since its permanence is guaranteed through verse; and verse, like name, renders personality immortal.

The passage reflects a number of themes from the *Dedication*: lineage with its suggestion of antiquity and inviolability; fame and its spur of virtuous action; house with its connotations of stability and privilege. If their elevation seems defensive on the part of a poet who in his last years was often reduced to something like elegant beggary, the psychological motive should not simplify the ideological and political character of these themes. For Dryden in the 1690s, the idea of name was charged with suggestion and meaning that went far beyond the traditional topos, and the exploration of the Ormond family and name in the *Dedication* gave Dryden an aristocratic exemplar for his theme. The Ormonds are celebrated as the true aristocratic locus of name and family now that usurpation has deprived England of the Stuart line.

And such themes are central to *Fables*—significant, as we might expect, in the dedicatory verse to the duchess of Ormond, with its reiteration of that family's antiquity and nobility. The duchess is invoked as "true *Plantagenet*," and cel-

ebrated as a descendant of the line of longest unbroken rule
in English history. She is as well promise of the Ormond
succession, a "precious Mould, / Which all the future *Ormonds*
was to hold" (IV, 1467, 142-143). But the Ormond succes-
sion argues more than an extension of the family line; it prom-
ises the restoration of the nation and the race, "An Heir from
You, who may redeem the failing Kind" (IV, 1467, 145). The
language is reminiscent of Marvell's tribute to the Fairfaxes in
Upon Appleton House, the imagery of restoration and apoca-
lypse in Dryden's poem arguing the same conviction about
the place of family in national and sacred history:

> As when the Dove returning, bore the Mark
> Of Earth restor'd to the long-lab'ring Ark,
> The Relicks of Mankind, secure of Rest,
> Op'd ev'ry Window to receive the Guest,
> And the fair Bearer of the Message bless'd;
> So, when You came, with loud repeated Cries,
> The Nation took an Omen from your Eyes,
> And God advanc'd his Rainbow in the Skies,
> To sign inviolable Peace restor'd;
> The Saints with solemn Shouts proclaim'd the new accord.
> (IV, 1465, 70-79)

But the method of *Fables* is not primarily figural or histor-
ical; its mode is not analytical; and its procedures are not an-
tithesis and dialectic. The pace is leisured and digressive; the
method is accrued example, theme and variation. The self-
consciously loosened structures of both *Preface* and collection
suggest not so much an effort at persuasion as a record of
passions and ideals. The context of *Fables* is not political crisis
as it had been for *Annus Mirabilis, Absalom and Achitophel*, and
The Hind and the Panther, but poetry and eternity, and the
high degree of literary self-consciousness recorded in the *Pref-
ace* argues the sense of place and tradition in literary terms.

The thematic issues for *Fables* are displayed in the *Dedica-
tion*, but it is the *Preface* that by argument and example sug-
gests the method and poetics of the verse. The self-conscious
delineation of method begins at the very opening of the *Pref-*

ace. This is Dryden in high digression: " 'Tis with a Poet, as with a Man who designs to build, and is very exact, as he supposes, in casting up the Cost beforehand: But, generally speaking, he is mistaken in his Account, and reckons short of the Expence he first intended: He alters his Mind as the Work proceeds. . . . So has it hapned to me; I have built a House, where I intended but a Lodge" (IV, 1444, 1-7). The whole has had the most casual of genesis; the collection grew bit by bit; the poet stumbled from one invention to another, at times almost against his will, certainly against his better judgment. We are sufficiently familiar with these gestures to consider them with some suspicion, for while the temper has changed, *Fables*, whatever its genesis, is not a haphazard collection. Dryden suggests digression and disarray, but he also allows that, if we press hard enough, we will find that the choice is not random, that these fables are not just disparate pleasures: "I have endeavour'd to chuse such Fables, both Ancient and Modern, as contain in each of them some instructive Moral, which I could prove by Induction, but the Way is tedious; and they leap foremost into sight, without the Reader's Trouble of looking after them" (IV, 1447, 120-123).

And, indeed, some of these morals as ideals, examples, even imperatives, do come forward easily in the fables: the rewards of charity, constancy, and valor; the dangers and attractions of heroic and erotic love; the responsibilities of kingship and the consequences of tyranny. It is the last subject that is of special interest because it shows us how, under fable and through fiction, Dryden continued to meditate on civic themes and their transformations through fable and translation. In their most direct expression, the civic themes argue the necessity for balance and restraint, virtues that Dryden outlines most explicitly for his parliamentary cousin:

A Patriot, both the King and Country serves;
Prerogative, and Privilege preserves:
Of Each, our Laws the certain Limit show;
One must not ebb, nor t'other overflow:
Betwixt the Prince and Parliament we stand;

The Barriers of the State on either Hand:
May neither overflow, for then they drown the Land.
When both are full, they feed our bless'd Abode;
Like those, that water'd once, the Paradise of God.

(IV, 1534, 171-179)

Whether or not paradise was the constitutional monarchy that Dryden here imagines, dressed in the garb of the balanced constitution with the equable and flexible rhythms of prerogative and privilege, the ideal in *Honour'd Kinsman* is drawn to an English model that would appeal to country squire and parliamentarian. But the darker side of this figure, conquest and the consequences of tyranny, is more prominent than the civic ideal.

The admonitions against conquest and tyranny are quite explicit at the close of *The Character of a Good Parson*, a portrait that Dryden enlarged from Chaucer in order to politicize Chaucer's spiritual ideal and to decry the use of religious apologetics in the vindication of tyranny:[41]

A King can give no more than is his own:
The Title stood entail'd, had *Richard* had a Son.
    Conquest, an odious Name, was laid aside,
Where all submitted; none the Battle try'd.
The senseless Plea of Right by Providence,
Was, by a flatt'ring Priest, invented since:
And lasts no longer than the present sway;
But justifies the next who comes in play.
    The People's Right remains; let those who dare
Dispute their Pow'r, when they the Judges are.
    He join'd not in their Choice; because he knew
Worse might, and often did from Change ensue.

(IV, 1739, 113-124)

The political themes of the 1690s are openly stated and moralized: lineal succession cannot be altered where there is an heir; William's invasion ought to be recognized as conquest even though his troops had no need to raise arms against James's deserting army; and the low-church explanations of legitimacy through the arguments of providence ought to be recognized for the casuistry and base flattery that they were. Once the political fabric has been altered, once power is placed in the popular voice, there is no reversing that election.

In the collection as Dryden finally assembled it, the verses to the duchess of Ormond follow the *Dedication* and *Preface* and precede *Palamon and Arcite*; they link poet and patron with their lineal and spiritual heirs and, by invoking Chaucer's heroic figures, they prepare for the opening fable. But in the *Preface*, Dryden points out that these adaptations began with book 1 of the *Iliad* and that the matter of Troy suggested the succeeding translation projects, book 12 of the *Metamorphoses* and the speeches of Ajax and Ulysses. Of translating Homer, Dryden remarked that "the *Grecian* is more according to my Genius, than the *Latin* Poet"; the evidence of book 1 certainly suggests the ease and assurance with which Dryden handled the *Iliad*: the translation free and vigorous, at once suggesting but not compelling contemporary political application. Here is Dryden's Achilles rebuking an Agamemnon not quite Homer's own:

What Wrong from *Troy* remote, cou'd I sustain,
To leave my fruitful Soil, and happy Reign,
And plough the Surges of the stormy Main?
Thee, frontless Man, we follow'd from afar;
Thy Instruments of Death, and Tools of War.
Thine is the Triumph; ours the Toil alone:
We bear thee on our Backs, and mount thee on the
 Throne.
For thee we fall in Fight; for thee redress
Thy baffled Brother; not the Wrongs of *Greece*.
And now thou threaten'st with unjust Decree,
To punish thy affronting Heav'n, on me.
To seize the Prize which I so dearly bought;
By common Suffrage giv'n, confirm'd by Lot.
Mean Match to thine: For still above the rest,
Thy hook'd rapacious Hands usurp the best.

(IV, 1590, 233-247)

This is, of course, Achilles' complaint, but as in Dryden's *Virgil*, the ancient text is carried over and transformed both through a language and a political consciousness. Without attempting topical complaint, Dryden shaded the language so that we can, if we would, hear personal and political cadences that are not Homer's. Nor is it simply cadences that are shaded; domestic and rural particulars are dropped and political subjects heightened and extended. The earlier (IV, 1589, 227-228) contrast between Agamemnon's "Sovereign Sway" and the Greeks as "abject Slaves" is Dryden's own; moreover, the harsh rebuke in which Achilles piles grievance after grievance is Dryden's invention: "Thy Instruments of Death, and Tools of War. / Thine is the Triumph; ours the Toil alone: / We bear thee on our Backs, and mount thee on the Throne." The language is not particular to King William's wars, but the details conjure the figure in such a way that the translation carries an additional burden. The whole of suggestion and innuendo comes to sharp and sudden resolution in the line that Dryden interpolated at 246-247: "For still above the rest, / Thy hook'd rapacious Hands usurp the best." This is a particularly interesting transformation of Homer, since the hands of the original are those of laboring Achilles ("Never have I prize like to thine, when the Achaeans sack a well-peopled citadel of the Trojans; nay, the brunt of tumultuous war do my hands bear . . .").[42] Not only has the hand migrated in translation from Achilles to Agamemnon, but in migration it focuses the charges of rapaciousness and greed, and colors the whole subject of war spoils with the issue of usurpation. Such an issue then collects details throughout the confrontation so that phrases like "Sovereign Sway," "scepter'd Slaves," "pretended Right," "lawless Pow'r"—often Dryden's own rather than direct translation or expansion from Homer—are given an explicitly political turn though not necessarily a topical focus. And yet for those who would hear topical comment, the phrase "hook'd rapacious Hands" was a stinging reminder of the personal attacks on William that were especially common in the early years of the reign.[43]

For Calchas, Agamemnon is "the Tyrant, whom none dares

resist"; and Atrides warns and rebukes Agamemnon, stressing
the limits of sovereignty in a way that includes and rebukes
the English king as well:

> But this proud Man affects Imperial Sway.
> Controlling Kings, and trampling on our State
> His Will is Law; and what he wills is Fate.
> The Gods have giv'n him Strength: But whence the Style,
> Of lawless Pow'r assum'd, or Licence to revile?
>
> (IV, 1594, 406-410)

But the method is not parallel history; it is suggestion and
innuendo; the language allows but does not insist on appli-
cation. It could not have been Dryden's intention, by the close
of the decade, to attempt a series of parallel histories; and yet
it would also have been quite unlike the poet to allow these
narratives to remain wholly Greek, Italian, or Roman in char-
acter and meaning. What Dryden saw in Homer, he translates
into a language that permits, indeed at points suggests and
even argues, that honor and valor, right kingship and lawless
tyranny, are recorded in fables but enacted throughout time.

Homer's *Iliad* looks toward the later seventeenth century;
Boccaccio's tale of Sigismonda and Guiscardo glances obliquely
in the same direction. Passionate love and jealous fatherhood
are timeless motifs, and Dryden honors the texture of Boccac-
cio's romance; but he also has Boccaccio's characters ponder
such issues as justice and fate in a way that reflects the trans-
lator's concern:

> Or call it Heav'ns Imperial Pow'r alone,
> Which moves on Springs of Justice, though unknown;
> Yet this we see, though order'd for the best,
> The Bad exalted, and the Good oppress'd;
> Permitted Laurels grace the Lawless Brow,
> Th' Unworthy rais'd, the Worthy cast below.
>
> (IV, 1558, 493-498)

Dryden's Sigismonda recoils at Tancred's justice and against
all such miscarriage; the pressure of Dryden's own experience
can be felt through the texture of this story:

>   . . . he whose Mind
> Is Vertuous, is alone of Noble Kind.
> Though poor in Fortune, of Celestial Race;
> And he commits the Crime, who calls him Base.
>   (IV, 1558-1559, 519-522)

And again,

> . . . for 'tis not Baseness to be Poor;
> His Poverty augments thy Crime the more;
> Upbraids thy Justice with the scant Regard
> Of Worth: Whom Princes praise, they shou'd reward.
> Are these the Kings intrusted by the Crowd
> With Wealth, to be dispens'd for Common Good?
> The People sweat not for their King's Delight,
> T' enrich a Pimp, or raise a Parasite;
> Theirs is the Toil; and he who well has serv'd
> His Country, has his Countrys Wealth deserv'd.
>   (IV, 1559, 547-556)

Not only does the story insist that the true character of virtue is independent of fortune—a theme that Dryden explores throughout *Fables*—but Dryden also reflects steadily on the character of tyranny:

> . . . For, (Slaves to Pay)
> What Kings decree, the Soldier must obey:
> Wag'd against Foes; and, when the Wars are o'er,
> Fit only to maintain Despotick Pow'r:
> Dang'rous to Freedom, and desir'd alone
> By Kings, who seek an Arbitrary Throne.
>   (IV, 1560-1561, 596-601)

The language of this fourteenth-century Italian romance is made to reflect specific concerns of the late 1690s, when the standing army was repeatedly attacked by those Tory opponents of King William's wars who saw in the maintenance of a standing force a threat to their own liberty and property.[44] Dryden is not using Boccaccio to argue the political issue in an English context—though the interplay between Tancred and William as kings who seek an arbitrary throne is suggestive—but is reflecting through Boccaccio's tale his own awareness of the character, the injustice, and the consequences of the revolutionary settlement.

But it is not only politics, virtuous and corrupt, that are on Dryden's mind at the end of the decade. He sees in the flux of politics a larger specter, and he sees in Ovid's "Of the Pythagorean Philosophy" an ideal text for contemplating the meaning of change and the possibility of reconciliation to a universe in flux. Book 15 of *Metamorphoses* is Ovid's summary of Pythagorean natural philosophy, the wisdom that Numa seeks in order to guide the Roman state. The political content is obvious and general; Dryden's praise of Numa's wisdom, temperance, love of charity and justice render a figure of the ideal ruler. Moreover, the connections between this book of Ovid and the general themes of *Fables* are manifold. Book 15 continues the debate over the character of virtue from the preceding translation of Chaucer, underscoring the theme of selfless generosity in *Baucis and Philemon*, and stressing the natural economy in which Dryden also places the human figure in his epistle to John Driden. There are specific slights administered to priests (IV, 1722, 165 ff.), and a specific critique of political and social tyranny that Dryden has added to Ovid. But there is a more important encounter in this fable, an attempt to penetrate and appreciate the "mighty Mysteries, / Of Truths conceal'd" (IV, 1723, 210-211).

Through the encounter with Ovid's "Pythagorean philosophy" Dryden came to some accommodation with the changes that had come over his own life and with those that had come over the nation in the 1690s. The attempt to understand the Pythagorean mysteries is less a celebration of pagan religious philosophy than an attempt to derive consolation from the mysterious laws of flux. The reconciliation is first with an individual sense of mortality. Seen from the perspective of eternally shifting forms, death is but temporary change, not cessation:

> Mistaken Mortals wandring from the way,
> And wanting Wisdom, fearful for the state
> Of future Things, and trembling at their Fate!

> Those I would teach; and by right Reason bring
> To think of Death, as but an idle Thing.
> Why thus affrighted at an empty Name,
> A Dream of Darkness, and fictitious Flame?
> . . . .
> Nor dies the Spirit, but new Life repeats
> In other Forms, and only changes Seats.
>
> > (IV, 1723, 218-224, 229-230)

The personal consolation is then raised to the condition of nature:

> Thus all Things are but alter'd, nothing dies;
> And here and there th' unbodied Spirit flies,
> By Time, or Force, or Sickness dispossest,
> And lodges, where it lights, in Man or Beast;
> Or hunts without, till ready Limbs it find,
> And actuates those according to their kind;
> From Tenement to Tenement is toss'd;
> The Soul is still the same, the Figure only lost.
>
> > (IV, 1724, 239-246)

And flux and sway in the natural world are exalted as a universal principle, a definition of all experience:

> Ev'n Times are in perpetual Flux; and run
> Like Rivers from their Fountain rowling on;
> For Time no more than Streams, is at a stay:
> The flying Hour is ever on her way.   (IV, 1724, 266-269)

And it is from this perception of universal flux that Dryden derives a political consolation:

> . . . For former Things
> Are set aside, like abdicated Kings:
> And every moment alters what is done,
> And innovates some Act till then unknown.
> Darkness we see emerges into Light,
> And shining Suns descend to Sable Night;
> Ev'n Heav'n it self receives another die,
> When weari'd Animals in Slumbers lie.
>
> > (IV, 1725, 274-281)

Within this vision of flux and change, even the violations of usurpation and conquest are accommodated to the mysterious law of nature, indeed to the nature and perception of human experience. "All suffer change" (IV, 1735, 672); within that sweeping formula lies a reconciliation with a universe that is disturbing, at points incomprehensible, but whose change and contingency yield a set of moral principles, "all Things have an equal right to live. / Kill noxious Creatures, where 'tis Sin to save; / This only just Prerogative we have" (IV, 1736, 706-708). Armed with such consolation and such precepts, Numa ascends the Roman throne, "Himself a Saint, a Goddess was his Bride, / And all the Muses o'er his Acts preside" (IV, 1736, 719-720). The vision of true monarchy restored is reminiscent of the many prophetic restorations which Dryden had provided for his political poems, but the conclusion of this fable, Dryden must have known late in the 1690s, was possible only in poetry.

Dryden spoke out clearly against political violation, but I think he also accepted the Pythagorean consolation; he had come to a new understanding not only of the impracticability of nostalgic politics but also of the way in which such a reconciliation to change might at once allow political criticism and yet enable him to rise above its particulars. *The Character of a Good Parson* is at points minutely topical and at points a harsh condemnation of the revolutionary settlement, but it is also an effort to immortalize a particular kind of spirituality; and as always in Dryden the edge of particularity heightens the idealization. The texture of *Fables* pulls more in the direction of idealization, but there is a fine balance between romance and reality in these poems.

In the final poem of *Fables*, Boccaccio's *Cymon and Iphigenia*, Dryden makes a very delicate assay of the relation between romance and history. The adaptation begins with a long passage in which the poet speaks in his own voice, answering charges of indecency and scandal, and the apology closes with a celebration of the duchess of Ormond, Dryden returning us at the end of this collection to the subject of initial praise. The tale itself is a complex series of triumphs and disappointments of passion; it illustrates the heights of virtue and barbarity to

which love will drive its victim. The passion for Iphigenia
civilizes the rude Cymon, but it is the same passion that drives
him to conquest by arms:

> In *Iphigene* I claim my rightful Due,
> Rob'd by my Rival, and detain'd by you:
> Your *Pasimond* a lawless Bargain drove,
> The Parent could not sell the Daughters Love;
> Or if he cou'd, my Love disdains the Laws,
> And like a King by Conquest gains his Cause:
> Where Arms take place, all other Pleas are vain,
> Love taught me Force, and Force shall Love maintain.
>
> (IV, 1748-1749, 296-303)

The language argues an enduring issue for Dryden. He does
not mean us to hear the conquest as an allegory of politics,
but rather as a shadowy reflection on the inevitability of con-
quest and its consequences. Hence, the conquest that has oc-
curred is reversed in the tale, for what is brought in by force
can by force be removed. The theme reflects Dryden's steady
conviction on this subject, but it also nicely accommodates
the vision of perpetual change in Pythagoras. Where right is
founded in conquest, only the law of arms holds sway:

> *Cymon* inslav'd, who first the War begun,
> And *Iphigene* once more is lost and won.
>
> (IV, 1751, 413-414)

Hence from violence to violence the story turns, nor can Dry-
den restrain himself from comment:

> Unprais'd by me, tho' Heav'n sometime may bless
> An impious Act with undeserv'd Success:
> The Great, it seems, are priviledg'd alone
> To punish all Injustice but their own.
> But here I stop, not daring to proceed,
> Yet blush to flatter an unrighteous Deed:
> For Crimes are but permitted, not decreed.
>
> (IV, 1753, 469-475)

And it is to such a conclusion that the poet has come at
last: "Crimes are but permitted, not decreed." On this theme

the story turns another variation, for both lovers recognize that the quarrel will be settled not by right but by force. The poet cannot celebrate such conclusion, but he recognizes and, indeed, seems reconciled to its truth:

> 'Tis Force when done must justify the Deed:
> Our Task perform'd we next prepare for Flight;
> And let the Losers talk in vain of Right.
>
> (IV, 1754, 521-523)

The tale of passion and force concludes in the exercise of such passion and force. Dryden acknowledges the reality of such integers, and yet he is no blithe celebrant of a world in which these truths are more powerful than laws and rights. The poem concludes with a glimpse of the world left by such passion and violence:

> What should the People do, when left alone?
> The Governor, and Government are gone.
> The publick Wealth to Foreign Parts convey'd;
> Some Troops disbanded, and the rest unpaid.
> *Rhodes* is the Soveraign of the Sea no more;
> Their Ships unrigg'd, and spent their Naval Store;
> They neither could defend, nor can pursue,
> But grind their Teeth, and cast a helpless view.
>
> (IV, 1757, 615-622)

It seems an especially touching conclusion for a poem that so finely balances the truths of romance against those of history. The Revolution had taught Dryden, and he had at last become reconciled to, the inevitability and irreversibility of change; the world moved to a law which he finally could admit but not fully comprehend. Yet while acknowledging the force of such laws, the force of passion and violence, he could not help asking and indeed interpolating into Boccaccio's text, "What should the People do, when left alone?" Perhaps all they could do was cast a helpless view, but this poet found another exercise as well. By meditating on those truths and wrongs, the poet finally transcended them through fable, through fiction, through a world in which the powers of the imagination reconciled change with constancy.

The beauty and delicacy of this adjustment is nowhere more exactly expressed than in that enigmatic lyric from the *Secular Masque*:

> *All, all, of a piece throughout;*
> *Thy Chase had a Beast in View;*
> *Thy Wars brought nothing about;*
> *Thy Lovers were all untrue.*
> *'Tis well an Old Age is out,*
> *And time to begin a New.* (IV, 1765, 92-97)

The chorus from the *Secular Masque* brings together the disparate elements of Dryden's lyric style in the late poetry. It is political commentary and fable of the highest order; the poet reflects on the particulars of his age but he also rises above them to see in the futility and change and disappointment of his own life a pattern more beautiful than its frustrations. The tone is melancholy; but the lyric ends in return and renewal. It would be pleasant to think that the chorus expresses the reconciliation to which Dryden had come in his last years.

6. Politics and Translation

VIRGIL'S ÆNEIS

DRYDEN's *Fables* reflects the political and ideological preoccupations of his last years, but political themes in *Fables* are mediated by translation, by adaptation, by the exigencies of lyric and narrative, and perhaps most importantly by the poet's own reconciliation to the disturbing fact of a revolution that he knew, late in the 1690s, would not be reversed in his lifetime. The most sustained political meditation of the last decade came a few years before *Fables*, and it occurred not as lyric or narrative but in the epic mode, in the translation of Virgil's *Aeneid*. Dryden began translating Virgil in 1693,[1] and the years between the initial contract and publication were a time when William's reign was not fixed with the certainty it assumed late in the decade, a time when Stuart restoration might still be contemplated, and not wholly as fantasy.[2] The 1697 *Virgil* is a meditation on the language and culture of Virgil's poetry, but it is also a set of reflections on English politics in the aftermath of the Glorious Revolution, and it is the interplay between Rome and England and the ways in which Rome at once conceals and expresses England that form my subject. In the materials that Dryden attached to his edition, as well as in the translation, the poet both directly and obliquely argued the connections of Trojan, Roman, and English histories. The ways in which Dryden thought about Virgil and about his own task as translator can be approached by reading together the prefaces and postscripts, the plates and subscriptions, and the translation itself. What emerges from such a reading is an understanding of the continuities in theme and anxiety among the "texts" of this book, an understanding of the task and achievement of the translator as Dryden might have conceived them and as his readers in 1697 might have experienced them.

The *Dedication of the Æneis* is one of the longest and least esteemed of Dryden's critical essays. By the poet's own admission—indeed frequent insistence—the *Dedication* is a rambling discourse without the shape or method of the work that he claims as his model (III, 1020, 655 ff.). Nor is shape the only problem. There are, as well, questions of Dryden's originality as a theorist, his handling of critical commonplaces, and the lengthy digressions. Approached in these terms, the essay is disappointing and enigmatic. The remarks on heroic verse are often literal translations and transciptions from the authorities,[3] and what Dryden does develop as his own suggests idiosyncrasy rather than originality. What, for example, are we to make of Dryden's remarks on the rival claims of Aeneas, Helenus, and Priamus to the Trojan crown (III, 1016, 541 ff.), his assertion that Aeneas's sovereignty is an example of elective kingship (III, 1018, 588), or the peculiar reading of book 4, which Dryden construes as Virgil currying favor with a Roman public that despised Carthage and with a Roman emperor who had recently arranged his own divorce (III, 1031-1033, 1088-1161)?

The asides and apologies in the *Dedication* indicate the poet's own discomfort over critical performance. Self-doubt is, of course, one of the standard poses in the critical essays, but the topos here, nervously repeated through the essay, bears the imprint of a stronger anxiety, an anxiety not wholly misplaced. By the standard of his own work, the *Dedication* is a disappointment. Dryden's encounter with Virgil began in the 1660s and culminated with this translation, whose introduction is Dryden's most extended work on the epic. It is not surprising that an essay devoted to the poet and literary form that had so long held his interests and ambitions should raise high expectations.

But the *Dedication* is not wholly a patchwork of commonplaces and crotchets. There is an argument and a poetics of some interest here. To see them, however, we must approach the essay from a new direction. The force and originality of this piece are not to be found where we might assume that they lie. Dryden's contribution is not a theory of the epic or an appreciation of the splendors of Virgil's poetry, but a reading of Virgil's politics that enables us to see how the translator understood and used the *Aeneid*.

"A Heroick Poem, truly such, is undoubtedly the greatest Work which the Soul of Man is capable to perform. The Design of it, is to form the Mind to Heroick Virtue by Example" (III, 1003, 1-3). But of this ennobling art we hear, in fact, very little in the *Dedication*. For Dryden, the business of Virgil's poem is not the condition of the soul but politics in Augustan Rome, not the mythology of empire but political revolution. The ostensible subject of Virgil's poem is the myth of Aeneas, but for Dryden the identity of Aeneas is Augustus Caesar. The function of Virgil's poem is to celebrate Augustus Caesar, and its moral is political obedience. Virgil's intention was to be useful to his government, to argue the necessity of union and to confirm the Romans in their obedience to Caesar (III, 1015, 470 ff.). And into this scheme Dryden fits the whole of the *Aeneid*: its most famous and frequently translated episodes, its minor characters, its central action, its mythology, its remaking of Homer, and its conclusion.

The commonplaces of critical theory with which Dryden opens the essay and which he frequently invokes are not, however, entirely disjunctive from the political reading of Virgil that is the *Dedication*'s central argument. The role of these commonplaces is twofold: they act as conventional scaffolding, gestures one would expect in such a preface, and they lead by design and by indirection to the poet's lifelong preoccupation with politics, with the bearing of ancient on contemporary affairs of state. The sorts of connections that Dryden explored and their implications for reading the translation fall into three groups: the contemporary meaning of Roman politics; the specific bearing of Aeneas and Augustus on William III; and the figure of Virgil as self-portraiture.

But it is not with Roman politics that Dryden opens the *Dedication*. Dryden begins with that most familiar and most exalted of commonplaces on epic poetry. Yet the opening remarks have a bearing on the political meaning of Virgil, for they conflate moral and political issues by introducing the epic as a poem strictly concerned with moral conduct, and then discovering that such conduct reflects, in fact, a variety of political and pragmatic behavior. The epic forms "the Mind to Heroick Virtue" (III, 1003, 3); it "raises the Soul and hardens it to Virtue" (III, 1003, 18). Virgil's poem is by definition aimed at the moral character of the nation, yet that character is not conceived in relation to such ideals as justice, charity, or honor but in relation to political goals. For Dryden, Virgil throughout had an eye on Augustus Caesar as he drew his epic hero (III, 1017, 554); Dryden too had an eye on his contemporaries, on their political acts and political ideals, as he translated this epic and Virgil's condition into his own.

England and Rome are the central analogues in the *Dedication*, and that equation is first suggested some few hundred lines into the essay, at a point where Dryden begins a defense of the Roman poet: "I must now come closer to my present business: and not think of making more invasive Wars abroad, when like *Hannibal*, I am call'd back to the defence of my own Country. *Virgil* is attack'd by many Enemies: He has a whole Confederacy against him, and I must endeavour to defend him as well as I am able" (III, 1011, 318-322). Virgil was, of course, the most esteemed of ancient poets, this epic revered as the culmination of a form that expressed for Renaissance poets and theorists the highest attainment of the literary intellect. The defensive posture follows not so much from Dryden's understanding of Virgil's condition as from the translator's sense of his own embattled circumstance. The letters that Dryden wrote in the 1690s convey the self-portrait sharply and poignantly.[4] By defending Virgil, Dryden undertakes a reading of the Roman poet and a justification of his own circumstance. The coincidence of poet and translator emerges from the large analogy that Dryden pursues through his description of politics in Augustan Rome, "we are to consider him [Virgil] as writing his Poem in a time when the Old Form of Government was subverted, and a new one just Established by *Octavius Caesar*: In effect by force of Arms, but seemingly by the Consent of the *Roman* People" (III, 1012, 366-369). Dryden is describing Roman politics in the century of the Caesars, but the language also argues another century and another revolution.

Stuart loyalists maintained that the Revolution was effected by force of arms, that it was an invasion conducted under the pretense of a protection of property and liberty, a subversion of the government that had altered fundamental laws and constitutions. Through the summary of Roman political history, Dryden outlines the course of politics in late seventeenth-century England:[5]

> The Commonwealth had receiv'd a deadly Wound in the former Civil Wars betwixt *Marius* and *Sylla*. The Commons, while the first prevail'd, had almost shaken off the Yoke of the Nobility; and *Marius* and *Cinna*, like the Captains of the Mobb, under the specious Pretence of the Publick Good, and of doing Justice on the Oppressours of their Liberty, reveng'd themselves, without Form of Law, on their private Enemies. *Sylla*, in his turn, proscrib'd the Heads of the adverse Party: He too had nothing but Liberty and Reformation in his Mouth; (for the Cause of Religion is but a Modern Motive to Rebellion, invented by the Christian Priesthood, refining on the Heathen:). . . . Such was the Reformation of the Government by both Parties. The Senate and the Commons were the two Bases on which it stood; and the two Champions of either Faction, each destroy'd the Foundations of the other side: So the Fabrique of consequence must fall betwixt them: And Tyranny must be built upon their Ruines. This comes of altering Fundamental Laws and Constitutions. . . . Thus the *Roman* People were grosly gull'd; twice or thrice over: and as often enslav'd in one Century, and under the same pretence of Reformation. (III, 1012-1013, 370-420)

The application of English political history from the civil wars through the end of the century would have been difficult for Dryden's audience to resist. Not only do key words and phrases argue those connections, but the whole scheme of political history as disguise fits both the conduct and perception of politics in the later seventeenth century.[6] Conspiracy as a theory of history and mode of political analysis dominated the English political mind from the outbreak of the civil wars through the Sacheverell trial in the early years of the next century. The subversion of government under the pretense of reform, the use of arms under the guise of public consent, the tyranny consequent on altering fundamental laws and constitutions—none who spoke the language of seventeenth-century politics could have mistaken the English meaning of this Roman history. Some among Dryden's audience would have resented or scorned his implications in this narrative, but all would have recognized the contemporary meaning of those words and phrases, the special fit of Roman history to English politics. Men who engaged in political acts and political speech in this age commonly assumed that politics was the triumph of disguise; not only was the general frame accepted but the banners and catchwords were common property. The "fundamental laws and constitutions" belonged to all who would claim them, and there was little abstinence in the use of such language. The assertion that James II had violated those fundamental laws and constitutions was urged as resolutely by those who came to oppose his regime as it was by Jacobites who resisted the imposition of William III.

Roman history afforded general analogies with English politics; it allowed as well more daring particulars, and occasionally in the *Dedication* Dryden risks such particulars:

> The last *Tarquin* was Expell'd justly, for Overt-Acts of Tyranny, and Male-Administration; for such are the Conditions of an Elective Kingdom: And I meddle not with others: being, for my own Opinion, of *Montaigns* Principles, that an Honest Man ought to be contented with that Form of Government, and with those Fundamental Constitutions of it, which he receiv'd from his Ancestors, and under which himself was Born: Though at the same time he confess'd freely, that if he could have chosen his Place of Birth, it shou'd have been at *Venice*: Which for many Reasons I dislike, and am better pleas'd to have been born an *English* Man. (III, 1014, 444-453)

The initial application of the passage is obvious; the confla-
tion of tyranny and elective kingship is an insult to William
III and to his supporters. The satiric literature of the 1690s
had made current the identification of William and Mary with
Tarquin and Tullia,[7] those models of despotism and filial im-
piety; but the slur of elective kingship aims at constitutional
rather than personal issues. The parliamentary convention of
1689 that had scrupled so minutely over the language with
which to describe James's departure from England took such
care with words to avoid two implications: that William's de-
scent into England was an invasion, and that his title was
founded on election or conquest.[8] The parliamentary bill for
the Exclusion of James, duke of York, from succession had
been defeated in 1680 on the strength of the argument that
such exclusion would turn the kingship into elective mon-
archy; none who supported William's kingship would have
had his title hinged on so precarious a term. But this argu-
ment by slur and implication does not close with the reference
to Tarquin. The citation from Montaigne raises the same is-
sue, though in more oblique fashion. The contentment of
Montaigne's "Honest Man" is not simple piety, it is a form of
civic virtue that recognizes the binding force of personal and
national inheritance. Dryden insists on these principles in *Ab-
salom and Achitophel*, where they are buttressed by a fuller moral,
legal, and theological argument. The position in the *Dedica-
tion*, although suggested with greater tact, is the same.

There is one additional point to be made about this pas-
sage, and that concerns the patriotic gesture that closes the
argument. Perhaps Montaigne longed for the glories of the
Venetian republic, but Dryden prizes England over all such
fantasies. The assertion of patriotic pride is a familiar topos in
Dryden's works in the 1690s, and its psychology and polem-
ical value are not difficult to grasp. What is interesting about
this version is that the whole passage has migrated almost
word for word from Dryden's *Preface* to *The Character of Po-
lybius*, which was published in 1692. There is, however, one
important change:

I cannot hold from breaking out with Montagne into this expression: "It is just," says he, "for every honest man to be content with the government and laws of his native country, without endeavouring to alter or subvert them; but if I were to choose, where I would be born, it should have been in a commonwealth." He indeed names Venice, which, for many reasons, should not be my wish; but rather Rome in such an age, if it were possible, as that wherein Polybius lived; or that of Sparta, whose constitution for a republic is by our author compared with Rome, to which he justly gives the preference.[9]

In the 1697 *Virgil*, the most public of Dryden's productions in the 1690s, a book issued by subscription and one that had the names of distinguished patrons attached to it, there could be no toying with Rome and Sparta as ideal constitutions. Here Dryden had to assert his English identity as a counterbalance to a passage that took some liberties with the character and administration of William III. The stance of loyal opposition afforded some protection, but it turned on the unimpeachable patriotism of that opposition.

Nor is Tarquin the only analogue for the English king. There are comparisons with Aeneas and Augustus, and a rather pointed contrast with Latinus, that paradigm of kingly legitimacy. The ways in which Aeneas and Augustus are used to think about William is one of the most complex issues in the *Dedication* and translation. We are not to construe the narrative as a point-by-point allegory, no simple conflation to be effected, as Tonson would have liked, by hooking the Roman hero's nose.[10] Dryden's strategy in the *Dedication* is not to analogize either Aeneas or Augustus directly with William but to present the ancient figures in a language that would argue the circumstances of William's kingship. Hence, the long and peculiar passage on succession and title as they bear on Aeneas's claims to the Trojan office:

Æneas cou'd not pretend to be *Priam's* Heir in a Lineal Succession: For *Anchises* the Heroe's Father, was only of the second Branch of the Royal Family: And *Helenus*, a Son

of *Priam*, was yet surviving, and might lawfully claim be-
fore him. It may be *Virgil* mentions him on that Account.
Neither has he forgotten *Priamus*, in the Fifth of his *Æneis*,
the Son of *Polites*, youngest Son to *Priam*; who was slain
by *Pyrrhus*, in the Second Book. *Æneas* had only Married
Creusa, Priam's Daughter, and by her could have no Title,
while any of the Male Issue were remaining. In this case,
the Poet gave him the next Title, which is, that of an Elec-
tive King. (III, 1016-1017, 541-551)

For Dryden, Virgil is instructing and warning Augustus on
the nature of the Roman emperor's title: elective kings rule at
the pleasure of the people. Dryden has Virgil raise this subject
so that he, Dryden, can scorn the legitimacy of William's rule
and warn those who claimed for the Dutchman the sanctity
and rights of lineal descent that they had in fact sanctioned
revolution and usurpation. The debate over the nature of Wil-
liam's title had not been settled in 1689; it was raised
throughout his kingship, and with special force in the year
before the *Virgil* publication. The assassination plot of 1696
had caused parliament to vote an Association proclaiming loy-
alty to William as rightful and lawful king.[11] But in the debate
over the Association, even so late as 1696, and even in the
face of the plot, members of parliament still scrupled over the
title.

Dryden's Virgil depicts Aeneas's Trojan office as elective
kingship so that Augustus Caesar might be instructed in the
character and dangers of such a title; the analogy is twofold.
First, between the Virgilian models of elective kingship—
Aeneas, Mezentius, and Tarquin—and William III; second,
between the Roman emperor and the English king. The Vir-
gilian models, pious and restrained in the person of Aeneas
but brutal and corrupt in the persons of Mezentius and Tar-
quin, demonstrate the extremes. Augustus Caesar, conqueror
and despot, needs the instruction of Virgil's poem so that he
might become the best of the bad lot to which he belongs. By
arguing that Virgil draws Aeneas to the measure of Augustus
Caesar, Dryden is free to raise the problems of Caesar's king-

ship as they are illustrated in Virgil's epic. The distortion is curious, but with William in mind we can see its point. "Our Poet, who all this while had *Augustus* in his Eye, had no desire he should seem to succeed by any right of Inheritance, deriv'd from *Julius Caesar*; such a Title being but one degree remov'd from Conquest. For what was introduc'd by force, by force may be remov'd" (III, 1017, 553-557). In this complex arrangement of poetic models and historical figures, William falls somewhere between Aeneas and the worst examples, Mezentius and Tarquin. One assumes that Dryden found a greater affinity between Tarquin and William than between Aeneas and the English king, but perhaps the closest analogue is Caesar. The language in which Dryden casts Virgil's deliberation over the character of Aeneas's sovereignty and the nature of Caesar's role is strikingly appropriate to the debate over the revolutionary settlement: under what conditions had William entered the country and by what rights did he now wield power? The whole of this problem is, of course, reflected in the translation, especially book 7 (Aeneas's entry into Latium), where the steady shading of the language, the consistent impulse to render entry as conquest, can only be the translator brooding over the injustice and perhaps the inevitability of such conquest of Latium by Aeneas and of England by William III.

The contemporary application of the whole discussion of legitimacy and sovereignty is sharpened by the introduction of Latinus:

> Our Author shews us another sort of Kingship in the Person of *Latinus*. He was descended from *Saturn*, and as I remember, in the Third Degree. He is describ'd a just and a gracious Prince; solicitous for the Welfare of his People; always Consulting with his Senate to promote the common Good. We find him at the head of them, when he enters into the Council-Hall. Speaking first, but still demanding their Advice, and steering by it as far as the Iniquity of the Times wou'd suffer him. And this is the proper Character of a King by Inheritance, who is born a Father of his Coun-

try. *Æneas*, tho' he Married the Heiress of the Crown, yet claim'd no Title to it during the Life of his Father-in-Law. (III, 1017, 561-571)

Perhaps the idea of Latinus as James II—gracious father to his people and sage parliamentarian—would have roused the scorn of much of Dryden's audience, but who could have missed the analogy between Aeneas and William, the thrust of the end of this passage? Aeneas claimed no title during the life of his father-in-law, but William certainly did.

Not all contemporary issues are argued so openly as this. Some topics are raised only by allusion and not pursued through extended analogy. But we can hear the contemporary harmonies in Dryden's handling of such themes as ingratitude and constancy. Gratitude as a political virtue had been frequently extolled by those Stuart apologists who saw in the system of patronage and in the generosity of Charles II an ideal of governance and kingship.[12] Dryden was hardly alone in the Exclusion Crisis when he scored the ingratitude of those who had battened on the king's largesse and then turned against their benefactor. Gratitude was, in fact, a linchpin of Stuart politics, and the language of Dryden's *Dedication* in 1697 conjures a powerful political argument that takes meaning not only from the disloyalty of those who raised arms against James II but from the whole history of disloyalty to Stuart kings, from that highest crime of regicide which gave particular force to this theme: "want of Constancy, and Ingratitude after the last Favour, is a Crime that never will be forgiven" (III, 1027, 953-955).

Nor is gratitude the only theme thus handled. There are glancing references to "dispensing powers," a subject that Dryden treats in purely literary terms, but none who heard the phrase could ignore its political meaning: the long history of a struggle between two Stuart kings and truculent parliaments that were unwilling to allow their laws to be suspended at will by kings bent on what they thought was the destruction of the Protestant religion and the imposition of Catholic slavery.[13] "Any thing might be allow'd to his Son *Virgil* on the account of his other Merits; That being a Monarch he had a dispensing Power, and pardon'd him. . . . To Moralize this Story, *Virgil* is the *Apollo*, who has this Dispensing Power. His great Judgment made the Laws of Poetry, but he never made himself a Slave to them" (III, 1030, 1046-1054). Virgil, like Apollo, could supersede mechanical rules for the same reason that a "Monarch may dispense with, or suspend his own Laws, when he finds it necessary so to do; especially if those Laws are not altogether fundamental" (III, 1031, 1080-1082). If this seems a slightly offhand way of conducting a political argument, the mode is explained by its history. The battle had been long and bitterly fought, and Dryden's use of Virgil's looseness with chronology and fables to demonstrate the inevitable rights of monarchy is not so much an argument as it is a memory of a political contest.

Similarly, the reference to the coinage crisis is made under the guise of poetics: "Words are not so easily Coyn'd as Money: And yet we see that the Credit not only of Banks, but of Exchequers cracks, when little comes in, and much goes out" (III, 1058, 2105-2107). The enormous expenditures that supported William's land wars are clearly alluded to here and in the following passage on the "coining" of words: "I carry not out the Treasure of the Nation, which is never to return: but what I bring from *Italy*, I spend in *England*: Here it remains, and here it circulates; for if the Coyn be good, it will pass from one hand to another. I Trade both with the Living and the Dead, for the enrichment of our Native Language" (III, 1059, 2167-2172).[14] Taken individually, such references—and there are more in the *Dedication*[15]—do not account for the political argument of this preface, but seen in the context of the general analogy that Dryden explores between ancient and contemporary politics, they become part of a larger argument whose structure must occasionally be inferred, but whose meaning cannot be in doubt.

But Virgil's text was more than an occasion for glancing reference to contemporary political topics, more than a vehicle for criticizing William III, more even than a way of running a commentary on the character of the Glorious Revolution. Dryden saw in Virgil an image of himself as court poet: a man of letters sustaining and criticizing the mythology of empire, analyzing political issues, and praising and blaming those patrons, statesmen, and ideologues who shaped and enacted the affairs of state. Indeed, for Dryden politics and empire were always seen in terms of personality; and, in what Dryden construed to be Virgil's practice of rewarding friends and punishing enemies,[16] the translator saw or imposed his own powerful instincts as panegyrist and satirist. Virgil used his poem as the text for such allusion, but Dryden, who intended no continuous allegory by his translation, found another way of binding his contemporaries to Virgil. The whole problem of contemporary reference emerges most clearly in Dryden's discussion of book 5 in the *Dedication*:

> Neither were the great *Roman* Families which flourish'd in his time, less oblig'd by him than the Emperour. Your Lordship knows with what Address he makes mention of them, as Captains of Ships, or Leaders in the War; and even some of *Italian* Extraction are not forgotten. These are the single Stars which are sprinkled through the *Æneis*: But there are whole Constellations of them in the Fifth Book. And I could not but take notice, when I Translated it, of some Favourite Families to which he gives the Victory, and awards the Prizes, in the Person of his Heroe, at the Funeral Games which were Celebrated in Honour of *Anchises*. I, Insist not on their Names: But am pleas'd to find the *Memmii* amongst them, deriv'd from *Mnestheus*, because *Lucretius* Dedicates to one of that Family, a Branch of which destroy'd *Corinth*. I likewise either found or form'd an Image to my self of the contrary kind; that those who lost the Prizes, were such as had disoblig'd the Poet, or were in disgrace with *Augustus*, or Enemies to *Mecenas*: And this was the Poetical Revenge he took. For *genus irritabile Vatum*, as *Horace* says. When a Poet is throughly provok'd, he will do himself Justice, however dear it cost him, *Animamque, in Vulnere ponit*. I think these are not bare Imag-

inations of my own, though I find no trace of them in the Commentatours: But one Poet may judge of another by himself. The Vengeance we defer, is not forgotten. (III, 1015-1016, 496-516)

There can be no question of the personal significance of this issue for the translator. Praise and blame were central imaginative modes for Dryden; and whether or not he simply imagines them in Virgil, the very discovery or imposition of likeness—"one Poet may judge of another by himself"—argues their significance in the translation and their importance for understanding the role of the plates in Dryden's book. These plates allowed Dryden the same play of contemporary reference that he insisted that Virgil had once enjoyed.

Little is known of this aspect of the 1697 *Virgil*.[17] What I offer is speculation, but sufficiently congruent with Dryden's reading of book 5 in the *Dedication* and with the character of the plates and subscriptions themselves to justify exploration. The publication of books by subscription was not new in 1697.[18] Since early in the century, scientific texts had been issued by subscription, and by mid-century some entrepreneurs were publishing books by subscription for profit. Chief among them was John Ogilby, who had himself translated Virgil in 1649 and issued this translation in 1654 in folio with engravings and subscriptions from a number of important royalists.[19] In the last two decades of the century, the number of subscription books grew considerably. The most important literary publication by subscription before the *Virgil* was a 1688 edition of *Paradise Lost* that Tonson published with great commercial success. In the Milton, subscribers are listed at the front; in the *Virgil*, a two-guinea pledge bought the subscriber a position in such an alphabetical list, and a five-guinea subscription entitled the patron to have his name and crest attached to one of the 101 plates in the book.[20] The plates of the *Virgil* are those originally engraved for Ogilby,[21] but with two modifications: the nearly consistent hooking of Aeneas's nose so that the hero might bear a likeness to William III— Tonson's idea of a compliment[22]—and the addition of line numbers to the lower portion of the plates interleaved through the *Æneis*.[23]

From correspondence between Dryden and Tonson, we know that both poet and publisher sought subscribers for the project, but we do not know which of the two sought specific subscribers or who matched plate with patron.[24] What we can see is that in a number of instances the fit of plate and text to subscriber clearly argues the function of the plate and text as commentary on the subscription. The ties of patronage, friendship, and politics allow us to speculate on where Dryden may have designated plate for subscription.

There are, to begin, some cases in which the plate obviously joins with the text to compliment the subscriber. In the "Postscript" to the *Aeneis*, Dryden praises the generosity of William Bowyer, at whose country estate he had translated parts of the *Georgics* and *Aeneid* (III, 1425-1426, 75-80); the second *Georgic*, Virgil's great praise of country life, is prefaced with a pastoral scene dedicated to Bowyer (plate 16).[25] The third plate of this *Georgic*, attached to the lines, "I teach thee next the diff'ring Soils to know; / The light for Vines, the heavyer for the Plough" (III, 944, 309-310) is dedicated to George London, "of his Majesties Royall Garden" (plate 18).[26] Anthony Henley, wit and politician, known for his generous patronage, is given the lavish picnic in book 7 of the *Aeneid* (plate 71);[27] and George Stepney, amateur poet, translator of Juvenal, member of Dorset's circle and, in the language of the dedication, "His Majesties Envoy Extraordinary to Severall Princes in Germany," is given the plate illustrating Ilioneus's embassy to Latinus (plate 72).[28] The plate for *Pastoral* 5 (plate 5), which illustrates the apotheosis of Daphnis, is dedicated to James Bertie, earl of Abingdon, perhaps a reminiscence of the themes of *Eleonora* (1692), Dryden's poem commemorating the death and celebrating the apotheosis of Bertie's wife. The most complex of these assignments of personal compliment is the plate given to Kneller in book 8 of the *Aeneid* (plate 79). The plate depicts Aeneas contemplating the radiant arms Venus has given her son for combat with Turnus. At the center of the plate is the massive shield that Vulcan has embossed with the history of Rome. There is an elaborate play in the lines attached to the plate between verbal and visual art, between shield and poem as emblems of Roman history, and the plate and subscription carry the play forward to include translator and portrait painter in the ancient rivalry of poetry and painting.[29] As personal compliment, the plate acts as intermediary text, focusing the poem momentarily on the subscriber, a reading of past in present, the very trope on which Dryden's poem to Kneller had turned in 1694.

In addition to plates of individual compliment, there are a group of engravings with altars, sacrifices, and divining scenes dedicated to Roman Catholics.[30] One, however, was reserved for Nathaniel Crewe, Bishop of Durham. Crewe was assigned an engraving that depicts Anius, priest and king (plate 44); in light of Crewe's career, the complimentary force of the plate and the linkage with Roman Catholics is not difficult to grasp. Crewe was first chaplain to the duke of York, then a member of James's ecclesiastical commission and one of the king's most obliging instruments in the campaign against the Anglican Church.[31] The most interesting of these assignments is, however, the plate dedicated to James Cecil, fourth earl of Salisbury. His plate depicts Laocoon struggling with serpents to save his children (plate 38; Figure 1); in 1697 the current earl was the six-year-old James Cecil, son of James, fourth earl of Salisbury, who had turned Catholic in 1688, plotted against William, and was jailed in the Tower of London until 1692, shortly before his death. Perhaps the plate is intended as a memorial to Salisbury, Catholic and Jacobite, wrestling with the fates on behalf of his son. Although the facts of Salisbury's life might be construed in other terms,[32] the commemorative design of the plate seems plausible, given Dryden's religion and politics.

More complex yet are those assignments in which both political and personal compliment are paid. One of the most interesting of these is the dedication of the third plate in the *Pastorals* (plate 3; Figure 2) to Charles Sackville, earl of Dorset, longtime patron and friend of Dryden. Dorset was the man to whom Dryden had dedicated the *Essay of Dramatic*

Poesy (1668) and the *Discourse concerning Satire* (1693). In both, Dorset is cast as arbiter of literary taste. In the *Pastoral* to which his subscription is fixed, Dorset can be understood as Palaemon, the figure called to judge the singing contest of Damaetas and Menalcas. The assignment echoes Dorset's role as Eugenius in the *Essay*, and is neatly folded into the assignment of the next plate to Lord Buckhurst, Dorset's nine-year-old son (plate 4; Figure 3). Virgil dedicated his fourth *Pastoral* to Pollio—consul, patron, and critic—and in the assignment to Buckhurst, Dryden suggests that the child is Salonius and the father Pollio, thus extending the compliment of the earlier plate. Dorset is the generous patron imagined now not only as arbiter of taste but also as the civic personality which the minister of state certainly was. Moreover, Dorset and Buckhurst as Pollio and Saloninus allow Dryden to become Virgil to this generous patron and man of great affairs. Finally, in book 7 of the *Aeneid*, the plate that illustrates the wounding of Silvia's stag is dedicated to Mary Sackville, Dorset's daughter (plate 74; Figure 4). In this dedication, Mary Sackville is the tenderhearted Latian maid and Dorset becomes "*Tyrrheus*, chief Ranger to the *Latian* King" (III, 1251, 676), hence loyal retainer of Stuart monarchy, an allusion to a happier past that Dryden shared with Dorset.

The use of plates to compliment patrons and reward friends is the most obvious allusive facet of the subscription list, a way for the translator to see Virgil's themes of loyalty, virtue, and friendship expressed in his own social and political world, and the number of such complimentary assignments is large. I have not touched on the assignment of plates depicting a valiant though doomed Turnus to Ailesbury (plate 76) and Ormond (plate 101), perhaps Dryden's valediction to a noble though fated cause. But compliment was not the only function of these plates. Dryden claims that Virgil's poem not only rewarded friends but also punished enemies. Indeed, Dryden insists on this aspect of Virgil's poem, though he confesses singularity in that perception: "I think these are not bare Imaginations of my own, though I find no trace of them in the Commentatours" (III, 1016, 513-515). The subscription assignments afforded Dryden the occasion to act on the same impulse, to fit plates to subscribers so that the assignment might function ironically or derisively. Such cases are more difficult to establish than the complimentary assignments because the ironic mode had of necessity to function more obliquely. But how else would the translator have hoped to effect revenge if not in such a way as to veil insult in ambiguity? Dryden understood that he would have to proceed with caution in this way, but he also insisted on the compulsion: "When a Poet is thoroughly provok'd, he will do himself Justice, however dear it cost him."

We do not know what, if anything, such assignments might have cost Dryden, but it is inviting to speculate on Sir Robert Howard's response to the plate that his five-guinea subscription had bought. A recent biography of Howard argues that old enmities between the poet and his brother-in-law had been resolved in the 1690s;[33] there had been feuds and skirmishes for three decades and clearly some reconciliation took place. But one wonders with Dryden if personal resentments were ever completely abandoned, and what effect Howard's quite vocal role in the Convention parliament might have had on Dryden's feelings. Howard was a member of the parliament meeting in 1689, and in its proceedings his voice is heard stridently denouncing James II and arguing in the most extreme and insulting language that James had abdicated the throne and that William rightfully succeeded him as king.[34] It seems unlikely that Dryden would have been wholly ignorant either of such opinions or of the vehemence with which they were held and expressed.

Howard's subscription resulted in the most personally insulting of the assignments. The plate, which appears in book 10 and is referred to line 450 (plate 87; Figure 5), depicts the battle of Aeneas with Cydon's seven brothers:

> Then wretched *Cydon* had receiv'd his Doom,
> Who courted *Clytius* in his beardless Bloom,
> And sought with lust obscene polluted Joys:
> The *Trojan* Sword had cur'd his love of Boys,

Had not his sev'n bold Brethren stop'd the Course
Of the fierce Champion, with united Force.

(III, 1332, 449-454)

Not only is the assignment damaging and insulting in the way
it focuses the plate and hence the figure of Howard on Cydon,
but Dryden's translation coarsens that figure, makes specific
and harsh a condemnation which in Virgil is certainly oblique.
Virgil's discreet, "dum sequeris Clytium infelix, nova gaudia,
Cydon" ("You too, unfortunate Cydon, as you kept close to
Clytius, your latest delight")[35] becomes, in Dryden's transla-
tion harsher and more detailed; and Dryden's next line (452)
makes quite explicit the threatened castration of the figure.
We do not know that Dryden translated these lines with
Howard in mind, nor have we evidence that Dryden made
the assignment. But the relations between Dryden and How-
ard suggest that Dryden's "vengeance deferred" had not been
forgotten in this plate.

Personal insult was not, of course, the only derisive use to
which the plates were put; as in the case of complimentary
assignment, those plates which could be treated in political
terms offered Dryden a way of thinking about contemporary
politics in relation to his great task as translator. An exemplary
case is the assignment to Henry Viscount Sydney of the first
plate of book 7 (plate 70; Figure 6) which depicts Janus, keeper
of the gate.[36] The subject of this book is Aeneas's entry into
Latium; that and such subsidiary themes as lineage, succes-
sion, and conquest which are developed through the book as
a whole allowed Dryden to read Virgil very closely here as a
commentary on the politics of the Glorious Revolution. On
the translation of the book I shall comment shortly, but the
assignment of the initial plate to Sydney we might consider in
terms of these facts of Sydney's political career: that he was
one of the seven men who signed the invitation to William,
that the invitation was in his own hand, that he joined Wil-
liam in Holland before the invasion, that he was one of the
few Englishmen whom William trusted over the whole of his
administration, and that he was a politician famed as "the great

wheel on whom the revolution turned."[37] The only other sub-
scriber who signed the invitation to William, Charles Talbot,
duke of Shrewsbury, is given the first plate of book 11 (plate
91; Figure 7) which depicts the head and armor of the dead
Mezentius, Virgil's atheist and tyrant, "curs'd *Mezentius*, in a
fatal Hour, / Assum'd the Crown, with Arbitrary Pow'r" (III,
1279, 630-631). In the plate that opens book 7, Sydney is
linked with Janus who in Virgil's language is simply "bifron-
tis"; for Dryden, he is "ancient *Janus*, with his double Face, /
And Bunch of Keys, the Porter of the place" (III, 1240, 245-
246). The details of key and office Dryden seems to have in-
vented; they appear in neither the Lauderdale nor the Ogilby
translation.[38] But if Dryden conceived of Sydney in terms of
his political career, then to characterize him as keeper of the
gate certainly sharpens our perception of his role in the Rev-
olution. Sydney's titles as Master Generall of the Ordinance and
Warden of the Cinque Ports, both recorded in the legend to
the subscription, allow a blameless meaning for Dryden's de-
tails, but they do not deny the suggestive and damaging alli-
ance between Sydney and Janus as wardens who have be-
trayed the palace to foreign guests. Swift wrote of Sydney in
the 1690s, "he was an old vitious illiterate Rake without any
sense of Truth or Honor."[39]

I have attempted thus far to delineate a poetics of transla-
tion in a specific political circumstance, to show the bearing
that Virgil's Roman history might be seen to have on English
political life in the later seventeenth century, and to suggest
how Dryden's book as a whole can be understood as an inter-
pretation of Virgil. Central to my thesis about translation as
commentary is, of course, the translation itself. And the evi-
dence here is striking. Not only is there a steady shading of
the translation, a heightening of political themes and topics
throughout the poem, but at crucial points—at points where
the subject matter of Virgil's poem could be brought directly
to bear on contemporary political issues—Dryden's attention
to that contemporaneity is unfailing.

To the Right
Earle of

Hon:ble James
Salisbury &

FIGURE 1: LAOCOON

FIGURE 2: PALAEMON

To the Right Honble Sackvill Lord Buck. Charles Earle of

Lionel Cranfeild hurst, eldest son of Dorsett & Midlesex.

Pag:4

FIGURE 3: POLLIO AND SOLONINUS

To y̓ Right Hon:ble e y̓ Lady Mary Sackvile daughter
to Charles Earle of Dorset & Middlesex

FIGURE 4: THE WOUNDING OF SILVIA'S STAG

To ye Right Hon.ble Sr. Robert Howard
Auditor of his Ma.ties Exchequer; and one of ye
Lords of his Maj.ties most Hon.ble Privy Councill

FIGURE 5: CYDON

F. Clyn in.   E. g. li.   Lombart   sculpsit londini

To the Right Hoble Henry   Earle of Romney Viscount
Sydney of Shippy Baron   Milton Master Generall
of the Ordinance Ld Warden   of the Cinque Ports &ct

FIGURE 6: JANUS

To ỹ Right: Noble Charles Duke of of Shrewsbury Westford & Water- Blackmere Gifford of Brimsfield & most Honble Privy Councill Principall of ỹ most Noble Order

Shrewsbury Marquis of: Alton Earle ford, Baron Talbot Strange of One of the Lords of his Maties Secretary of State, and Knight of the Garter.

FIGURE 7: MEZENTIUS

To make a translation is not, of course, to write an allegory, but for Dryden the contemporary point of reference must frequently have pressed near the text. Even in what is taken to be the most hurried of his jobs, the translation of book 1 of Tacitus's *Annals*,[40] a comparison of Latin, French, and English texts reveals some striking instances where Dryden is rethinking Tacitus so that the *Annals* reflect political issues of special concern to Dryden in the 1690s. In translating Virgil, a task that Dryden invests with enormous personal and professional significance, there can be no doubt of the steady pressure that his own political concerns exerted on the rendering of this political epic.

While there is hardly space to consider the whole of the *Virgil*—although passages of radical departure from the Latin when grouped together create something of a glossary of Dryden's political concerns—I should like to look at his translation of some passages from the *Aeneid*. Book 7, with its attention to foreign settlement, lineal descent, and the role of fate in politics, must have been of special interest to Dryden.

The book opens with a memorial to Caieta, a name fixed to the shore of the bay where Aeneas anchors his ship before entering Latium:

> Tu quoque litoribus nostris, Aeneia nutrix,
> Aeternam moriens famam, Caieta, dedisti
> Et nunc servat honos sedem tuus; ossaque nomen
> Hesperia in magna, si qua est ea gloria, signat.
>
> (Virgil 7, 1-4)[41]

In Dryden's translation there is a slight departure in the last line quoted, and this turn points a theme important to the translation as a whole and recurrent in Dryden's late poetry. Virgil invokes Caieta as a "name" giving deathless fame to the shore, if there is any glory at all after death. Dryden renders the passage:

> And thou, O Matron of Immortal Fame!
> Here Dying, to the Shore hast left thy Name:
> *Cajeta* still the place is call'd from thee,

The Nurse of great *Æneas* Infancy.
Here rest thy Bones in rich *Hesperia*'s Plains,
Thy Name ('tis all a Ghost can have) remains.

(III, 1233, 1-6)

The initial line is invention and the first rhyme coupling declares Dryden's theme, but the turn in line 6 is particularly interesting, as it is an example of Dryden thinking directly on Virgil's language. Virgil's construction is conditional; Dryden's is declarative. The change is slight, but not so the glory that attaches to name, a glory underscored by Dryden's insertion of "still" in line 3, and a glory that had come to have considerable force for Dryden in the 1690s. In his work of these years there appears a constellation of remarks on name.[42] The variations on this theme often appear in obvious places: dedications to those great families still able or willing to oblige the poet, where the celebration of name is a standard panegyric topic. But now it seems to have a special urgency, and is invariably linked to succession and lineal descent. Name embodies the virtues of family, virtues heritable, passed from one generation to the next as estates—as indeed crowns—ought to be passed. But name takes a new precedence over estate and over office. Place and name are not always antipodal, of course, but when Dryden now contemplates these themes, name is the bulwark against the vagaries of fortune; it has a substance beyond anything it had previously been invested with.

A more obvious turn from Virgil's language and a more explicitly political theme emerges at the close of the prophecy concerning Lavinia:

Id vero horrendum ac visu mirabile ferri.
Namque fore illustrem famâ fatisque canebant
Ipsam, sed populo magnum portendere bellum.

(Virgil 7, 78-80)

What Dryden does with these lines is to turn war into political revolution:

The Nymph who scatters flaming Fires around,
Shall shine with Honour, shall herself be crown'd:

But, caus'd by her irrevocable Fate,
War shall the Country waste, and change the State.
(III, 1236, 117-120)

The crown of line 118 is a new and suggestive detail, but the significant change is the revolution of line 120. Virgil prophesies war, "magnum bellum," Dryden prophesies waste and "change of State." The transformation picks up a slight change at line 103 above, where Virgil's "externum virum" (7, 69), a stranger, becomes Dryden's "foreign Prince." In Virgil this stranger rules in a lofty citadel, "& summa dominarier arce"; in Dryden, "The Town he conquers, and the Tow'r commands" (Virgil 7, 70; III, 1236, 106). The first half line draws our attention. Even if Dryden had not intended to press a connection between Aeneas and William as foreign princes, fated to rule, conquerors and revolutionaries, the introduction of these details was not adventitious. The right construction is not exactly analogy; Dryden is not running a parallel between historical events but rather turning Virgil toward the 1690s, and the congruence is not solely at the level of implication.

At line 253, Virgil's Latinus dwells upon marriage rites, "thalamo"; Dryden has him ponder "Succession, Empire, and his Daughter's Fate" (III, 1242, 346). The extension is deliberate, the preoccupation again political, and the issue succession. And Juno's dark prophecy of Trojan and Rutulian blood for Lavinia's dowry (Virgil 7, 318) is similarly extended:

With Blood the dear Alliance shall be bought;
And both the People near Destruction brought.
So shall the Son-in-Law, and Father join,
With Ruin, War, and Waste of either Line.
(III, 1244-1245, 438-441)

What in Virgil is suggestion, Dryden makes particular and disastrous. Amata's foreign heir in Virgil (Virgil 7, 367) becomes Dryden's "usurper" (III, 1249, 595). What is passive in Virgil becomes active in translation; what is fate in Virgil and hence inscrutable, Dryden turns to conquest, to personal ambition, to political revolution.

Similar themes are explored in other books, and Dryden's preoccupations as translator are those that he reveals in book 7. At the opening of book 10, Venus and Juno rehearse the causes and character of the war that now unfolds between Trojans and Rutulians. Again, Trojan entry is made to conjure the image of invasion and conquest. In part the translation is exact; but Dryden also invents, and at points shades the political idiom to accommodate his own concerns with the injustice of the Revolution: "Hard and unjust indeed, for Men to draw / Their Native Air, nor take a foreign Law" (III, 1323, 114). The tone is resentful and xenophobic; the language has no original in Virgil. Nor does the following line: "Realms, not your own, among your Clans divide" (III, 1323, 120). Dryden is translating "avertere praedas," to carry off plunder, with the phrase above; and the closing lines of this passage draw the *Æneis* close to the charges laid against the expanding European war which Dryden and others claimed was draining the English treasure in an endless European adventure, resulting moreover in the awards of lavish grants and estates to foreigners.[43] The topics derive from Virgil, but the particular thrust of the language is Dryden's own:

> You think it hard, the *Latians* shou'd destroy
> With Swords your *Trojans*, and with Fires your *Troy*:
> Hard and unjust indeed, for Men to draw
> Their Native Air, nor take a foreign Law:
> That *Turnus* is permitted still to live,
> To whom his Birth a God and Goddess give:
> But yet 'tis just and lawful for your Line,
> To drive their Fields, and Force with Fraud to join.
> Realms, not your own, among your Clans divide,
> And from the Bridegroom tear the promis'd Bride:
> Petition, while you publick Arms prepare;
> Pretend a Peace, and yet provoke a War.
>
> (III, 1323, 112-123)

The same issues of legitimacy and conquest are to be found in Dryden's translation of book 6. At the opening Dryden

makes significant changes where Aeneas ponders his fate and
begs of the gods something like peaceful retirement:

Tuque ô sanctissima vates
Praescia venturi: da (non indebita posco
Regna meis fatis) Latio considere Teucros,
Errantesque Deos, agitataque numina Trojae.

(Virgil 6, 65-68)

Dryden translates these lines:

And thou, O sacred Maid, inspir'd to see
Th' Event of things in dark Futurity;
Give me, what Heav'n has promis'd to my Fate,
To conquer and command the *Latian* State:
To fix my wand'ring Gods; and find a place
For the long Exiles of the *Trojan* Race.

(III, 1204, 100-105)

Virgil's Aeneas begs shelter and settlement; he specifically re-
jects empire. Dryden's Aeneas would "conquer and command
the *Latian* State." Virgil's qualifications are ignored, and the
whole passage is rendered in a language charged with the po-
litical currents of the 1690s. These are not random turns in
the translation, but a consistent way of seeing Aeneas's entry
as conquest and violation, not the gift of a benign heaven, but
the will of unsearchable fate.

At the close of book 6, Dryden takes another such occasion
to sharpen the political and topical meaning of Virgil's poem.
In the underworld, Aeneas sees the cheats and frauds who
violate domestic and civic bonds, abuse clients, and profane
sacred rites:

Hic quibus invisi fratres, dum vita manebat,
Pulsatusve parens, & fraus innexa clienti;
Aut quis divitiis soli incubuêre repertis,
Nec partem posuêre suis, quae maxima turba est;
Quique ob adulterium caesi, quique arma secuti
Impia, nec veriti dominorum fallere dextras:
Inclusi poenam expectant.   (Virgil 6, 608-614)

The passage offered Dryden an interesting temptation:

> Then they, who Brothers better Claim disown,
> Expel their Parents, and usurp the Throne;
> Defraud their Clients, and to Lucre sold,
> Sit brooding on unprofitable Gold:
> Who dare not give, and ev'n refuse to lend
> To their poor Kindred, or a wanting Friend:
> Vast is the Throng of these.   (III, 1222, 824-830)

It is hard to avoid the conclusion that Dryden was thinking directly on the royal family at the beginning of this passage:[44] the disclaiming of a brother's right, the expulsion of parents, the usurpation of a throne. At each juncture Dryden turns the language so that the application is exact. Virgil's brothers suffered hatred, Dryden's brother is defrauded of a claim; Virgil's parent is beaten, Dryden's parents are expelled; and the half line at 825, the usurpation of the throne, which focuses the first two violations, is Dryden's invention. The reshaping of the lines is so obvious here that we seem not to be dealing with Dryden's political anxieties simply pushing forward in the act of translating, but with a specific and rather sharp rebuke being administered by the clear changes in Virgil's language. Nor is this quite all. Virgil's misers brood over their wealth and neglect to lay aside part for their own. Dryden's misers neither give nor lend, denying both friend and family. Does the poet imagine his own neglect here? The linking of royal and personal misfortune is certainly not beyond him, and whereas the suggestion of his own misfortune is oblique, it is characteristic.[45]

Conquest, imposition, violation, and usurpation are steady themes in Dryden's translation; and it is a consistent act of the translator to use such language in rendering passages that in Virgil seem neutral or only obliquely political. Nor, of course, is Dryden's impulse to translate one set of terms with another peculiar to the transformation of entry into conquest. There are a number of related themes, and to grasp their interconnections we need examine the whole translation at length;

however, a striking example that complements the language we have looked at is Dryden's handling of the concept of fate.

The role of fate in the disposition of governments was much debated after the Glorious Revolution.[46] As in the Engagement Controversy, men were both privately and publicly concerned with discovering or disputing those sanctions that allowed the disavowal of sacred oaths and the swearing of loyalty to a new regime. Those who favored a providential view of the Glorious Revolution, a view which allowed them to abjure oaths of nonresistance and loyalty to the person and government of James II, argued that the Revolution was providential, that this providence was benign, that indeed William of Orange was swept across the channel by a Protestant wind. But Jacobites and nonjurors scorned such argument; common theft could also be justified by this logic. And though Jacobites acknowledged the turn of fortune's wheel, they refused to understand the Revolution as the design of heaven. In Dryden's translation it is hardly surprising that we should experience Virgil's gods in somber terms. The neutral future, the promised day, the destined land—these and a number of Virgil's other topoi are consistently darkened and undercut. We are made to feel the active malignance of gods who in Virgil are detached or indifferent. Such language as "dark futurity," "fates irrevocable doom," and "fatal place of rest" shapes our perception of the fates in Dryden's translation. Throughout, we experience Dryden's response to the idea of gods as political agency, and on such a subject it is not surprising that the temperament is melancholy. The language suggests not so much the construct of historical analogy through which Dryden might intend to parallel the furies in English and Roman politics, but rather a general and philosophical point of view that I think could hardly be detained from expression. Here is Aeneas from book 2, contemplating the fall of Troy:

> Apparent dirae facies, inimicaque Trojae
> Numina magna Deûm.
> Tum vero omne mihi visum considere in ignes
> Ilium, & ex imo verti Neptunia Troja.

CHAPTER 6

Ac veluti summis antiquam in montibus ornum
Cum ferro accisam crebrisque bipennibus instant
Eruere agricolae certatim; illa usque minatur,
Et tremefacta comam concusso vertice nutat:
Vulneribus donec paulatim evicta, supremum
Congemuit, traxitque jugis avulsa ruinam.

(Virgil, 2, 622-631)

And here is Dryden's version of this scene:

I look'd, I listen'd; dreadful Sounds I hear;
And the dire Forms of hostile Gods appear.
Troy sunk in Flames I saw, nor could prevent;
And *Ilium* from its old Foundations rent.
Rent like a Mountain Ash, which dar'd the Winds;
And stood the sturdy Stroaks of lab'ring Hinds:
About the Roots the cruel Ax resounds,
The Stumps are pierc'd, with oft repeated Wounds.
The War is felt on high, the nodding Crown
Now threats a Fall, and throws the leafy Honours down.
To their united Force it yields, though late;
And mourns with mortal Groans th' approaching Fate:
The Roots no more their upper load sustain;
But down she falls, and spreads a ruin thro' the Plain.

(III, 1113-1114, 842-855)

There are a number of small, quite delicate changes here, and
the shifts of emphasis and slight additional generalizations have
the effect of enlarging Virgil's scene. Dryden acknowledges
the way in which Virgil uses the fall of the ash as an emblem
for the destruction of Troy,[47] but he also uses Virgil's simile
to suggest the fate of Stuart monarchy, the fall of that "nod-
ding Crown" whose demise "spreads a ruin thro' the Plain."
The vocabulary in this scene is tinged with the fate of Stuart
monarchy.

Such a tempering of language is characteristic of the trans-
lation as a whole, overt when Virgil's poem touches such sub-
jects as conquest and lineage, subtler and less pressing when
Dryden treats the gods or the bonds of oath and nature. Here

political and ideological preoccupations are suggested by a slight movement of language toward the translator's own concerns. What is striking about the political axis along which this translation was made is the diversity of tone that it allowed. Dryden's intimacy with, indeed possession of, Virgil's text was so complete and so powerful that the movement of Virgil's poem into English came at a constantly changing pace and over a very broad spectrum of suggestion, implication, and argument.

When Dryden began *The Works of Virgil* for Tonson, he had been ejected from the laureateship, he had converted to Roman Catholicism, and he was maintaining what can only seem to us a preposterous loyalty to James II; for these principles he had lost favor and patronage. He was a man precarious in his safety, his health, and his finances, dependent on the leavings of a few minor gentry and loyal patrons who bore him no grudge in what he himself perceived as rather shabby circumstances. And yet he now chose to make an English *Virgil*, to translate a poem of empire and sublimity, not perhaps the most likely enterprise for this old age. Dryden took up the translation because he needed money; but he also knew that an English *Virgil* would honor the Roman poet and enshrine the translator who thought himself Virgil's likeness and heir.

By maneuvering the *Aeneid* into an oppositional stance, such a work gave this Jacobite a way of asserting his literary and political identity under cover of epic enterprise. The translation of Virgil allowed Dryden to see himself as patriot; it allowed him to celebrate as the Roman nobility those families that still obliged him, and to scorn the Revolution that had displaced the legitimate king and poet laureate with tyranny and the mob. The analogy with Rome that Dryden pondered through the *Dedication* and over the long course of his translation of Virgil provided a language and a history for such assertion. How clearly the political assertions were heard is difficult to say; but Dryden's *Virgil* also suggested eternity, and in that invocation, the poet was not wrong.

Epilogue

IN THE *Epistle to Bathurst*, Pope celebrates one John Kyrle, model of charity and virtue, exemplar of honor and forthrightness; and he begins the portrait of Kyrle by invoking the "honest Muse." Honest, because this praise might be clear and artless, but also because Pope wants to show that Kyrle embodies the social and the moral meanings of honesty. The portrait couples an older social sense of the word, even its slightly archaic connotations, with a more contemporary and increasingly powerful moral definition of honesty. Both definitions were available to Pope, but one had begun to fade by 1733, and the other was just beginning an ascendancy. In the transformation of "honest" from social to moral epithet there lies a history, yet fully to be written, of changing social ideals, of new literary values and a new literary language. The history of honesty will connect Empson's meditations on honest Iago with Lionel Trilling's reflections on Jane Austen and George Eliot. But such a history, particularly for the years between the English civil wars and the Glorious Revolution, cannot be written solely from literary texts. For these years, honesty must be conceived as both literary and political history.

More than a decade ago, Rachel Trickett began her book on the honest muse by writing about Dryden; for reasons that I hope are clear, the dating is too early, the figure mistaken. But the issue is not just dating; it is the nature of political culture in the later seventeenth century and the effect of its imperatives on poetry. The later seventeenth century thrived on deception; its politicians understood that after civil war and political revolution, deception would enable men to approximate civic stability. And its most representative writer, its poet laureate, practiced those enabling arts, though not always with high-minded aims. And yet, professional and sophisticate that he was, Dryden must have been aware, by the end of his life, of the cost of such arts. In his last years he wrote plaintively, "I can neither take the Oaths, nor forsake my Religion, because I know not what Church to go to, if I leave the Catholique." It was not only an exhausted credibility that worried Dryden; the later poetry also suggests that the whole age had succumbed to dishonesty, that it was not only difficult to know where truth lay, but whether it might be found at all.

I have written about a particular political culture and its foremost poet, but I hope to have argued broader implications, to have suggested that in thinking about public poetry, we must not only understand the public nature of the poet's subject, the languages appropriate to and appropriated by such subjects, but also the political valence and politicized nature of those languages. Words express and conceal convictions; the second event is more difficult to grasp and describe than the first, but in an age when convictions forced men to arms, the role of language in such concealment and the interplay between obliqueness and articulation are crucially important. The history of the honest muse might be written from the poetry of the eighteenth century, but it must be written with an understanding of how the arts of political management, how the growth of political stability and the triumph of what J. H. Plumb has described as the Venetian oligarchy of early eighteenth-century England not only allowed the development of a new political culture but also created the civic and psychic leisure necessary for an honest muse.

Notes

1. LANGUAGE AS DISGUISE

1. Donald Wing, *Short-Title Catalogue . . . 1641-1700* (New York, 1964).

2. See Howard Nenner's excellent study of language and politics, *By Colour of Law: Legal Culture and Constitutional Politics in England, 1660-1689* (Chicago, 1977), chapters 3, 4, and 6. Although this chapter was first written before reading Nenner's book, the whole of my study has benefited from *By Colour of Law*.

3. On this vast subject see, especially, Keith Thomas, *Religion and the Decline of Magic* (London, 1971), and Carol Weiner, "The Beleaguered Isle, a Study of Elizabethan and Early Jacobean Anti-Catholicism," *Past and Present*, LI (May 1971), 27-67.

4. David Underdown, *Royalist Conspiracy in England, 1649-1660* (New Haven, 1960).

5. The best study of the political uses of plots and alarms in the early years of the Restoration is Michael McKeon's *Politics and Poetry in Restoration England: The Case of Dryden's 'Annus Mirabilis'* (Cambridge, Mass., 1975).

6. On the Jacobite plots and conspiracies, see Jane Garrett, *The Triumphs of Providence* (Cambridge, 1980).

7. On language theory in the later seventeenth century, see Murray Cohen, *Sensible Words, Linguistic Practice in England, 1640-1785* (Baltimore, 1977), chapter 1; Hans Aarsleff, *From Locke to Saussure, Essays on the Study of Language and Intellectual History* (Minneapolis, 1982), "Introduction," "Leibniz on Locke on Language," "Thomas Sprat," "John Wilkins," and "An Outline of Language-Origins Theory since the Renaissance"; and Vivian Salmon's introduction to *The Works of Francis Lodwick* (London, 1972).

8. Cohen, *Sensible Words*, 21, 40; Aarsleff, *From Locke to Saussure*, 25-27; David S. Katz, "The Language of Adam in Seventeenth-Century England," *History and Imagination*, edited by Hugh Lloyd-Jones, Valerie Pearl, and Blair Worden (London, 1981), 132-145; and, for more detail, Katz, *Philo-Semitism and the Readmission of the Jews to England, 1603-1655* (Oxford, 1982), chapter 2.

9. Cohen, *Sensible Words*, 32.

209

10. Thomas Hobbes, *English Works*, 10 volumes (London, 1839), I, 13-16, "Of Names."

11. *An Essay Concerning Human Understanding*, edited by Peter Nidditch (Oxford, 1975), 408.

12. See, for example, John Wilkins' preface to the *Essay towards a Real Character and a Philosophical Language* (London, 1668), b^r, "The design will likewise contribute much to the clearing of some of our modern differences in *Religion*, by unmasking many wild errors, that shelter themselves under the disguise of affected phrases. . . . And several of these pretended mysterious, profound notions, expressed in great swelling words . . . being this way examined, will appear to be, either nonsense, or very flat and jejune."

13. The thesis is, of course, William Haller's in *Foxe's Book of Martyrs and the Elect Nation* (London, 1963) and has been much refined and developed in the literature of the past twenty years on English Puritanism; the most recent correctives and rejoinders are those of John W. McKenna, "How God Became an Englishman," *Tudor Rule and Revolution* (Cambridge, 1982), 25-43, and Anthony Fletcher, "The First Century of English Protestantism and the Growth of National Identity," *Studies in Church History*, edited by D. Baker (Oxford, 1982), XIX, 309-317.

14. *The Stuart Constitution, 1603-1688, Documents and Commentary*, edited by J. P. Kenyon (Cambridge, 1966), 366.

15. Ibid., 368-376.

16. See Clarendon and Burnet on this theme in Joan Thirsk, *The Restoration* (London, 1976), 5-6; on clerical vindictiveness, see J. R. Jones, *Country and Court* (Cambridge, Mass., 1979), 146.

17. William Cobbett, *Parliamentary History of England*, 36 volumes (London, 1806-1820), IV, 127, "But, my lords and gentlemen, whilst we conspire together to execute faithfully this part of the Bill, to put all old names and terms of distinction into utter Oblivion, let us not find new names and terms to keep up the same, or a worse distinction. If the old reproaches of Cavalier, and Round-Head, and Malignant, be committed to the grave, let us not find more significant and better words, to signify worse things; let not piety and godliness grow into terms of reproach, and distinguish between the court, and the city, and the country; and let not piety and godliness be measured by a morosity in manners, an affectation of gesture, a new mode and tone of speaking; at least, let not our constitutions and complexions make us be thought of a contrary party;

and because we have not affected austerity in our looks, that we have not piety in our hearts."

18. *Journals of the House of Lords*, XI, 242-243.

19. Cobbett, *Parliamentary History*, IV, 252-253.

20. Kenyon, *Stuart Constitution*, 357-358.

21. Cobbett, *Parliamentary History*, IV, 131.

22. Ibid., 265.

23. *Journals of the House of Lords*, XI, 625.

24. Cobbett, *Parliamentary History*, IV, 442; cf. IV, 429, 496.

25. Marvell, "Second Advice to a Painter," in *Poems on Affairs of State*, 7 volumes (New Haven, 1963-1975), I, edited by George deF. Lord, 43, "Our seventh Edward, and his house and line! / Who, to divert the danger of the war / With Bristol, hounds us on the Hollander." The Articles of Impeachment can be found in Cobbett, *Parliamentary History*, IV, 377-379.

26. *Poems on Affairs of State*, I, 51.

27. Anchitell Grey, *Debates of the House of Commons from the Year 1667 to the Year 1694*, 10 volumes (London, 1769), I, 21.

28. Cobbett, *Parliamentary History*, IV, 381, "If we proceed only by the common law, we may be censured at some of the bars below; we must do it to satisfy, and then not satisfy by doing it. Though common law has its proper sphere, 'tis not in this place, we are in a higher sphere."

29. *The History and Proceedings of the House of Commons from the Restoration to the Present Time*, 6 volumes (London, 1742), I, 113.

30. Clarendon, *The Life of Edward Earl of Clarendon*, 3 volumes (Oxford, 1759), III, 906.

31. Grey, *Debates*, I, 65.

32. Cobbett, *Parliamentary History*, IV, 404.

33. Grey, *Debates*, I, 160.

34. Cobbett, *Parliamentary History*, IV, 516.

35. *The History and Proceedings of the House of Commons*, I, 164.

36. Ibid.

37. Ibid.

38. Grey, *Debates*, II, 26 ff.

39. Ibid., 31.

40. Ibid., 30.

41. Ibid., 32.

42. Ibid., 43.

43. Ibid., 55.

44. Ibid., 60.

45. Ibid., 111.

46. Ibid.

47. Cobbett, *Parliamentary History*, IV, 598.

48. Ibid., 565.

49. Ibid., 577.

50. Ibid., 581.

51. Ibid., 586.

52. Ibid., 588.

53. Thomas Lamplugh, *A Sermon Preached . . . on the Fifth of November* (London, 1678), 220.

54. *The Character of a Rebellion* (London, 1681), 70.

55. *Philanax Misopappas, The Troy Plot* (London, 1682), "To the Royal Reader," A2ʳ.

56. *The Poems of John Dryden*, edited by James Kinsley, 4 volumes (Oxford, 1958), I, 215-216; unless otherwise indicated, all citations from Dryden's poetry and prose are from this edition and indicated by volume, page, and line numbers in the text.

57. The partisan responses can be followed in Hugh Macdonald's "The Attacks on Dryden," *Essays and Studies by Members of the English Association*, XXI (1936), 41-74; and the "Drydeniana" section of Macdonald's *John Dryden: A Bibliography of Early Editions and of Drydeniana* (Oxford, 1939).

58. *The Observator* (no. 247, Nov. 25, 1682); cf. George deF. Lord, editor, *Anthology of Poems on Affairs of State, 1660-1714* (New Haven, 1975), 364.

59. *Poems on Affairs of State*, III, edited by Howard Schless, xxxii-xxxiii and 448-449.

60. David Jenner, *The Prerogative of Primogeniture* (London, 1685), A6ᵛ.

61. Cf. James Tyrell's letter to Locke on this subject, *The Correspondence of John Locke*, edited by E. S. de Beer, 6 volumes (Oxford, 1978), III, 191-193.

62. Cobbett, *Parliamentary History*, IV, 1342.

63. Kenyon, *Stuart Constitution*, 410.

64. Ibid., 411.

65. Cobbett, *Parliamentary History*, IV, 1357.

66. Ibid., 1353-1354.

67. Ibid., 1370-1371.

68. See George McFadden, *Dryden, the Public Writer, 1660-1685* (Princeton, 1978), 88-94.

69. See M. H. Pritchard, "Fables Moral and Political: The Adap-

tation of the Aesopian Fable to English Social and Political Life, 1650-1772," Ph.D. dissertation, University of Western Ontario, 1976.

70. The "Debate on the Word Abdicated" can be followed in Cobbett, *Parliamentary History*, V, 61-108.

71. *An Essay*, 405.

72. Cohen, *Sensible Words*, 38.

73. In his introduction to Locke's *Two Treatises of Government* (Cambridge, 1960), 82-88, Peter Laslett discusses the relationship between the *Essay* and the *Two Treatises*.

74. Clarendon, *History of the Rebellion*, 6 volumes, edited by W. Dunn Macray (Oxford, 1888), I, 222, 385, 404, 448, 456, 493, 506, 537, 549; II, 26, 56, 84.

75. *The History and Proceedings of the House of Commons*, II, 138-139, "There is one Opinion which prevails much in the World, which as it is false, so it does a great deal of hurt, and that is this; that every Government in the World was constituted by God himself: But that cannot be so; for it would follow, that God is unjust, which he cannot be. There neither is nor was any Government of that sort but only that of the Jews; the rest of the World were left to themselves, to frame such a Government as suited best their Inclinations, and to make such Rules and Laws as they could best obey and be governed by."

2. TROPES AND STRATEGIES

1. See Dr. Johnson on Dryden as panegyrist, *Lives of the English Poets*, edited by G. B. Hill, 3 volumes (Oxford, 1905), I, 398-401; Macaulay's abrasive essay first appeared in the *Edinburgh Review* (1828), cf. *The Works of Lord Macaulay, Complete*, 8 volumes, edited by Lady Trevelyan (London, 1866), II, 29 ff.

2. Bredvold's reading of Dryden's career in terms of Pyrrhonist skepticism has repeatedly been challenged. The most recent critiques are those of Phillip Harth, *Contexts of Dryden's Thought* (Chicago, 1968), 1-31, and Sanford Budick, *Dryden and the Abyss of Light* (New Haven and London, 1970), 6-8; but the "unity" of Dryden's criticism has been a theme in John Sherwood's "Precept and Practice in Dryden's Criticism," *JEGP*, LXVIII (1969), 432-440, and Robert Hume's *Dryden's Criticism* (Ithaca, N.Y., 1970). Edward Pechter in *Dryden's Classical Theory of Literature* (Cambridge, 1975) uses the notion of doubleness or dialectic in order to see the unity of both theory and practice in Dryden's work.

3. For a more sympathetic reading of Marvell's Restoration career

see Annabel Patterson, *Marvell and the Civic Crown* (Princeton, 1978), chapters 3 through 5.

4. See Christopher Hill on *Samson* in *Milton and the English Revolution* (New York, 1977); Mary Ann Radzinowicz is particularly good on political imperatives in *Samson, Toward Samson Agonistes* (Princeton, 1978), 167-179.

5. George Watson argues a similar theme in his Introduction to *Of Dramatic Poesy and Other Critical Essays*, 2 volumes (London, 1962), I, v-xvii.

6. E. N. Hooker, "The Purpose of *Annus Mirabilis*," *HLQ*, X (1946), 49-67; Michael McKeon in *Politics and Poetry in Restoration England, The Case of Dryden's 'Annus Mirabilis'* (Cambridge, Mass., 1975), argues that these apocalyptic schemes are rhetorical commonplaces and not peculiarly devices of dissent.

7. See Hooker, "The Purpose of *Annus Mirabilis*"; and Patterson, *Marvell and the Civic Crown*, 144-147.

8. See Valerie Pearl, *London and the Outbreak of the Puritan Revolution* (London, 1961), chapters 5 and 6.

9. The composition of the *Essay* seems to have taken place between the summer of 1665 and 1668; see *The Works of John Dryden*, edited by H. T. Swedenberg, Jr. et al., 20 volumes (Berkeley and Los Angeles, 1956-), XVII, edited by Samuel Holt Monk, 331-332.

10. Mary Thale argues a general patriotic purpose for the *Essay*, "The Framework of 'An Essay of Dramatic Poesy,' " *PLL*, VIII (1972), 362-369; cf. Watson, *Of Dramatic Poesy*, I, xi.

11. *Essays of John Dryden*, edited by W. P. Ker, 2 volumes (Oxford, 1900).

12. *The Works of John Dryden*, edited by Sir Walter Scott, revised by George Saintsbury, 18 volumes (Edinburgh, 1882-1893), II, 288.

13. The fact that the *Essay* was indeed composed at the country estate of his father-in-law does not of course deny either the literary or strategic implications of this information.

14. On Dryden's use of Sidney and on the play between *The Defence* and the *Essay*, see Swedenberg, *The Works*, XVII, 342 n., 359, 373; and Edward Pechter, *Dryden's Classical Theory*, 124-125.

15. Scott-Saintsbury, *The Works*, II, 288.

16. Ibid., III, 375.

17. See for example *The Character of a Rebellion* (London, 1681); *The Phanatic in His Colours* (London, 1681).

18. On the rhetorical function of modesty in this preface, see Harth, *Contexts*, 196.

19. Swedenberg, *The Works*, II, 350; Harth, *Contexts*, 149 ff.; William Empson, "Dryden's Apparent Skepticism," *Essays in Criticism*, XX (1970), 172 ff.

20. In his commentary on the *Preface*, Swedenberg cites some materials relating to Athanasius, but the references are to works from the 1640s and 1650s; Swedenberg, *The Works*, II, 352-353.

21. Harth in *Contexts*, 228, tries to deny the political content of *Religio Laici* altogether.

22. William Myers argues, like Harth, that *Religio Laici* does not emerge from a political context. "It is a relief to turn back to 1682 and *Religio Laici*, a poem mercifully free from the pressures of Exclusionist controversy and tory triumphalism," *Dryden* (London, 1973), 102.

23. On dialectic in Dryden's work, see Martin Price, *To the Palace of Wisdom* (New York, 1964), 29-30; Budick, *Dryden and the Abyss of Light*, 104 ff.; and Pechter, *Dryden's Classical Theory*, especially chapter 1.

24. R. F. Jones in "The Originality of *Absalom and Achitophel*," *MLN*, XLVI (1931), 211-218, was the first to argue the precedents; since Jones's article, the literature on sources and analogues has grown considerably, see Swedenberg, *The Works*, II, 230 ff.

25. Hugh Macdonald, *John Dryden: A Bibliography* (Oxford, 1939), 18-21, 223-228.

26. Robert Gould, *The Laureate. Jack Squabb's History* (London, 1687), 4, put the case succinctly, remarking of *The Hind and the Panther*, "What in that Tedious Poem has thou done, / But cramm'd all *Aesops* into one."

27. Cf. Swedenberg, *The Works*, III, edited by Earl Miner, 350-352.

28. Cf. Swedenberg, *The Works*, III, edited by Earl Miner, 484-485 and XIX, edited by Alan Roper, 490.

29. Anicius Manlius Severinus Boethius, *Of the Consolation of Philosophy. Made English and Illustrated with Notes, by the Right Honourable Richard Lord Viscount Preston* (London, 1695), "To the Reader," iii A3ʳ, "In the worst of these Times this good Man endeavoured to maintain the Rights of his Country, and was the great Supporter of that small Part of the Roman Liberty which remained, desiring nothing more than to see it one day restored. . . . It is true that this way of treating Unfortunate, though Good, Men, as it had a Beginning long before the Times of Boethius, so daily experience shews that it hath been carefully continued since, even to our own, and will be

carried on, doubtless, till all things shall have an End." Graham's use of Roman history to press a Jacobite argument bears an interesting relation to Dryden's uses of that same history in the *Dedication* to and translation of the *Aeneid* [see Chapter 6]. It seems not by accident that in his account to the reader Graham should mention the "ingenius and learned Mr. Dryden."

30. See Dryden's remarks on Juvenal and Persius in the headnotes to his translation of the satires, *The Poems of John Dryden*, edited by James Kinsley, 4 volumes (Oxford, 1958), II, 671, 741, 742, 751; the classic essay on this theme is, of course, Leo Strauss's "Persecution and the Art of Writing," *Persecution and the Art of Writing* (Glencoe, Ill., 1952), 22-38.

3. AMBIGUITIES AND UNCERTAINTIES

1. Hugh Macdonald, *John Dryden: A Bibliography* (Oxford, 1939), 4; Sir Walter Scott, *The Life of John Dryden*, edited by B. Kriessman (Lincoln, Neb., 1963), 31-32.

2. Hooker and Swedenberg put this case best, *The Works of John Dryden*, edited by H. T. Swedenberg, Jr. et al., 20 volumes (Berkeley and Los Angeles, 1956-), I, 187-191; cf. Charles E. Ward, *The Life of John Dryden* (Chapel Hill, N.C., 1961), 18-19.

3. Paul Ramsey, *The Art of John Dryden* (Lexington, Ky., 1969), 54-55, sees the ambiguities as a loss of poetic control; Alan Roper, *Dryden's Poetic Kingdoms* (London, 1965) argues a point similar to my own, that the poem is distanced from persuasion, but he senses a clarity of image and design, a "cautious selection of detail," in the poem that does not, I think, survive the poem's paradoxes and problems.

4. Cf. S. Carrington, *The History of the Life and Death of Oliver, Late Lord Protector* (London, 1659); *An Account of the Last Houres of the late Renowned Oliver Lord Protector* (London, 1659); *The Perfect Politician* (London, 1660); J. H., *Flagellum: Or, the Life and Death of Cromwell* (1663).

5. *The Perfect Politician*, 349; a century later, David Hume had a rather different conclusion to draw about Cromwell's style, *The History of England*, 8 volumes (London, 1787), VII, 272-273: "While the protector argued so much in contradiction both to his judgment and inclination, it is no wonder that his elocution, always confused, embarrassed, and unintelligible, should be involved in tenfold darkness, and discover no glimmering of common sense or reason. . . . But what a contrast, when we pass to the protector's replies! After

so singular a manner does nature distribute her talents, that in a nation abounding with sense and learning, a man who, by superior personal merit alone, had obliged parliament to make him a tender offer of the crown, but in a manner which a peasant of the most ordinary capacity would justly be ashamed of."

6. C. V. Wedgewood's portrait is an economical account of these paradoxes, *Oliver Cromwell* (London, 1939), especially chapter 9; and, of course, Marvell's *Horatian Ode* repeatedly turns on the paradoxes of Cromwell's career. Marvell's defense of the Lord Protector in *The First Anniversary* gives some sense of the vulnerability of Cromwell's rule, especially in its attack on sectaries.

7. *An Account of the Last Houres of the late Renowned Oliver Lord Protector*, "To the Reader," A3ʳ-A4ᵛ, "To limn him to the Life in all these Colours, is too much for one Pencil; therefore I onely present you the Epitome of great *Cromwels* Actions, from his home near *Huntington*, to his Tomb in *Westminster*. The Work is not unlike *Homers Iliads* in a nut-shel, yet may it serve for a *Momento* of our ever-to-be lamented unnatural divisions. The main scope of this Discourse, is a continued series of Tragical Scenes, with Comic Interludes lately acted in *England, Ireland*, and *Scotland*: herein I indeavour to keep pace with *Truth*, so near as possibly it may be traced. My aim is *Moderation*, as the surest way to hit *Affection*; therefore have I chosen it before partiality or egregious Encomiums, which do not become an Historian. . . ."

8. Cf. Roper, *Dryden's Poetic Kingdoms*, 60-62, on the Roman closing of this poem.

9. Jackson Cope in his note "Science, Christ, and Cromwell in Dryden's 'Heroic Stanzas,' " *MLN*, LXXI (1956), 483-485, claims to see christic references in the poem, as for example in the "sacred eagle" of line 4, but these references can be understood in the Roman context more easily than in a scriptural sense.

10. Swedenberg, *The Works*, I, 206, and *The Poems of John Dryden*, edited by James Kinsley, 4 volumes (Oxford, 1958), IV, 1812, note the story and its source, but the editors are silent on the meaning of the analogy.

11. Ramsey, *The Art of John Dryden*, 59-60, comments on the verbal techniques.

12. See Roper, *Dryden's Poetic Kingdoms*, 58-59, for commentary on the constitutional meaning of the opening antitheses.

13. [Henry Fletcher,] *The Perfect Politician*, A4ʳ.

14. See commentary of W. C. Abbott, and Cromwell's letters and

speeches on the kingship question in *The Writings and Speeches of Oliver Cromwell*, 4 volumes (Cambridge, Mass., 1947), IV, chapters 7 through 10.

15. The phrase was a crucial demonstration for Dryden's enemies of the poet's political opportunism; cf. Macdonald, *Bibliography*, 5, items 3b, 3c, "An Elegy on the Usurper O. C. by the Author of *Absalom and Achitophel*. Published to shew the Loyalty and Integrity of the Poet" (London, 1681).

16. The weighted palm was an emblem for the martyr king; see Kinsley, *The Poems*, IV, 1810; the visual materials can be consulted in Arthur Hind, *Engravings in England in the Sixteenth and Seventeenth Centuries*, 3 volumes (Cambridge, 1952-1964), III, 73.

17. *The Perfect Politician*, 348-349: "In the choyce of his Privie-Council, much cunning might be seen; yet he never relyed so much on their Counsels, as to have it said, *England* was governed by a *Council* and *Protector*: for he made the world know, it was by *Protector* and *Council*. In his rise, he never cut down one step before another was built to support him. . . . In all these Changes, he took time by the foretop, not suffering such an *Interregnum* as might encourage the Peoples minds to work him any mischief. . . . Secrecie in carrying on Designs, is the principal part of a Prince: at this he was excellent, both in Military and Civil Affairs." Carrington, *The History of the Life and Death*, A3ᵛ: "His late Highness like unto an expert Physician, was first put to read the Temperament of *England*, her former way and manner of actings, before the Current of her Humors, and the Symptoms of all the Evils and Malignities which threatened her."

18. See commentary by Hooker and Swedenberg, *The Works*, I, 203-206.

19. Macdonald, *Bibliography*, 3-4.

4. POLITICS AND RELIGION

1. John Evans, *Moderation Stated* (London, 1682), 8: "There was never more need, never greater occasion for the exercise of Moderation, than now in our Age. It's much in the common talk, and in the wishes of all sorts of men, all seem to desire and court it; and yet I believe it was never less understood, less practised."

2. See, for example, George deF. Lord, "*Absalom and Achitophel* and Dryden's Political Cosmos," in *John Dryden*, edited by Earl Miner (London, 1972), 182-183: "yet if we would understand Dryden's moderation it is important for us to see how closely it resembles in

principle the moderation of Marvell, a chief spokesman for the op-
position. 'God send us moderation and agreement,' Marvell wrote in
1671, and this prayer 'may stand as an epigraph to all his efforts
during the last years of his life.' But the prayer might equally well
represent Dryden's political position at the time of writing *Absalom
and Achitophel.* . . . He shared with Marvell a deep aversion to the
'party-color'd mind.' " Lord's statement of the poet's political mod-
eration represents the explicit claims or implicit assumptions of much
recent criticism of *Absalom and Achitophel*, including Schilling's lengthy
study of the poem, *Dryden and the Conservative Myth* (New Haven,
1961). Although Schilling describes Dryden as a political conserva-
tive, his reading of the poem's corrective dialectic implies that Dry-
den's politics were an ideological middle ground, a belief in order
that transcended party. Similar notions can be found in William Frost's
introduction to the Rhinehart edition, *Selected Works of John Dryden*
(New York, 1971), 12; Isabel Rivers' general characterization of
Dryden's politics in *The Poetry of Conservatism* (Cambridge, 1973),
134-135; Sanford Budick's analysis of the poem's opening lines in
Poetry of Civilization (New Haven, 1974), 88-89; David Farley-Hills
in *The Benevolence of Laughter* (London, 1974), 114-131; and in the
exchange between A. E. Dyson and Julian Lovelock, *Masterful Images*
(London, 1976), 71-97. These readings share an assumption that the
poem moves from the lamentable real (opening lines) to the sup-
posed ideal (closing fiat), and that this dialectical quest itself repre-
sents Dryden's real beliefs, moderate and nearly apolitical, essentially
honest in their inability to subvert the truth of history to party needs.
An older generation of scholars, as, for example, Keith Feiling in the
History of the Tory Party (Oxford, 1924), tacitly assumed the partisan
nature of Dryden's arguments in *Absalom and Achitophel*, although
they, in turn, paid little attention to the rhetoric of moderation in
the poem.

3. On Bredvold's thesis that Dryden is a Pyrrhonist, see Phillip
Harth, *Contexts of Dryden's Thought* (Chicago, 1968), 30-31; but see
as well Michael McKeon's critique of Harth's formulation of mod-
erate rhetoric as moderate beliefs, *Politics and Poetry in Restoration
England* (Cambridge, Mass., 1975), 28-29.

4. The boldest of such confusions between political language and
political convictions can be found in William Myers' study, *Dryden*
(London, 1973), 86, 92, 94. Myers identifies the narrator's claims
of independence with his own notion of Dryden's political beliefs,
86: "He is too ready to identify integrity with balanced, ironic truth-

telling, to be a great propagandist. . . . even in this overtly propagandist poem his approach is a carefully balanced one." In Myers' reading, David is "an ageing, bribable adulterer [who] is every bit as disgusting as a bankrupt, toiling politician. With thoroughly un-Burkean coldness, Dryden shows 'Royal' manners to be as inconsistent and blasphemous as the temptation speeches of Achitophel." And of the poem's conclusion, this critic observes, "Dryden is asserting once again that political success is almost inevitably based on unprincipled nastiness."

5. See Hugh Macdonald, "The Attacks on Dryden," *Essays and Studies by Members of the English Association*, XXI (1936), 41-74; and the "Drydeniana" section of Macdonald's *John Dryden: A Bibliography* (Oxford, 1939).

6. H. T. Swedenberg argued the interesting point that the praise of Achitophel as judge might well have been taken ironically by Dryden's seventeenth-century reader, *The Works of John Dryden*, edited by H. T. Swedenberg, Jr. et al., 20 volumes (Berkeley and Los Angeles, 1956-), II, 250-251; George McFadden, *Dryden the Public Writer* (Princeton, 1978), 258, sees the passage as an "expression of gratitude" on Dryden's part for Shaftesbury's role in authorizing the payment of a claim owed to Dryden's wife.

7. See, for example, the debate on minor matters of electoral reform surveyed in J. Cannon, *Parliamentary Reform 1640-1832* (Cambridge, 1972), 27, or the lord chancellor's speech, February 15, 1677, in *A Collection of the Parliamentary Debates in England*, 6 volumes (London, 1741), I, 191: "Now 'tis a great and dangerous mistake in those, who think the peace at home is well enough preserved, so long as the sword is not drawn; whereas in truth nothing deserves the name of peace but unity: Such an unity as flows from an unshaken trust and confidence between the King and his people, from a due reverence and obedience to the laws, and to his government, from a religious and awful care, not to remove the ancient landmarks, not to disturb those constitutions which time and the public convenience hath settled, from a zeal to preserve the whole frame and order of the government upon the old foundations, and from a perfect detestation and abhorrency of all such as are given to change: Whatever falls short of this falls short of peace too."

8. Feiling, *History of the Tory Party*, 199-200.

9. Cf. Chester Cable, "*Absalom and Achitophel* as Epic Satire," *Studies in Honor of John Wilcox*, edited by A. D. Wallace (Detroit, 1958), 51-60; Morris Freedman, "Dryden's Miniature Epic," *JEGP*, LVII

(1958), 211-219; and R. G. Peterson, "Larger Manners and Events: Sallust and Virgil in *Absalom and Achitophel*," *PMLA*, LXXXII (1967), 236-244.

10. See John Wallace on benefits and gratitude, "John Dryden's Plays and the Conception of a Heroic Society," in *Culture and Politics from Puritanism to the Enlightenment*, edited by Perez Zagorin (Berkeley and Los Angeles, 1980), 113-134.

11. R. Willman, "The Origins of 'Whig' and 'Tory' in English Political Language," *HJ*, XVII (1974), 263-264; it is interesting that in a portrait of Catherine of Braganza in *Fidelis Achates* (London, 1699), 42, the same issue and language of ingratitude should be raised: "The Royal Choice does on the Billows ride, / And now to *Caesar*'s Arms present the Bride: / But ah! th'unhappy Soil was barren grown, / Like fruitless *Libya* scorch'd by too much Sun. / Caesar's Endeavours and our Hopes are vain, / The ungrateful Glebe makes no returns again. / No pregnant Show'rs cou'd urge a smiling Bloom, / No ripen'd Sheafs by all the Tillage come. / But this defect was not on Caesar's side; / 'Twas not his Fault this Blessing was deny'd."

12. It is worth noting that the men whom Dryden singles out as not only Charles's staunchest allies but also as ideal patrons should all have, at one point or another in Dryden's career, acted as the poet's patrons. Further, it may be more than coincidental that Amiel, Edward Seymour, who was reported to have commissioned the writing of this call for stern measures (*HMC Ormonde*, new series, VI, 233), should, it is now thought, have been the mastermind of the Court's repressive policy in the aftermath of the Oxford parliament; J. P. Kenyon, *Stuart England* (London, 1978), 222. Although Dryden clearly could not have known this in 1681, the link nevertheless raises the interesting question of how closely the poem expresses Court policy. Wallace Maurer reviewed the evidence for Seymour's involvement in "Who Prompted Dryden to Write *Absalom and Achitophel*," *Philological Quarterly* XL (January 1961), 130-138.

13. See, for example, Frost, *Selected Works*, 12.

14. J. R. Jones, *The First Whigs* (London, 1961), 196.

15. See J. P. Kenyon, *Revolution Principles* (Cambridge, 1977), chapter 5.

16. Quoted by M. C. Jacob, "Millenarianism and Science in the Late Seventeenth Century," *JHI*, XXXVII (1976), 339-340.

17. J. R. Jones, *The Revolution of 1688 in England* (London, 1972); J. R. Western, *Monarchy and Revolution* (London, 1972).

18. On the significance of scriptural figuralism in *Absalom and*

Achitophel see Steven Zwicker, *Dryden's Political Poetry* (Providence, 1972), 83-101.

19. It has been argued by J. M. Wallace, " 'Examples Are Best Precepts': Readers and Meanings in Seventeenth-Century Poetry," *Critical Inquiry*, I (1974), 273-91, that seventeenth-century readers could exercise their discretion in choosing to draw parallels between historical examples and the contemporary world. Although Wallace excepts *Absalom and Achitophel* from this account, he argues that in general Dryden was content to have metaphors open-ended; this argument also implies that the reader need not have made the contemporary application. My own sense is that rather than an exception, *Absalom and Achitophel* is simply the most obvious and most insistent example of a poem demanding application, and that many of Dryden's other histories and fables require similar attentiveness to application.

20. Although we must allow for the very different political climate of 1684, Dryden's "Postscript" to his translation of *The History of the League* (1684) makes an interesting commentary on the problems and solutions argued by *Absalom and Achitophel*. See, for example, Dryden's application of Maimbourg's remarks on Huguenots to the sectaries, Swedenberg, *The Works*, XVIII, edited by Alan Roper, 405: "They are a malicious and bloody Generation, they bespatter honest Men with their Pens when they are not in power; and when they are uppermost, they hang them up like Dogs. To such kind of people all means of reclaiming, but only severity, are useless, while they continue obstinate in their designs against Church and Government: For tho' now their claws are par'd, they may grow again to be more sharp; they are still Lyons in their Nature, and may profit so much by their own errors in their late managements, that they may become more sanctify'd Traytors another time."

21. Macdonald gives the evidence for dating in his *Bibliography*, 18-20, 26.

22. E. N. Hooker's political reading of *Religio Laici*, "Dryden and the Atoms of Epicurus," was published in 1957, *ELH*, XXIV, 177-190; and Donald Benson has made some interesting contributions to Hooker's account in "Theology and Politics in Dryden's Conversion," *SEL*, IV (1964), 393-412. An earlier generation had tacitly assumed the poem's political content; for example, A. W. Verrall, *Lectures on Dryden* (Cambridge, 1914); but more recently the explicit and implicit political meanings of the poem have been all but denied. See Harth, *Contexts*, 228: "The fact that politics and religion were

closely connected in the Restoration period does not mean that Englishmen could not separate the two when they became topics for discussion. To see *Religio Laici* as a political poem and its publication as a political act is to fail to appreciate this distinction"; Myers, *Dryden*, 102: "It is a relief to turn back to 1682 and *Religio Laici*, a poem mercifully free from the pressures of Exclusionist controversy and tory triumphalism."

23. Shadwell's attack can be consulted in *Dryden, The Critical Heritage*, edited by J. and H. Kinsley (London, 1971), 156-158; two other pamphlets were published contemporaneously with the play: *A Defence of the Charter* and *The True History of Guise*; see Macdonald, *Bibliography*, 241-242.

24. *Religio Laici in a Letter to John Dryden* (London, 1683), A4^v. In order to support his thesis about the character of Dryden's attack on the Deists, Harth construes Blount's pamphlet as an attack on Dryden, *Contexts*, 92-94; but see Budick's reading of the evidence, *Dryden and the Abyss of Light*, 16 n.13, and William Empson on Dryden and Blount, "A Deist Tract by Dryden," *Essays in Criticism*, XXXV (1975), 77-78.

25. In arguing for the essentially religious purpose and subject of *Religio Laici*, Harth asserts that although many seventeenth-century Englishmen took their politics from their religion, "neither Dryden nor his contemporaries were in the habit of suggesting that many Englishmen took their religion from their politics," *Contexts*, 228. In fact, quite the opposite is the case; Dryden and his contemporaries were in the habit not only of suggesting that many men took their religion from their politics but that they used religion as a cover for politics, and Dryden argues such repeatedly in his political satires, nowhere more obviously than in *Absalom and Achitophel*. The political literature of the age offers innumerable examples, from the speeches of the king and lord chancellors (see Cobbett, IV and V), to partisan hacks writing political pamphlets. I offer here a few titles and examples: James Duport, *Three Sermons . . . upon the Three Anniversaries* (London, 1676), 42: "But then again, is it not easie to pretend it, where it is not? for have not we known the most horrid and devilish designs, carry'd on under a shew and pretence of conscience, and the Caus of God, and Religion? The truth is, Conscience is made a saddle for every hors, a bush or sign to hand at every door"; Thomas Lamplugh, *A Sermon Preached* (London, 1678), 8: "How have Incendiaries, like Jewish Zealots, urged Texts for Bloodshed, and undertaken to prove the slaughter of their Brethren, (yea, of their own

lawful Prince and Soveraign) warrantable by the Word of God. . . . Was not a most unnatural Civil War called, The Burthen of the Lord, and undertaken upon the pretence of Religion?"; *An Impartial Survey* (London, 1679), 2: "It is probable that they may again make long harangues for the liberty and property of the subject (which they invaded and destroyed), redress of grievances, which they multiplyed a 1000 times over, reformation of church government, which they turn'd into a chaos of confusion; and though they have laid aside (as a State-device out of date) their religious mask, with which they cover'd such multitudes of horrid impieties, (as would make a pagan blush) yet they have found out fresh slights to debauch the people from their allegiance"; *Babylon Blazon'd, or, the Jesuit Jerk'd* (London, 1681), 4-5: "Now my *Alecto*, let's advance and view / The frauds that lurk under Religions shew; / For though to Heav'n their fair pretences swell, / The root lies deep and dark as in thy Cell. / . . . / *Rome's* Doctrine is a secular Device, / Mere trick of State in rev'rend Disguise." J. Williams, *The History of the Powder-Treason* (London, 1681), 1: "There are no Conspiracies and Insurrections more dangerous to the States and Governments, than those that the name of Religion is made to patronize"; *A Protestant Plot No Paradox* (London, 1681), 1: "Names make not things, but shew them; and forms and appearances alter not nature: The Lyon is still a Lyon, though he have the Foxes skin; and the Devil is still the Devil, though he transform himself into the appearance of an Angel of light. Men are not Protestants for calling themselves so"; and David Jenner, *Beaufrons; or, A New Discovery of Treason under the Fair-Face and Mask of Religion* (London, 1685).

26. Hooker, "Dryden and the Atoms of Epicurus," 177-190.

27. Swedenberg, *The Works*, II, 343: "There is no evidence that Dryden knew either the 1678 edition of the *Histoire critique du Vieux Testament*. . . . Furthermore, we cannot be certain when he became acquainted with Dickinson's translation. . . . Dryden had ample time to examine the *Critical History* before writing *Religio Laici*, but it is unlikely that he gave his days and nights to a study of Father Simon before composing his poem."

28. See *The Poems of John Dryden*, edited by James Kinsley, 4 volumes (Oxford, 1958), IV, 1932.

29. G. Lyon Turner, *Original Records of Early Nonconformity*, 3 volumes (London, 1914), III, 39: "It is abundantly clear, therefore, that throughout the quarter of a century through which the Nonconformists had to suffer, it was not from the pressure of the hand

of the King. The persecution was Parliamentary and Ecclesiastical, not Royal."

30. On general distinctions between Tory political interests and the crown in the 1680s, see J. R. Jones, "Parties and Parliament," in *The Restored Monarchy*, edited by J. R. Jones (London, 1979), 67-69; on the tension between High Church policy and the crown's interests, see R. A. Beddard, "The Restoration Church," in *The Restored Monarchy*, 170-174; Beddard, however, implies that Charles came to share the convictions of Cavalier Anglicanism, which I do not believe is true. See, as well, *The History of Non-Conformity* (London, 1704), A3r, "But, notwithstanding all that the Royal Advocate Charles II could say in Favour of the Presbyterians, the High-Churchmen were resolv'd to make the Terms of Communion narrower than before the War, on purpose to drive them out of the Church."

31. David Ogg, *England in the Reign of Charles II*, 2 volumes (Oxford, 1956), II, 618-619; cf. *The Poems*, IV, 1980, where Kinsley notes that the Exclusion Bill carried to the Lords on November 15 was rejected by 63 to 30 votes, "every bishop present voting against it."

32. Ogg, *England in the Reign of Charles II*, II, 635-640; J. R. Jones, *Country and Court* (Cambridge, Mass., 1979), 219-220.

33. On dialectic in *Religio Laici* see Budick, *Dryden and the Abyss of Light*, 104 ff.; Budick, however, argues that the force of dialectic in this poem is made to yield "Sacred Truth," though in fact the climax of dialectic is the poem's discovery of "common quiet."

34. On the historical identity of that judicious friend see David Brown, "Dryden's *Religio Laici* and the 'Judicious and Learned Friend,'" *MLR*, LVI (1961), 66-69; Kinsley notes a difficulty with the identification of the friend as Tillotson, *The Poems*, IV, 1933. Perhaps the friend was Dryden's invention, a foil against whom he might display his daring charity.

35. Cf. William Empson, "Dryden's Apparent Skepticism," *Essays in Criticism*, XX (1970), 172.

36. See Macdonald, *Bibliography*, 33, 262-263.

37. Harth, *Contexts*, 192-193.

38. Harth takes the line "A Work so full with various Learning fraught" as a genuine tribute to Simon's book, *Contexts*, 193; the line seems to me as ironic as the whole of the preceding tribute.

39. Arthur Hoffman, *John Dryden's Imagery* (Gainesville, Fla., 1962), 57 ff., and Paul Ramsey, *The Art of John Dryden* (Lexington, Ky., 1969), 83-85, analyze the language and metrics of the opening lines.

225

5. Fables, Allegories, and Enigmas

1. Dryden's contemporaries, of course, pointed to the contradiction: see Hugh Macdonald, *John Dryden: Bibliography* (Oxford, 1939), 253-263; the case is nicely put by Thomas Heyrick, *The New Atlantis* (n.p., 1687), "I have been as cool and moderate as Truth would let me; and if there remains any bitterness, I had it from the Author of the Hind and the Panther in his Preface and Poem of Religio Laici, which indeed is a Confutation of the Hind and Panther before hand."

2. James's first and only parliament was called into session on May 19, 1685; in November of that year he was lecturing parliament on the standing army and Test Act, William Cobbett, *Parliamentary History of England*, 36 volumes (London, 1806-1820), IV, 1370-1371.

3. See James Miller, *Popery and Politics in England, 1660-1688* (Cambridge, 1973), chapters 10 and 11; on the attempt to court Anglican compliance see Douglas Lacey, *Dissent and Parliamentary Politics in England, 1661-1689* (New Brunswick, N.J., 1969), 165 ff.

4. See Dryden's letter to Etherege, Charles Ward, ed., *The Letters of John Dryden* (Durham, N.C., 1942), 26-27; comments of Donald Benson, "Theology and Politics in Dryden's Conversion," *SEL*, IV (1964), 406-407; and Thomas Fujimura, "The Personal Drama of Dryden's *The Hind and the Panther*," *PMLA*, LXXXVII (1972), 412.

5. Rosemary Freeman in *English Emblem Books* (London, 1948), 204-205, reads the satiric application of fable materials in *The Hind and the Panther* as evidence that the tradition of veiled meaning is dead by the end of the seventeenth century; this seems a simplification of both the tradition of allegorical writing and of the transformation of fable and allegory in the later seventeenth century.

6. Sanford Budick argues that "the element of the esoteric was one of the conscious goals in the poem," *Dryden and the Abyss of Light* (New Haven and London, 1970), 190; see as well Earl Miner on Dryden's invocation and uses of the Aesop tradition, *Dryden's Poetry* (Bloomington, Ind., 1967), 156 ff. Dryden's contemporaries suspected a polemical intention, cf. M. Clifford, *Notes upon Mr. Dryden's Poems in Four Letters* (London, 1687), 38: "But still I cannot imagin the reason, why He should make use of these tedious and impertinent Allegories, unless he thought that what was solid and argumentative, being imp'd with something more light and airy, might carry further, and pierce deeper: Unless in this time of Heat and Anger the Roman Catholicks may think fit to employ him, as being a spiteful Creature, or the good Fathers may divert themselves awhile with an Animal, that is unlucky, mimical, and gamesome."

7. Clarence Miller makes an attempt to connect the remarks on style in the preface to the three parts of the poem, "The Styles of *The Hind and the Panther*," *JEGP*, LXI (1962), 511-527.

8. Budick, *Dryden and the Abyss of Light*, chapter 9.

9. Ibid., 196-207, 218-223.

10. Ibid., 223-232.

11. Donald Benson argues the opposite position; he sees the material presence of Christ in the Eucharist as a coordinate of Dryden's "skeptical and reductive treatment of language," a signal for both a "new ontology" and a less figurative and less transcendent style; "Dryden's *The Hind and the Panther*: Transubstantiation and Figurative Language," *JHI*, XLIII (1982), 195-208. But, in fact, Budick seems more accurately to describe the poetic styles of *The Hind and the Panther*; and what poem of Dryden's could be described as less figurative and less transcendent than his Anglican *Religio Laici*?

12. Louis Bredvold, *The Intellectual Milieu of John Dryden* (Ann Arbor, 1934), 121: "*Religio Laici* and *The Hind and the Panther* are so closely allied in their philosophy that the earlier poem might be regarded as a sort of prelude or introduction to the later"; cf. Budick, *Dryden and the Abyss of Light*, 172.

13. J. R. Jones, *Country and Court* (Cambridge, Mass., 1979), 242; Jones, "Parties and Parliament," in *The Restored Monarchy*, edited by Jones (London, 1979), 50; James Miller, "The Later Stuart Monarchy," in *The Restored Monarchy*, 37.

14. Cf. *The Works of John Dryden*, edited by H. T. Swedenberg et al., 20 volumes (Berkeley and Los Angeles, 1956-), III, edited by Earl Miner, 371.

15. J. Miller, *Popery and Politics*, 214-215.

16. The attempt to achieve distance from the court is echoed in part 3: "Mean-time my sons accus'd, by fames report / Pay small attendance at the *Lyon's* court," II, 509, 235-236.

17. Lacey, *Dissent and Parliamentary Politics*, 180-181.

18. Jones, "Main Trends in Restoration England," in *The Restored Monarchy*, 19; cf. Sackville Tufton, *The History of Faction, Alias Moderation, From its first Rise, down to its Present Toleration* (London, 1705), 61: "Magdalene College in Oxford, was made a Seminary for Popish Priests and Jesuits, and the Bishops imprison'd. All by the Advice of the Earl of Sunderland, then Secretary of State, who, Judas like, betray'd his Master with a Kiss, and ventur'd his own Damnation, by turning Apostate from the true Religion."

19. Miner, *The Works*, III, 371.

20. Dryden's editors pass over these lines in silence; Fujimura, "The Personal Drama of Dryden's *The Hind and the Panther*," 413, senses a similar distortion and reads the passage as an instance of "unconscious pride."

21. Miner, *The Works*, III, 381.

22. J. P. Kenyon, ed., *The Stuart Constitution, 1603-1688* (Cambridge, 1966), 465, "I, A.B., do solemnly and sincerely, in the presence of God, profess, testify and declare that I do believe that in the sacrament of the Lord's Supper there is not any transubstantiation of the elements of bread and wine into the body and blood of Christ. . . ."

23. Though his subject is sixteenth-century French writing, Terence Cave's discussion of *lingua* and *cornucopia* is extremely suggestive for the later English texts: *The Cornucopian Text* (Oxford, 1979).

24. Budick argues the connections among theology, style, and literary mode in his discussion of "Sign and Substance: Icon and Divinity," in *Dryden and the Abyss of Light*, 223-237.

25. The language is widespread, and numerous examples can be found in *Poems on Affairs of State*, edited by George deF. Lord et al., 7 volumes (New Haven, 1963-1975), IV, edited by Galbraith Crump; but such language was not limited to satirical verse and broadsides; cf. Roger Coke's history, *A Detection of the Court and State of England*, 2 volumes (London, 1694). After denying the taint of partisanship, Coke goes on to write of the reign of James, II, 397: "What before King Charles the 2d acted in Masquerade, King James did barefac'd and here you see how plain and easy a passage, the Absolute Will and Pleasure-Men, and Passive Obedience Men had made, for this King to over-throw the whole Church and State of England; and by what steps he proceeded in it, the King's speeches looking one way, and he going quite contrary"; II, 413: "The King was a Profest Jesuited Papist, whose Principles are, That not only the Givers of this Revenue, but the whole English Nation (except the Popish Faction) are Schismaticks, Sacrilegious Persons and Hereticks, with whom no Faith is to be kept."

26. In stressing Dryden's role as humble and forgiving Christian in *The Hind and the Panther*, Fujimura seems to miss the sharpness and edge of the Hind's attack in part 3, "The Personal Drama of Dryden's *The Hind and the Panther*," 409.

27. Phillip Harth discusses the background for the attacks on Latitudinarians in *Contexts of Dryden's Thought* (Chicago, 1968), 155-

161; *The Poems of John Dryden*, edited by James Kinsley, 4 volumes (Oxford, 1958), IV, 1980 n.160.

28. On Dryden's accommodation to the Declaration for Liberty of Conscience, see Miner, *The Works*, III, 350, 449-450, 457.

29. Cf. Charles E. Ward, *The Life of John Dryden* (Chapel Hill, N.C., 1961), 231; Kinsley, *The Poems*, IV, 1983; Miner, *The Works*, III, 421, 423.

30. Francis Manley has an interesting reading of these lines in "Ambivalent Allusions in Dryden's Fable of the Swallows," *MLN*, LXXI (1956), 485-487.

31. Miner sees the *Aeneid* functioning here to strengthen the Catholic claims of antiquity and cultural superiority, *The Works*, III, 435.

32. The case is sharply if laboriously stated by David Jenner, *The Prerogative of Primogeniture: Shewing that the Right of Succession to an Hereditary Crown, Depends not upon Grace, Religion &c. But only upon Birth-Right and Primogeniture* (London, 1685); see as well Thomas Wagstaffe, *An Answer to a late pamphlet, entitled obedience and submission to the present government* (London, 1690), 18: "A Man can never be said to be settled in an Estate, who hath only an *usurped Possession* of it and when there are other and better Claims and Titles on Foot. . . . Have not Robbers as Good a Title to my Purse, as an Usurper to the Crown?"; *An Old Cavalier turned a New Courtier* (London, 1690), 2; *The Graves-End Boat* (London, 1699), 11. But those who defended the Revolutionary settlement argued against the analogy between property rights in civil law and the king's estate; *A Letter to a Gentlewoman concerning Government* (London, 1697), 15: "The difference between a Kingdom and a private Man's Estate lies in this, That a private Man is absolute Master of his Estate, and therefore can, without Injury to anybody, dispose of it, as he pleases. Whereas a King is intrusted with his Kingdom by God Almighty, to rule it by his Laws in the first place, and then by the Laws of the Land. . . . By reason of this essential difference, a King may, on many Accounts, lose his Title to his Kingdom, when a private Man does not lose his, to his Estate: In case of Total Absence from it; in these Cases, private Men enjoy still their Estates, whereas a King ceases Lawfully to be King."

33. Although I disagree with specific readings, Miner's commentary in *The Works*, III, is particularly full and helpful.

34. Macdonald makes the unequivocal identification, *Bibliography*, 257 n.3; see as well Ward, *The Life*, 232-233; and Fujimura, "The Personal Drama of Dryden's *The Hind and the Panther*," 411-412.

Miner speculates on the last-minute revisions, *The Works*, III, 350, 449-450, 457; it is Miner's thesis that the portrait was first modeled on William of Orange but that at the last minute, perhaps in response to Burnet's publication, in April of 1687 of a pamplet entitled "Reasons against the Repealing the Acts of Parliament concerning the Test," Dryden inserted additional details in the portrait of the Buzzard aimed at Burnet. Miner then cites textual evidence to support his thesis, noting that the passage from 1147 to 1173 is the "only one in the poem showing any important degree of press correction. The changes . . . suggest that Dryden was trying to put right this passage at the very last moment." This seems a plausible interpretation of the textual evidence which includes, for lines 1147 to 1173, four substantive changes; Miner's case would be stronger, however, if these substantive changes indicated an attempt to turn the portrait away from William toward Burnet. The changes do not suggest that; all they show is that Dryden was tinkering, but not that he was attempting a new characterization here.

35. Miner, *The Works*, III, 449-450, 457-458.

36. Ibid., 449.

37. Miner has suggestions for the Rubicon and the biblical allusions, but none for the two Czars, ibid., 457-458.

38. For an introduction to and overview of *Fables* see Earl Miner's *Dryden's Poetry* (Bloomington, 1967), chapter 7, "Thematic Variation and Structure in *Fables*"; and Judith Sloman, "An Interpretation of Dryden's *Fables*," *ECS*, IV (1971), 199-211.

39. Kinsley, *The Poems*, IV, 2074, in his commentary to *Sigismonda and Guiscardo*, notes the allusion to William at the poem's close.

40. The fullest political reading is J. A. Levine, "John Dryden's *Epistle to John Dryden*," *JEGP*, LIII (1964), 450-474; and see, as well, Elizabeth Duthie, " 'A Memorial of My Own Principles': Dryden's 'To My Honour'd Kinsman,' " *ELH*, XLVII (1980), 682-704.

41. On the historical and political content of the Chaucer paraphrase, see Kinsley, "Dryden's *Character of a Good Parson* and Bishop Ken," *RES*, n.s. III (1952), 155-158, and Kinsley, *The Poems*, IV, 2080.

42. Translation from the Loeb edition, A. T. Murray, *Homer. The Iliad*, 2 volumes (New York, 1924), I, 15, 163-165.

43. These are most easily consulted in volume 5 of *Poems on Affairs of State*, edited by William J. Cameron (New Haven, 1971).

44. The fullest treatment of the standing army question in the

1690s is Lois Schwoerer, *No Standing Armies* (Baltimore, 1974), chapters 6-8; the best known of the pamphlets were Trenchard's *An Argument Shewing That a Standing Army is Inconsistent with a Free Government and Absolutely Destructive to the Constitution of English Monarchy* (London, 1697), and *A Short History of Standing Armies in England* (London, 1698).

6. POLITICS AND TRANSLATION

1. Prior to the Tonson argeement, Dryden had translated passages from books 5, 8, 9, and 10 of the *Aeneid*, which were published in *Sylvae* (1685); cf. *The Poems of John Dryden*, edited by James Kinsley, 4 volumes (Oxford, 1958), IV, 2032. On Dryden's long engagement with epic, see H. T. Swedenberg, "Dryden's Obsessive Concern with the Heroic," *SP* (Extra Series, January 1967), 12-26.

2. See Jane Garrett, *The Triumphs of Providence* (Cambridge, 1980); the proceedings against Fenwick can be followed in William Cobbett, *Parliamentary History of England*, 36 volumes (London, 1806-1820), V, 995-1154. George Watson suggests the broad Jacobite themes of the *Virgil* and the relevance of *The Hind and the Panther* to the later project in "Dryden and the Jacobites," *TLS* (March 16, 1973), 301-302; see also W. J. Cameron, "John Dryden's Jacobitism," in *Restoration Literature, Critical Approaches*, edited by H. Love (London, 1972), 277-308; Cameron comments on some of the passages with which I am concerned in this chapter, but his conclusions about Dryden's relation to William and the Williamites are very different from my own.

3. For Dryden's uses of Segrais, Vida, Le Bossu, Dacier, Scaliger, Heinsius, and Bochart, see W. P. Ker, ed., *Essays of John Dryden* (Oxford, 1900), II, 293-306; and Kinsley, *The Poems*, IV, 2038-2048.

4. Charles Ward, ed., *The Letters of John Dryden* (Durham, N.C., 1942), especially those to his sons, 92-94, and to Mrs. Steward, 112-113, 122-124.

5. See commentary by William Cameron, "John Dryden's Jacobitism," 288.

6. See Howard Nenner, *By Colour of Law* (Chicago, 1977); J. R. Jones, *Country and Court* (Cambridge, Mass., 1979), 1-10; and chapter 1.

7. Arthur Mainwaring, "Tarquin and Tullia," in *Poems on Affairs of State*, edited by George deF. Lord et al., 7 volumes (New Haven, 1963-1975), V, edited by William J. Cameron, 46-54, 298.

8. See "Conference on 'abdicated' and 'vacant', 1689," in E. N.

Williams, *Eighteenth-Century Constitution* (Cambridge, 1960), 20-26; the proceedings can be followed at greater length in Cobbett, *Parliamentary History*, V, 31-110; cf. William Podsey, *A Political Essay* (London, 1698), 161: "The Case of King William in it self, is, perhaps, the most Glorious and Generous Cause that hath appeared on the Stage of Human Actions; yet hath been sullied by dire Representations, by poor-spirited and precatious Arguments, which have been brought in for its support. His Title to the Crown of Great Britain stands Firm, and is justifiable upon Natural and Sound foundations of Reason, without Props: But hath been so oddly maintained by the manner of its Defence, that it hath been the Jusification only that hath Disgrac'd the Revolution. . . . We have been running out of the way to fetch in Aids from Art and Learning, whilst Nature presents us with obvious and undefiled Principles of Reason. Thus the King's Accession to the Throne hath been introduced by shuffling between Providential Settlement, Conquest, Desertion, Abdication, and topping Protection of Power; whilst Men of Honour, and People of Honest Plain Understandings, stand Amazed, stead of being Convinced. . . ."

9. *The Works of John Dryden*, edited by Sir Walter Scott, revised by George Saintsbury, 18 volumes (Edinburgh, 1882-1893), XVIII, 51.

10. Ward, *The Letters*, 93.

11. The language of the Association can be found and the response followed in *A Collection of the Parliamentary Debates in England* (London, 1741), III, 58-63; or Cobbett, *Parliamentary History*, V, 987-992; see, as well, Garrett, *The Triumphs of Providence*, chapter 9.

12. On this theme, see John Wallace, "John Dryden's Plays and the Conception of a Heroic Society," in *Culture and Politics from Puritanism to the Enlightenment*, edited by Perez Zagorin (Berkeley and Los Angeles, 1980), 113-134.

13. A discussion of the suspending and dispensing powers and some of the documents in the conflict can be found in J. P. Kenyon, ed., *The Stuart Constitution, 1603-1688* (Cambridge, 1966), 401-413; cf. chapter 1.

14. On the coinage crisis see H. Horwitz, *Parliament, Policy, and Politics in the Reign of William III* (Manchester and Newark, 1977), chapters 7-8.

15. See, for example, the references to bribery and foreign influence, Kinsley, *The Poems*, III, 1052, 1880 ff.; the additional reference

to the coinage crisis, III, 1060, 2185; the reference to succession, III, 1018, 588; or the passage on the Dutch, III, 1052, 1883.

16. Dryden was hardly alone in his perception of the *Aeneid* as a party poem; Spence quotes Pope on this point: "The *Aeneid* was evidently a party piece, as much as *Absalom and Achitophel*. Virgil (was) as slavish a writer as any of the gazetteers," Joseph Spence, *Observations, Anecdotes, and Characters of Books and Men*, edited by James M. Osborn, 2 volumes (Oxford, 1966), I, 229-230; cf. Voltaire on Virgil, *Essai sur la poésie épique*, in *Oeuvres complètes*, edited by Louis Moland (Paris, 1877-1885), VIII, 326. The most elaborate reading of contemporary political reference in this period is a pamphlet entitled *Turnus and Drances: Being an attempt to shew, who the real Persons were, that Virgil intended to represent under those two characters* (Oxford, 1750).

17. William Frost, editor of the *Virgil* for the California *Dryden*, is concurrently working on this problem; we have arrived independently at a similar notion of the function of the plates and at similar readings of the plates dedicated to Howard and to Salisbury; on the financial aspects of the subscription *Virgil*, see J. Barnard, "Dryden, Tonson, and the Subscriptions for the 1697 *Virgil*," *PBSA*, LVII (1963), 129-151.

18. There are early essays on seventeenth-century book subscription by S.L.C. Clapp, *Modern Philology*, XXIX (1931), 199-224 and XXX, 365-379; and *Library*, 4th series (1932), 158-183. Recent and quite extensive work on book subscription has been undertaken by the Book Subscription Lists Project, School of Education, The University of Newcastle upon Tyne, directed by P. J. Wallis and F.J.G. Robinson; the Newcastle upon Tyne research is summarized in bibliographical bulletins issued by the Project; none of the material now in print from the Project applies, I believe, to subscription books published before 1720.

19. Annabel Patterson is currently at work on the politics of the Ogilby plates and translation. The plates of Tonson's 1688 edition of Milton's *Paradise Lost* and their topical argument have been recently examined by Estella Schoenberg, "The Face of Satan, 1688," *Ringing the Bell Backward: the Proceedings of the First International Milton Symposium*, edited by Ronald G. Shafer (Indiana, Pennsylvania, 1982), 46-59.

20. The title page of the 1697 edition announces, "Adorn'd with a Hundred Sculptures"; there are however 101 subscriptions and an additional plate, not found in the Ogilby edition, which acts as a

frontispiece; this number seems to accord with Dryden's remark in a letter to William Walsh, "I propose to do [the translation] by subscription; haveing an hundred & two Brass Cutts, with the Coats of Armes of the Subscriber to each Cutt. . . ." Ward, *The Letters*, p. 64.

21. The use of the Ogilby plates was noted first by Spence, *Observations* I, 27; cf. Kathleen M. Lynch, *Jacob Tonson, Kit-Cat Publisher* (Knoxville, Tenn., 1971), 120.

22. See Ward, *The Letters*, p. 93, "[Tonson] has missd of his design in the Dedication: though He had prepared the Book for it: for in every figure of Eneas, he has causd him to be drawn like K. William, with a hookd Nose." G. F. Papili in *Jacob Tonson, Publisher* (Auckland, New Zealand, 1968) quotes the following contemporary verse on Tonson and the *Virgil*: "Old Jacob, by deep judgement swayed, / To please the wise beholders, / Has placed old Nassau's hook-nosed head, / On poor Aeneas shoulders. / To make the parallel hold tack, / Methinks ther's little lacking; / One took his father pick-a-pack, / And t'other sent his packing," p. 165. The fullest commentary on the Ogilby plates is to be found in Eleanor Leach's "Illustration as Interpretation in Brant's and Dryden's Editions of Virgil," *The Early Illustrated Book*, edited by Sandra Hindman (Washington, D.C., 1982), 175-208; Leach seems, however, unaware that it was Tonson rather than Dryden who had the engravings retouched and that Tonson had done so with a specific argument in mind.

23. The only other significant change in the plates was the use of a new frontispiece; the frontispiece for the Ogilby *Virgil* depicts the poet reading his *Aeneid* to the court of Augustus Caesar, the emperor enthroned in the middle of the scene. The frontispiece to Dryden's *Virgil*, engraved by Vander-Gucht, a Flemish engraver working in London in the 1690s, shows a poet, presumably Virgil, holding a book, crowned by Apollo with a wreath of bays; hovering above, a putti holds a cartouche that reads, "Dryden's Virgil, Printed for Jacob Tonson."

24. See Ward, *The Letters*, 80 (note 4, 174); 85-86 (note 1, 176); and 88 (note 1, 176).

25. All plates are from and references are to *The Works of Virgil* (London, 1697); plates are referred to in this text by the plate number assigned in "The Names of the Subscribers to the Cuts of Virgil," ††r—††v. Figures are reproduced from the large paper copy of the 1697 edition held by the William Andrews Clark Memorial Library, University of California at Los Angeles.

26. London held the appointment of Master Gardener and Deputy

Superintendent of the Royal Gardens during the reign of William III; cf. Blanche Henry, *British Botanical and Horticultural Literature before 1800* (London, 1975), 181.

27. *DNB*, s.v. Henley.

28. On Stepney's life and work, see *George Stepney's Translation of the Eighth Satire of Juvenal*, edited with an introduction by Thomas and Elizabeth Swedenberg (Berkeley and Los Angeles, 1948), 1-15.

29. It was Kneller, among others, who had urged Dryden to translate Du Fresnoy's *De Arte Graphica*, which was prefaced by Dryden's *Parallel of Poetry and Painting* (1695); Dryden did the translation and the *Parallel* in two months "borrowed . . . from his translation of Virgil," Macdonald, *Bibliography*, 175-176; cf. Ward, *The Letters*, 172 n.3.

30. See, for example, plate 50 subscribed by Lady Giffard and *DNB* article on the Giffards, or plate 53 subscribed by Henry Tasburgh, and *The English Catholic Nonjurors of 1715*, edited by E. E. Estcourt (London and New York, 1885), 193.

31. *DNB*, s.v. Crewe.

32. *DNB*, s.v. Salisbury (James Cecil); *Poems on Affairs of State*, V, edited by William J. Cameron, 335, 417n.

33. H. J. Oliver, *Sir Robert Howard* (Durham, N.C., 1963), 297-299.

34. Lois Schwoerer, "A Journal of the Convention of Westminster begun the 22 of January 1688/9," *Bulletin of the Institute of Historical Research*, XLIX (1976), 242-263; Dryden would probably have known as well of Howard's virulently anti-Catholic *The History of Religion* (London, 1694).

35. English prose translation by Gordon Williams, *Technique and Idea in the Aeneid* (New Haven, 1983), 193, and see commentary on this passage by Williams, 192-193; the strength and tact of Virgil's line is conveyed by Allen Mandelbaum, *The Aeneid of Virgil*, 2nd ed. (Berkeley and Los Angeles, 1981), 264: "You, too, sad Cydon, / while you were following your latest darling— / your Clytius, his cheeks blond with first down— / would then have fallen headlong by the Dardan's / right hand and lain, a miserable corpse, / forgetful of the boyish loves that always / were dear to you, had not your seven brothers / assailed the enemy with compact ranks." See, as well, commentary on these lines by T. W. Harrison, "Dryden's *Aeneid*," *Dryden's Mind and Art*, edited by Bruce King (Edinburgh, 1969), 164-165.

36. See *DNB*, s.v. Sidney; Jones, *Country and Court*, 246, 265;

Horwitz, *Parliament, Policy and Politics in the Reign of William III*, 66-67, 93, 218; and *Poems on Affairs of State*, V, 62, 165-166, 460-462.

37. Jones, *Country and Court*, 246.

38. The Ogilby translation and its influence on Dryden have been treated by L. Proudfoot, *Dryden's Aeneid and Its Seventeenth-Century Predecessors* (Manchester, 1960); the use that Dryden made of the Lauderdale translation, which he knew in manuscript, has been studied by Margaret Boddy, "Contemporary Allusions in Lauderdale's 'Aeneid'," *Notes and Queries*, IX (1962), 386-388; "Dryden-Lauderdale Relationships," *Philological Quarterly*, XLII (1963), 267-272.

39. Jonathan Swift, *The Prose Writings*, 14 volumes, edited by H. Davies (Oxford, 1951-1968), V, 194-195.

40. Dryden's translation of book 1 of Tacitus's *Annals* was part of a composite translation of the *Annals* published in 1698 by Matthew Gillyflower. What little attention has been given to this translation seems all to derive, directly or indirectly, from Thomas Gordon's derisive remarks in the preface to his own translation of Tacitus, *The Works of Tacitus . . . translated by T. Gordon* (London, 1728). The mistaken notion that Dryden worked directly and exclusively from a French translation by Amelot de la Houssaye comes from Gordon, "Dryden has translated the first Book; but done it almost literally from Mr. Amelot de la Houssaye, with haste and little exactness, that besides his many mistakes, he has introduced severall Gallicisms: he follows the French master servilely, and writes French English . . . at best 'tis only the French Translator ill translated, or ill imitated" B1^r-B1^v. Gordon was presumably trying to enhance his own claims as translator, but this judgment reappears in *The Critical Review* for June 1793 (London, 1793), 121, which in turn is quoted by J. W. Moss in *A Manual of Classical Bibliography* (London, 1825), II, and is repeated in so recent a work as Howard Weinbrot's *Augustus Caesar in "Augustan" England* (Princeton, 1978), 29: "Ignorance of Dryden's sources—Amelot rather than Tacitus—has led to some curious generalizations regarding the development of English prose style." In fact, Dryden must have had both the Latin and French in front of him and even a cursory comparison of texts reveals that he translated from the Latin, at times using de la Houssaye, but often rendering Tacitus into an English translation that exactly reflects Tacitus's diction and syntax. The very opening sentences of the translation yield examples of both the choice of Tacitus over de la Houssaye and of the introduction of the translator's own language. I quote first

from a modern edition of the *Annals*, then from the French transla-
tion, and finally from Dryden's translation. "Urbem Romam a prin-
cipio reges habuere; libertatem et consulatum L. Brutus instituit. dic-
taturae ad tempus sumebantur; neque decemviralis potestas ultra
biennium, neque tribunorum militum consulare ius diu valuit. non
Cinnae, non Sullae longa dominatio; et Pompei Crassique potentia
cito in Caesarem, Lepidi atque Antonii arma in Augustum cessere,
qui cuncta discordiis civilibus fessa nomine principis sub imperium
accepit. sed veteris populi Romani prospera vel adversa claris scrip-
toribus memorata sunt; temporibusque Augusti dicendis non defuere
decora ingenia, donec gliscente adulatione deterrerentur. Tiberii Gai-
que et Claudii ac Neronis res florentibus ipsis ob metum falsae,
postquam occiderant, recentibus odiis compositae sunt" [*The Annals
of Tacitus*, edited by H. Furneaux, 2 volumes (Oxford, 1897), I, 43].
"Rome, dans son commencement, eut des Rois, & après le
bannissement des Tarquins, Lucius Junius Brutus introduisit le Con-
sulat & la Liberté. La Dictature ne se donnoit que pour un tems, &
la puissance des Decemvirs ne dura pas plus de deux ans. L'autorité
Consulaire des Tribuns militaires ne fut pas longtems en vigueur. La
domination de Cinna, ni celle de Silla ne furent pas longues, & César
ne tarda guére à ruiner Crassus & Pompée, ses colégues; ni Auguste
à vaincre Lepidus & Marc-Antoine, ses rivaux. Et comme les guerres
civiles avoient épuisé toutes les forces de la Republique, Auguste en
prit le gouvernement sous le nom modeste de Prince du Sénat. Tout
ce qui est arivé de bonheur ou de malheur à l'ancienne République
a été raconté par de célébres Ecrivains. Et Auguste même n'a pas
manqué de beaux esprits, pour écrire son histoire, avant que la né-
cessité de flater, qui croissoit de jour en jour, les eût abatardis.
Lorsque Tibére, Caligula, Claudius & Néron, regnoient, la crainte de
les ofenser, fesoit écrire des mensonges; mais dés qu'ils furent morts,
la haine toute récente fit composer des invectives" (*Tacite avec des
Notes Politiques et Historiques* . . . par Amelot de la Houssaie, The
Hague, 1692, 1-9). "Rome was govern'd at first by Kings. Liberty
and the Consulship were introduc'd by Lucius Brutus: the Dictator-
ship was granted, but as necessity requir'd, and for some time: And
the Authority of the Decemvirate continu'd only for two Years. The
Consular Power of the Military Tribunes remain'd in force but for a
little space. Neither was the Arbitrary Dominion of Cinna, or that
of Sylla, of any long continuance. The Power of Pompey and Cras-
sus, were soon transferr'd to Julius Caesar; and the Arms of Marc
Anthony and Lepidus, gave place to those of his Successor, Augus-

tus. Then it was, that the Civil Wars having exhausted the Forces of the Common-wealth, Augustus Caesar assum'd the Government, under the Modest Title of Prince of the Senate.

"But all the good or adverse Fortune, which happen'd to the Ancient Republique of the Romans, has already been related, by great Authors. Neither were there wanting Famous Wits to transfer the Actions of Augustus to future Ages, till they were hinder'd by the Growth of Flattery. During the Reigns of Tiberius, Caligula, Claudius, and Nero; their several Actions were falsify'd through fear, while they were yet living; and after their Decease, were traduc'd through the recent hate of their Historians" (*The Annals and History of Cornelius Tacitus . . . In Three Volumes*, London, 1698, I, 1-6). In the very first sentence, Dryden clearly seems to follow Tacitus's syntax and not Amelot's; in his second sentence, Dryden introduces his own language in the phrase, "as necessity requir'd," which has no original in either Tacitus nor Amelot; and again in Dryden's fourth sentence the epithet "arbitrary" belongs to the English translator. In the remarks on Pompey, Crassus and Mark Antony, Dryden follows Tacitus very closely, but he adopts Amelot's language in describing Augustus's acquisition of title. Dryden's last two sentences are very close to Tacitus, adopting neither Amelot's syntax nor diction. And Dryden's "falsify'd through fear" is a direct and handsome rendering of "ob metum falsae" that hardly seems indebted to—or mediated by —Amelot. And such examples abound in this translation; the whole of Dryden's rendering of book 1 of the *Annals* needs careful study not only for the ways in which Dryden moves between the Latin and French, why and where he adopts Amelot's language, but as well to see how Dryden turns Tacitus toward the political issues of the 1690s. What is clear however even from the opening sentences is that Dryden's English is a rendering of Tacitus and not of Amelot de la Houssaye.

41. Virgil's Latin is quoted from the Delphin edition that Dryden used in preparing his translation, P. Virgilii Maronis, *Opera . . . Secunda Editio*, Amstelodami, 1690; cf. Arvid Losnes, "Dryden's *Aeneis* and the Delphin Virgil," in M. Sofie Rostvig et al., *The Hidden Sense* (Oslo, Norway, 1963).

42. See, for example, *Eleonora*, 193-204; the *Dedication* of *Fables*, 10-16, 24-50, 60-63, 180-182; *To Her Grace the Dutchess of Ormond*, 141-150, 165-168; and, of course, *To my Honour'd Kinsman, John Driden, of Chesterton*; cf. Chapter 5 above.

43. On the question of William's grants to his Dutch compatriots,

see Frank H. Ellis, *A Discourse on the Contests and Dissentions Between the Nobles and the Commons . . . by Jonathan Swift* (Oxford, 1967), 14-27; and the debates in the 1695 parliament, *A Collection of the Parliamentary Debates*, III, 52-57.

44. See comments by William Cameron, "John Dryden's Jacobitism," 290-291.

45. See, for example, the passage in *The Hind and the Panther*, part 3, 304-305, "That suff'ring from ill tongues he bears no more / Than what his Sovereign bears, and what his Saviour bore"; and Chapter 5 above.

46. See, for example, Thomas Wagstaffe, *An answer to a late pamphlet, entitled obedience and submission to the present government* (London, 1690), 43; John Kettlewell, *Of Christian Prudence, or Religious Wisdom; not Degenerating into Irreligious Craftiness, in Trying Times* (London, 1691), 84.

47. Hobbes read the passage in Virgil in the same manner, "To the Reader, Concerning the Virtues of an Heroic Poem," in *The English Works*, edited by W. Molesworth (London, 1844), X, ix.

Index

Library of Congress Cataloging in Publication Data

Zwicker, Steven N.
Politics and language in Dryden's poetry.

Includes bibliographical references and index.
1. Dryden, John, 1631-1700—Political and social views. 2. Politics
in literature. 3. Politics and literature—Great Britain. 4. Great Brit-
ain—Politics and government—1660-1714. I. Title.

PR3427.P6Z94 1984   821'.4   84-42550
ISBN 0-691-06618-3 (alk. paper)